Mother Tongues

Mother Tongues

Sexuality,

Trials,

Motherhood,

Translation

Barbara Johnson

HARVARD UNIVERSITY PRESS
Cambridge, Massachusetts, and London, England 2003

P. 200 constitutes an extension of the copyright page

Library of Congress Cataloging-in Publication Data

Johnson, Barbara, 1947–
Mother tongues : sexuality, trials, motherhood,
translation / Barbara Johnson.
  p.   cm.
Includes bibliographical references and index.
ISBN 0-674-01187-2
1. Sex differences (Psychology) in literature.
2. Sex role in literature.
3. Feminism and literature.   I. Title.

PN56.S52J64 2003
809'.93353—dc21   2003051077

Designed by Gwen Nefsky Frankfeldt

To my regular e-mail correspondents

    Judith Butler

    and

    Barbara Rietveld,

who have taught me everything I know about e-construction

Contents

Acknowledgments

Thus I set pen to paper with delight,
And quickly had my thoughts in black and white.
For having now my method by the end,
Still as I pulled it came, and so I penned
It down, until it came at last to be
For length and breadth the bigness that you see.

With minor technological adjustments, what John Bunyan says about how he wrote *The Pilgrim's Progress* applies to the origins of this book. As I typed, it seemed to come according to its own logic. Of course, none of us really writes alone: my two constant e-mail companions are those the book is dedicated to. In addition, I took the play on e-construction from Jane Gallop's "E-constructing Sisterhood," given at the 1999 English Institute and published by Routledge in *Time and the Literary* in 2002. And of course, the long-suffering default reader of drafts, Marjorie Garber, has also made this book possible for me in every way. Several of the book's chapters have appeared elsewhere: "Doing Time" in *Time and the Literary* (New York: Routledge, 2003); "L'Esthétique du Mal" (initially "Bad Writing") in *Just Being Difficult?* (Stanford: Stanford University Press, 2002), part of the chapter called "Construction Work—entitled "Ode on a Public Thing"—in *Field Work*, edited by Marjorie Garber, Paul B. Franklin, and Rebecca L. Walkowitz (New York: Routledge, 1996), and a chapter of a book on Benjamin's *Arcades* in which I was invited by Beatrice Hanssen to think about Benjamin's relation to Baudelaire, and which is perhaps where this book started.

Mother Tongues

Now all the earth was of one language and one set-of-words. And it was when they migrated to the east that they found a valley in the land of Shinar and settled there. They said, each man to his neighbor: Come-now! Let us bake bricks and let us burn them well-burnt! So for them brick-stone was like building-stone, and raw-bitumen was for them like red-mortar. Now they said: Come-now! Let us build ourselves a city and a tower.

—Genesis 11:1–4, The Schocken Bible

And the name of God the father would be the name of that origin of tongues. But it is also that God who, in the action of his anger, . . . annals the gift of tongues, or at least embroils it, sows confusion among his sons, and poisons the present (*Gift*-gift). This is also the origin of tongues, of the multiplicity of idioms, of what in other words are usually called mother tongues.

—Jacques Derrida, "Des tours de Babel"

ONE
_____

Correctional Facilities

I. Trials

The police have blundered. They thought they were attacking a run-of-the-mill
novel and some ordinary little scribbler; whereas now (in part thanks to the
prosecution) my novel is looked on as a masterpiece.
—Gustave Flaubert, letter of January 20, 1857

The two most famous French literary works published in 1857,
Flaubert's *Madame Bovary* and Baudelaire's *Les Fleurs du Mal,* were
both indicted for outraging public morality and religion. With the
advantage of historical hindsight, one can easily feel superior to
those officers of the court who wanted to silence or cut up two great
works of art. Or perhaps one can admire them for recognizing, even
negatively, the revolutionary nature of their targets. The stance of
superiority and hindsight is a little more difficult to maintain when
the officer of the court is Plato, and when the expulsion of poetry
from the Republic is an indictment of imitative arts in general. Surely
this is going too far. Plato must be referring to popular or unrefined
things like *bad* poetry, romance novels, television—the kind of thing
a susceptible person like Emma Bovary would be affected by.[1] Corruption by images may be widespread, the argument would go, but
it *can* be contained and corrected.

Nevertheless, our uncertainty increases if we remember that Socrates will be—indeed *has been,* by the time Plato is writing—condemned to death for something like the same things he held against
poetry: seducing, leading astray, creating belief in false images. How
can we save Socrates and condemn Athens without casting doubt
upon what that same Socrates said in *The Republic?* At least in Benjamin Jowett's translation.[2] Or at least what Plato alleged, in writing,
that Socrates said. The same Plato who wrote, however, in Hugh

Tredennick's translation of *Phaedo,* that Socrates spent his final days composing poetry.[3] So even if Athens is a bad example of the public sphere and Socrates a bad example of poetry, which side is he on? If the culmination of Socratic irony lies in the invention of *that very difference,* does Socrates have to die in order for this statement to be true? What can be said about this validation of a truth that is necessarily other than life? Is death a good thing? Is Socrates' death his last and best teaching? Of course, there is a whole religion around that kind of paradox. Public executions seem to be useful in creating cultural authority. But even if Socrates and Christ have a lot in common (or at least *come to have* a lot in common in the construction of Neo-Platonism), would the Apostles have written *The Republic?* What can be said about a polis that cares enough about poetry to expel it? Or if we want to save poetry, should we applaud those officers of the Second Empire court, finally, for discerning the greatness of works they single out for prosecution?

The more one studies the trials of Flaubert and Baudelaire, the more one can't help noticing that the prosecutor (the same in both cases, Ernest Pinard) is a better reader than the defense lawyers. His reasoning is simple: representation gives existence. No amount of condemnation can substitute for an image's nonexistence. Therefore even if the work in question evokes something in order to prove how bad it is (which was the reasoning of the defense, whether or not Baudelaire or Flaubert would have agreed), condemnation leaves a memory of the thing condemned, and that memory has an independent life. This is always the problem with pointing out something for censure. The representation works upon its reader despite or perhaps even because of the judgment pronounced against it. This is the basis of Catherine MacKinnon's argument against the sex-differentiated, educative function of pornography. It is also Michel Foucault's reading of the Victorian "repressive hypothesis." In Freud's terms, the image unrepresses something that the secondary revision cannot completely erase or control. In both the Freudian and the legal context, the force behind the secondary revision is called *censorship.*

In our present moment, the one thing all critics seem to agree about is the danger and political retrogradeness of Art for Art's

Sake—literature detached from any connection with a referent. If a representation is censored, it is presumably referential. That is, what is not wanted is something *in the world* that representation makes real. Political and historical criticism have become very sophisticated; the nonreferential dimension of literature can be historically subversive and disconcerting to such simple mimetic models. Thus, Dominick LaCapra can brilliantly analyze why Flaubert's *style indirect libre* was more upsetting to bourgeois models of realism than any immorality. But he nevertheless draws a line he will not cross:

> The danger of semiotics is the confinement of critical inquiry to metacriticism that politically and socially neutralizes itself by placing the analyst in a deceptive position above the conflict of interpretations.[4]

The consensus about the dangers of detachment from conflict and of political neutralization is, therefore, still the danger of behaving a certain way *in the world*. The danger is that the attention paid to the operation of the signifier will have necessary referential consequences. While you are parsing a sentence, analyzing a metaphor, or smiling over a meaning entirely produced by the magic of rhyme, you are not paying attention to what is going on in the world. The question I would like to ask is whether *not* paying attention to the signifier *automatically* keeps you there. The Marxist suspicion of formalism does not make a person suspicious of formalism into a Marxist. A Marxist is suspicious of formalism because the temptation to reify forms might arrest an analysis designed to lead to revolutionary action. Merely being suspicious of forms is itself a reification if it is not *for* something. Instead of formalism for its own sake, we would have an even more empty antiformalism for its own sake, not even capable of taking form itself seriously, and certainly not intent on intervening in the world.

Why is the fear of forgetting reality so great? It is a grandiose fantasy of omnipotence to fear that by forgetting reality, a person might damage reality. The fact that the fear of damaging reality cannot be averted should make us more humble, not more in search of mastery, about the consequences of our actions. Even though we know now that the Holocaust really happened—and happened in large part through an accumulation of small actions of many people seen now as people who could have done something to stop it—we have drawn the wrong conclusions, I think. It is not that now we see that the Holocaust happened because of the actions of individuals, but that it happened because those individuals did not see that they were part of a pattern. No individual could have produced or stopped it on his or her own, even though it was through the risky and sacrificial actions of individuals that it could be resisted at all.

Why is the taboo against focusing on rhetorical structures without grounding their effects in the world so strong? It has grown all the stronger with the aversive effects of Paul de Man's wartime journalism.[5] But it was when I realized that the Nazis were just as opposed to the play of forms for their own sake as contemporary critics are—including myself—that I began to wonder why I had bought into the universal disparagement of Art for Art's Sake. Surely the collaborationist journalism of Paul de Man argues at least as strongly against the dangers of politicized criticism as against the dangers of detachment. Why is it that his late work—directed as it is against the temptations he himself had succumbed to—has been taken as a pathway to the same dangers he was resisting? Is his resistance too absolute? Is there something about turning so absolutely against a former temptation that repeats it in a different form? I have no answers to these questions, but they are part of what led me to take the particular intellectual paths I have taken here.

Getting back to what may be just as outrageous as a defense of Art for Art's Sake and is somehow related to it, it will be my contention here that what is censored in the Western tradition derived from Plato is always the fact of sexual difference.

Of course, I realize that sexual difference is not a fact but an interpretation, and it may be an interpretation of something that has nothing to do with sexual difference. Nevertheless, I would say that what is censored is a fact. It becomes an interpretation in the act of getting past the censor.

Surprisingly, female specificity is represented in one of two ways to reduce the threat it poses: it is seen as either motherhood or lesbianism. These two images appear to have little in common, and, in fact, that is the point. The first allows for male and female to be complementary; the second allows for them to be equivalent. Everything else falls into the category of "attractive nuisance." These two images are either central to patriarchy or indifferent to it. Thus, motherhood can be held up as the standard a woman hasn't met ("She may be a CEO, but she's *childless*") or lesbianism an accusation so monstrous it provokes denial if at all possible ("We know what her problem is: she *doesn't like men*"). Of course, the number of women who have negative feelings about men are hardly confined to lesbians—in fact, lesbians should be rather impervious to those feelings. But the trace of bad conscience—sweeping something that can't be incorporated under the rug—remains.

Sexual difference is not censored simply by virtue of the fact that Plato lived in a world of men, but rather the opposite: a certain censorship of sexual difference—one that confined women to the duties of reproduction—permitted the birth of philosophy.

In Plato's warnings against poetry in Book X of *The Republic,* particular attention is paid to representations of overflowing feelings. Witnessing the spectacle of lamentation or terror, Socrates says, "Few persons ever reflect, as I should imagine, that the contagion must pass from others to themselves. For the pity which has been nourished and strengthened in the misfortunes of others is with difficulty repressed in our own."[6] In other words, poetry unrepresses the real through the habit of the simulacrum. Sympathy is an admirable thing, but the wise man recognizes the slippery slope. He prides himself on his lack of reaction when the sorrow happens to him: "This is considered the manly part, and the other which delighted us in the recitation is now deemed to be the part of a woman" (Adams, 36).

The poetry that is expelled from the city, then, is equated with femininity. It is perhaps not an accident that one of the greatest lyric poets at that time was Sappho, whom Plato mentions in the *Phaedrus* ("I'm sure I have heard something better [than Lysias's speech] from the fair Sappho maybe").[7] Expelling poets is expelling femininity; expelling femininity is expelling women. And yet, in the *Phaedrus,* as Page du Bois has pointed out, Socrates seems to borrow from Sappho the rhetoric of inflamed desire. "Plato echoes and appropriates the female position, and then uses the occasion to deny the body and to sublimate erotic desire into philosophy."[8] When Socrates' wife, Xanthippe, visits him in his prison cell on the day he is to die, he sends her away for crying hysterically. Women would seem to represent all that is weak and bodily, all that is not philosophy. Yet what is Xanthippe lamenting as she is dragged away? "Oh, Socrates," she says, "this is the last time that you and your friends will be able to talk together!"[9] It is when she says *that* that Socrates asks that she be taken home. She gives voice not to the body's grief but to philosophy's, not to her own lamentations but to the sadness of the scene of her exclusion. To feel sympathy for the loss felt by those who share something that excludes you, *that* is the role of women. She is taken out not for bringing into the cell the other of philosophy, but for seeing and saying that the other of philosophy is already there.

The condemnation of poetry in Baudelaire's case originally involved two kinds of outrage: as outlined by Jean Pommier, four poems were initially condemned for "atteinte à la morale religieuse" and ten for "atteinte à la morale publique."[10] ("Religious" and "public" make as strange an opposition as "self" and "full" in gas stations!) When the trial was over, the accusation of outrage to religion was dropped, and Baudelaire was required to remove six poems and pay a fine. Given that he was always in debt and that there were exactly 100 carefully placed poems in the 1857 edition, both parts of the penalty were experienced as harsh.

In the courtroom, the prosecutor Pinard argues that his role is not that of arbiter of literary quality (to which he has just shown himself to be sensitive) but that of a sentinel guarding the bounds of public decency. He says:

> Le juge n'est point un critique littéraire, appelé à prononcer sur des modes opposés d'apprécier l'art et de le rendre. Il n'est point le juge des écoles, mais le législateur l'a investi d'une mission définie: le législateur a inscrit dans nos codes le délit d'offense à la morale publique, il a punie ce délit de certaines peines, il a donné au pouvoir judiciaire une autorité discrétionnaire pour reconnaître si cette morale est offensée, si la limite a été franchie. Le juge est une sentinelle qui ne doit pas laisser passer la frontière.[11]

[A judge is no literary critic, called upon to pronounce on the opposite modes of appreciating art and making it. He is also not here to judge schools, but rather the legislature has given him a precise mission: the legislator has inscribed among our laws the crime of offending public decency, he has decided on the punishment to mete out for this crime, and he has given discretionary authority to the judiciary to recognize whether such decency has indeed been offended, whether the limit has been crossed. The judge is a border guard who must prevent illicit passages.]

The judge is thus a sentinel preventing illicit "passages." It is perhaps those same "passages" that both Baudelaire and Benjamin will associate with the nineteenth century's modernity. In Benjamin's long, unfinished *Passagen-Werk,* glass and iron arcades are the link between inside and outside, commerce and art, street and store. And in the poems Baudelaire would later add to his "mutilated" masterwork, that same "passage" becomes the very substance of the erotic. As he writes in "A une passante" to the woman who ignites his desire as she suddenly appears through the medium of the city crowd, "Ô toi que j'eusse aimée, ô toi qui le savais!" [O you I would have loved, O you who knew that!]

Pinard cites the dangers of textual promiscuity in the age of the feuilleton. He warns against what will happen to public decency with the mass circulation of cheap journals, an argument better suited to Flaubert than to Baudelaire (whose poetry was not cheap). The very existence of the argument, however, implies the presence of an expanding and commercialized readership that Baudelaire could not control. Not all readers would be able to withstand the temptations offered by representations in the service of the moral lesson that is to be derived from them. Taking a page out of Plato's book, Pinard argues:

> Mais la vérité, la voici: l'homme est toujours plus ou moins infirme, plus ou moins faible, plus ou moins malade, portant d'autant plus le poids de sa chute originelle, qu'il veut en douter ou la nier. Si telle est sa nature intime tant qu'elle n'est pas relevée par de mâles efforts et une forte discipline, qui ne sait combien il prendra facilement le goût des frivolités lascives, sans se préoccuper de l'enseignement que l'auteur veut y placer.[12]

[But here is the painful truth: man is always more or less wavering, more or less weak, more or less sick, carrying the burden of original sin the more he would like to doubt or negate it. If such is his intimate nature so long as it is not strengthened by male efforts and strong discipline, who knows how easily he will get a taste for lascivious frivolities and not give a damn for the lesson that the author means to place there.]

The senses will be awakened by the poems, and can thereafter never be securely contained. Clearly Pinard, as a representative of Second Empire bourgeois decency, is more afraid of being aroused than of being difficult to arouse, which was rather the danger Baudelaire was afraid of ("Je suis comme le roi d'un pays pluvieux. . . . Rien ne peut l'égayer" [I am like the king of a rainy country. . . . Nothing can arouse him]). I am taking *égayer* as a synonym for "arouse." That *égayer* should mean "arouse" to Pinard, too, is suggested by the condemnation of the poem "A celle qui est trop gaie." "To the woman who is too aroused"? As that poem suggests, it is *female* arousal that Pinard is most worried about. For him, arousal itself, as implicitly female, must be combated by the "male efforts" that the upright man expends. But, given the expanding market of *female* readers, what is to prevent these poems from falling into the hands of *women*? What if our daughters are even seduced by what Pinard learnedly calls "les plus intimes moeurs des tribades" [the most intimate customs of Tribades]? Pinard uses an archaic but explicit word meaning "female homosexual" (which Claude Pichois, in the notes to his edition of the works of Baudelaire, finds used in this sense in two dictionaries of the period). In fact, the attempt to understand whether or not the initial title of *Les Fleurs du Mal—Les Lesbiennes*— did or did not have what Pichois refers to as "the modern sense" pushes him into veritable feats of philology. Poetry? Or homosexuality? Geography? Or homosexuality? These same questions arise around the name Sappho. Was she or wasn't she? As Joan de Jean notes in her *Fictions of Sappho:*

If I learned anything while working on this study, something for which I was totally unprepared, it is quite simply that Sappho makes a great many people nervous.[13]

(While I was working on the first version of this paper on an airplane, surrounded by two translations and two studies of Sappho, I certainly felt as if I were exposing something that I normally hide!)

> One phenomenon I explain in this way is the recurrent, stubborn refusal to mention female homosexuality under any name. (Commentators thus find themselves in the delicate position of attempting to disprove Sappho's homosexuality without actually naming that which they claim she was not.) (de Jean, 2)

This is the logical extension of the logic of censorship: you treat the thing you are condemning as if it could not be represented without creating the harm you are trying to prevent. The resistance to naming is a good example of the attempt to deny existence to the thing to which one is attempting to deny existence. Which doesn't mean that the thing repressed can't be resistant to naming in another sense. But we are getting ahead of ourselves.

In any case, Pinard *does* name female homosexuality as a dangerous moral corruption that might really occur in the world of female readers. But nothing could be further from Baudelaire's mind. The idea that lesbians might be recruited out of the ranks of good bourgeois reading daughters never occurs to him. Several times in his attempts to draft a post-condemnation preface to his *Fleurs du Mal,* he repeats:

> Ce n'est pas pour mes femmes, mes filles ou mes soeurs que ce livre a été écrit; non plus pour les femmes, les filles ou les soeurs de mon voisin.[14]
>
> [It is not for my wives, my daughters, or my sisters that this book was written, nor for the wives, daughters, and sisters of my neighbor.]

Since Baudelaire never married, had no children, and had no sisters, this is clearly a generic warning. Instead of coveting his neighbor's wife, he is merely preventing her from reading.

So paradoxically it is Pinard, not Baudelaire, who takes lesbianism seriously *in the world*. Pinard's distaste for it does not exclude a certain sensitivity to its charms, which merely increases his desire to prosecute it. In fact, *Les Fleurs du Mal* was prosecuted for "realism."

As the court put it, in rendering its final decision to condemn six poems and to fine the author, the editor, and the printer of *Les Fleurs du Mal:*

> Attendu que l'erreur du poète, dans le but qu'il voulait atteindre et dans la route qu'il a suivie, quelque effort de style qu'il ait pu faire, quel que soit le blâme qui précède ou qui suit ses peintures, ne saurait détruire l'effet funeste des tableaux qu'il présente au lecteur, et qui, dans les pièces incriminées, conduisent nécessairement à l'excitation des sens par un réalisme grossier et offensant pour la pudeur. . . .[15]

> [Given that the poet's error, in the goal he envisaged and in the pathway he followed, whatever stylistic efforts he made, whatever blame precedes or follows his images, cannot destroy the deleterious effect of the tableaux he puts before the eyes of the reader, which, in the condemned poems, necessarily excite the senses through a gross realism offensive to modesty. . . .]

This condemnation for realism was a misunderstanding proudly corrected by a 1949 court. The 1857 court should never have taken those poems literally.

> Attendu que les poèmes faisant l'objet de la prévention ne renfermant aucun terme obscène ou même grossier et ne dépassant pas, en leur forme expressive, les libertés permises à l'artiste; que si certaines peintures ont pu, par leur originalité, alarmer quelques esprits à l'époque de la première publication des *Fleurs du Mal* et apparaître aux premiers juges comme offensant les bonnes moeurs, une telle appréciation ne s'attachant qu'à l'interprétation réaliste de ces poèmes et négligeant leur sens symbolique, s'est révélé de caractère arbitraire; qu'elle n'a été ratifiée ni par l'opinion publique, ni par le jugement des lettrés.[16]

> [Given that the condemned poems do not include a single obscene or even crude word and by no means go beyond, in their expressive form, what is permitted as poetic license; that if certain images could, in their very originality, have alarmed some readers at the time of the first publication of *The Flowers of Evil* and appeared to the initial judges as an offense to public decency, such a reading applies only to a realist interpretation of those poems and ignores their symbolic sense, appearing arbitrary in character—such an interpretation has been ratified neither by public opinion nor by the judgment of literary people.]

The judgment of people of taste was precisely what would not count as evidence in a later obscenity trial where it was again a question of lesbianism: the trial of Radclyffe Hall for *The Well of Loneliness*. That court had become aware that obscenity did not inhere in words, nor could it be protected by literary merit. But note the two senses of "judgment" here: it applies to the legal system, but also to the aesthetic system. Kant's *Critique of Judgment* was not an indictment of the legal system but an investigation of taste. The aesthetic domain is generally seen as that which *escapes* determination by the legal system. Nevertheless, both courts and readers are called upon to make judgments. Perhaps the legal and the aesthetic systems have more in common than we customarily think. The condemnation and rehabilitation of *Les Fleurs du Mal*, for example, depend entirely on the distinction between realism and symbolism.

So in 1949, Baudelaire was rehabilitated. But lesbianism was thereby doubly condemned. If it was real, it was awful; if it was symbolic, it wasn't real. "Realism" was reality unidealized; its realness was proven by its undesirableness. If any reality were desirable, why would we need realism to see it? It wouldn't have been repressed in the first place. If lesbianism connotes "realism," then, it must be because of an inability to repress completely what is undesirable. The possibility that real lesbianism could be idealized would have to wait another twenty years. And when it did become thinkable, it would not take Baudelaire with it.

If real, then condemned; if symbolic, then not real. What is rendered impossible is the idea that lesbians, like philosophers, could be both at once. Or neither.

II. *Translation*

> Thanks to you and your invention, your pupils will be widely read without benefit of a teacher's instruction; in consequence, they'll entertain the delusion that they have wide knowledge, while they are, in fact, for the most part incapable of real judgment.
>
> —the King to the Inventor of Writing in Plato's *Phaedrus*

This is where Sappho comes back in. In Sappho's case, as Page du Bois puts it, "There is no there there."[17] Her poems are preserved in fragments in other people's quotations, in Egyptian garbage dumps, in allusions. "Who is Sappho?" writes Dudley Fitts in his preface to the Mary Barnard translation. "A lyricist unparalleled, a great beauty, no great beauty, a rumor, a writer of cultist hymns, a scandal, a fame, a bitchy sister to a silly brother, a headmistress, a mystic, a mistress of the poet Alkaios, a pervert, a suicide for love of a ferryman, an androgyne, a bluestocking, a pretty mother of a prettier daughter, an avatar of Yellow Book neodiabolism, a Greek."[18] The question of Sappho's real identity gives rise to the very insatiability that lesbians are made to stand for in Baudelaire. Translators have sometimes responded to her incompleteness by filling out Sappho's fragments and thus making a couple with her. Willis Barnstone writes:

> Now a Cambridge don, Mr. Edmonds, had come to her rescue and filled in the lost lines with his own conjectured Greek verse. His inventions, often half or whole lines, were bracketed. He bequeathed us a co-authored Greek text by Sappho and Edmonds.[19]

Barnstone decides to treat Sappho's "badly mutilated" texts more respectfully, leaving them fragmentary wherever "reasonable guesses" are impossible. But his description of Sappho is no less flirtatious: the rhetoric of the amorous chase is everywhere.

> One day in the late autumn of 1959, I spent an unexpected evening with Sappho. . . . After meeting Sappho, I decided on the spot to know her better and chose a way. . . . She appears in her naked Greek and to read her abroad she requires an attractive outfit in English. . . . When I left Sappho—and at the time I knew her lines by heart—I strayed into koine Greek of the Septuagint and Gospels. Then here in California, thirty-five years after the first evening with her, I was happily visited by a similar *coup de foudre*. (Barnstone, 11, 12, 13, 14)

The plot of this retrospectively narrated tale is self-consciously that of an intense love affair with a somewhat elusive woman. But flirting with Sappho may not be as reassuring as this story makes it out to be. The naturalness of the assumption that Sappho would welcome such advances—on which the charm of Barnstone's writing relies—is unquestioned. Just raising the question attributes an independent will to her, whatever the answer turns out to be. And one begins to suspect that translation's difficulties with "fidelity" might turn out to have something to do with it. It is not a matter of retrieving the lost Sappho, but rather of conceptualizing poetry written from a nonorigin.

In Jacques Derrida's analysis of Plato's *Phaedrus,* reference is repeatedly made to a scene called "the trial of writing." Since we are here in the process of studying the trial of Baudelaire (and, by extension, Flaubert), it seems useful to look closely at a judgment pronounced about writing itself. The inventor of writing, Theuth, presents writing to the King for his judgment. Theuth says that writing is a good remedy for forgetfulness. (Let us not forget that one of Baudelaire's condemned poems was called "Le Léthé.") Writing is not a remedy for forgetfulness, says the King; it's a *recipe* for it. The division between remedy and recipe has to exist in order to make sense of this trial, but the Greek word is in both cases the same: *pharmakon.* The decision to translate the *word* according to "reasonable guesses" about the meaning of the context gives rise to "remedy" and "recipe," "poison" or "antidote." That decision *has to be made* by the translator, but then the translated text performs a judgment that the original suspends. In one of the most illuminating passages I know about translation, Derrida writes:

> It will [also] be seen to what extent the malleable unity of this concept, or rather its rules and the strange logic that links it with its signifier, has been dispersed, masked, obliterated, and rendered almost unreadable not only by the imprudence or empiricism of the translators, but first and foremost by the redoubtable, irreducible difficulty of translation. It is a difficulty inherent in its very principle, situated less in the passage from one language to another, from one philosophical language to another, than already, as we shall see, in the tradition between Greek and Greek; a violent difficulty in the transference of a nonphilosopheme into a philosopheme. With this problem of translation we will thus be dealing with nothing less than the problem of the very passage into philosophy.[20]

And what does that passage consist of? Of dividing the undivided. In the original language, it is as though the *pharmakon* is the medium that exists prior to division. Only the translators have to decide between "poison" and "remedy." Philosophy in its original state is not the union of opposites but that which engenders opposition in the first place. "All translations into languages that are the heirs and depositaries of Western metaphysics thus produce on the *pharmakon* an *effect of analysis* that violently destroys it," writes Derrida (99).

Derrida's reading of Plato's text recaptures the lack of division between the antithetical senses of the word *pharmakon*. But the King would still have pronounced judgment upon Theuth's invention, which Theuth would have presented to him for that purpose. That the separation between positive and negative judgments should be incomplete and ambiguous in Plato's text around the King's judgment does not imply that philosophy exists prior to that separation. After all, whether it was good or bad for philosophy that Socrates died by drinking his own *pharmakon* cannot be decided *within* philosophy. And that Socrates should be the victim of distinctions he himself instituted should not be surprising. Derrida's brilliant reading of Plato's *text* as opposed to its intentions makes visible the fact that philosophy's founding trick is to make us *believe* that it constitutes the prior medium in which translators and, after them, readers, will carve decision. It thus appears that all the founding polarities of the Western metaphysical tradition—good versus evil, health versus sickness, life versus death, and so on—are somehow oversimplifications of an originating ambiguity. But an originating ambiguity is not necessarily the same as a prior medium. Philosophy has thus instituted by back-formation the original unity from which it has fallen and to which it tries to return. But to have ambiguity or undecidability, there has to have already have been polarity. Derrida's "correction" of the deformations necessarily produced by translators is itself inevitably a metaphysical look. The text becomes uncanny to the extent that everything in it could point to its opposite. It is simply impossible to fix that uncanniness in an unambiguous way. In the beginning was undecidability?

Genesis says that the world was created by division. By separating the waters from the waters. The whole question is what was there before. It is easy to say "undifferentiation," but is undifferentiation

unity? Much later comes the act of separating philosophy from sophistry, of enacting the founding *krinein,* of pronouncing the founding
judgment. Philosophy will henceforth separate the serious from the
frivolous, truth from falsehood, literal from figurative. Also life from
death. Yet somehow philosophy is also the first discourse that does
not assume automatically that life is better than death. Philosophy's
founding separation may thus be counterintuitive: life is separated
from death, but death might henceforth not be entirely negative. After all, philosophy starts out not from biological life but from language.

Even if there had been no trial of writing in Plato's text, there
would still have been translation. The one thing we know for sure
about translation is that it comes after—and is dependent on—an
original. Or do we?

I was at this point in my thinking about trials of and in literary
texts when I suddenly thought it might be time to take a look at
Franz Kafka's *The Trial.* Since my German is too rudimentary for
reading, I turned to the old translation by Willa and Edwin Muir
that I happened to have on hand, and began. "Someone must have
traduced Joseph K., for without having done anything wrong he was
arrested one fine morning."[21]

"Traduced"? This is an English word I see only in lame attempts
to translate the Italian *traduttore, traditore* or the French *traduire,
trahir.* To translate is to traduce—the betrayal of the original in the
process of transmitting it is inherent in translation. In other words,
"traduce" is a bad translation of a pun on the inevitable badness of
translations. Joseph K. had been betrayed in exactly the same way. I
looked at the first sentence in a more recent edition in which the
Muirs' translation had been revised by E. M. Butler: "Someone must
have *been telling lies about* Joseph K., for without having done anything wrong he was arrested one fine morning."[22] In German the
sentence reads: "Jemand musste Josef K. verleumdet haben, denn
ohne dass er etwas Böses getan hätte, wurde er eines Morgens ver-
haftet."[23] One can see why the translator wanted to replace a somewhat archaic word with a more colloquial expression. My German-
English dictionary translates *verleumden* as "calumniate, slander,

defame, traduce, accuse wrongfully." But by writing "someone must have been telling lies," the translator has set up an opposition between truth and falsehood that, while it is called for by the context, cannot be stated without destroying the senselessness of the arrest. If someone had been telling lies about Joseph K., it makes perfect sense that he should be (falsely) arrested. The translation "traduce" is thus even better than the original in *not* performing on the ambiguous word a violent "effect of analysis." By making more sense of the arrest, the translator destroys its senselessness. *Only translation can betray* without necessarily instating the polarity from which it deviates. In fact the act of arresting Joseph K. cannot be better figured than by translation. The risk in translating Sappho is expressed in exactly this way by Willis Barnstone: "If a very fragmentary work is to be rendered into English it must function not only as a gloss for reading the original but come through with the dignity and excitement of an original text. *Anything less is to traduce Sappho*" (Barnstone, 12).

To introduce his German translation of "Tableaux Parisiens"—the section Baudelaire added to the original edition of *Les Fleurs du Mal* to make up for the loss of the condemned poems the court had forced him to remove—Walter Benjamin added a preface on the theory of translation. We shall have occasion to revisit this text at length later, but here, let me just quote one of Benjamin's key pronouncements. Translation, he writes, is "a somewhat provisional way of coming to grips with the foreignness of languages."[24] Only through translation does an original *become* an original. In saying this I think that Benjamin does not—or not only—mean to say that the original acquires some new authority from the process, but that the idea of the original is a back-formation from the difficulties of translation. Until one sees that from which something deviates, one does not think of that thing as a starting point. The trajectory from original to translation mimes the process of departing from an origin and thus enhances the belief that there *is* an origin. What translation allows us to see is also a fantasy language uniting the two works, as if all translations were falls away from some original language that fleetingly becomes visible. But nothing proves that this is not another back-formation from the difficulties of translation. We are so used to the model of wholeness falling into multiplicity that we read the effect of the effect as if it were a cause. A recent review of *The Power of Babel* in the *Financial Times* typifies our commitment to this belief: "Obviously, at the very beginning of human history there was just one language."[25] Obviously? To whom could such a thing be obvious?

It is not, as the myth of Babel would have it, that there was one original language that fell into multiplicity. Rather, the idea of that one original language might be a mere projection out of the process of translation. The inevitability of betrayal is the only evidence we actually have that there is something to betray.

III. *Difference*

> And the rib, which the Lord God had taken from man, made he a woman, and brought her unto the man. And Adam said, This is now bone of my bones, and flesh of my flesh: she shall be called Woman, because she was taken out of Man.
>
> —Genesis 2:22–23, King James Bible

> And, finally, need I add that I who speak here am bone of the bone and flesh of the flesh of them that live within the Veil?
>
> —W. E. B. Du Bois, *The Souls of Black Folk*

What work does sexual difference do for us intellectually? For Western metaphysics, "male" and "female" fit neatly into the pattern of polarities like "good" and "evil" or "life" and "death." Indeed, some theorists have considered that pattern to be *derived* from the heterosexual couple:

Where is she?
Activity/Passivity
Sun/Moon
Culture/Nature
Day/Night

Father/Mother
Head/Heart
Intelligible/Palpable
Logos/Pathos.
Form, convex, step, advance, semen, progress.

Matter, concave, ground—where steps are taken, holding—
and dumping—ground.
Man
_____
Woman
   Always the same metaphor: we follow it, it carries us, beneath all its
figures, wherever discourse is organized. If we read or speak, the same
thread or double braid is leading us throughout literature, philosophy,
criticism, centuries of representation and reflection.
Thought has always worked through opposition,
Speaking/Writing
Parole/Ecriture
High/Low
   Through dual, hierarchical oppositions.
Superior/Inferior. Myths, legends, books. Philosophical systems. Ev-
erywhere (where) ordering intervenes, where a law organizes what is
thinkable by oppositions (dual, irreconcilable; or sublatable, dialecti-
cal). And all these pairs of oppositions are *couples*.[26]

Sexual difference considered as the difference between male and
female has helped to organize—or been organized—by all other
pairs of difference. In some languages, sexual difference is tanta-
mount to difference itself ("Vive la différence!"). But although the
"facts of life" have presumably not changed much over time, the
historical conception of those facts has changed a great deal.[27] In
Aristotle's theory of reproduction, for example, woman was only the
formless receptacle, entirely shaped by the generativity of the man.
For Socrates, men and women could coexist because they were
not competing for the same space. He wouldn't have dreamed of
the possibility of falling in love with a woman—men were for that.
Romantic love for a woman—courtly love—was a breakthrough.
Women's value was raised enough that men could fall in love with
them (though both Girard's theory of mimetic desire and Sedg-
wick's reading of heterosexuality "between men" reveal how the
older model shows through). But at first women simply didn't have
enough value to worry about. Helen as the origin of the Trojan war
was like Eve as the origin of sin: somebody had to do it, and if everything bad could be blamed on women, men would look even better.
It is not for nothing that the counterfactual exercise most popular

among the sophists to show their rhetorical skills was the praise of Helen. The "bad" woman was the woman who could start a war, while the "good" woman (Penelope) waited faithfully at home. When seen as different from men, women's *only* function is to represent everything men don't want to attribute to themselves. For purposes of inheriting and owning both property and family names, men stood alone. Indeed, the equation between landed property and family names meant that aristocracy was the same as patriarchy.

Shakespeare offers an interesting twist on the metaphor of artistic creation: his sonnets are often seen these days as exemplifying bisexuality, but it seems to me they stick rather closely to the "men = eroticism, women = procreation" thesis in the beginning, but then the moment art and life begin to compete for the fair young man's posterity, the door is open for art to allow women back in as an aesthetic focus, not merely a biological function. The "one thing to my purpose nothing" initially reserves biological reproduction for heterosexuality and frees the subject to desire, love, write about men. But making texts and making babies do not equivalently produce "copies": the need for women's genes means the son will never be merely created in the image of the father. The question of "copies" that made Socrates nervous is bound to wreak havoc in reproduction as well, although patriarchy functions as if it were possible to forget it. Shakespeare's rhetoric sometimes encompasses the difficulty, but pre-Mendelian biological reproduction did not theorize the role of the mother.

> Mark how one string, sweet husband to another,
> Strikes each in each by mutual ordering;
> Resembling sire, and child, and happy mother,
> Who all in one, one pleasing note do sing;
> Whose speechless song, being many, seeming one,
> Sings this to thee: "Thou single wilt prove none."
>
> —Sonnet 8

With the idea that difference is complementary, many become parts of a whole. Biological reproduction restores unity and succession. Homosexuality is just a supplement. But if it is damned as sterile and as not admitting difference, then whenever there is a lack of unity in the couple—that is to say, *all the time*—the unity it is supposed to preserve breaks down. Two ceases to be equal to one. And the very fact that there are two people in a couple becomes a critique of the unity they are supposed to preserve. In homosexuality, because you do have two people, in fact, without the excuse of complementarity, the impossibility of making two perfectly equal one is fundamental. Homosexuality just makes the falseness of that ideal more inescapable.

Turning back to Shakespeare's sonnets, we see art starting to win over life when the question of how to ensure immortality starts to ally with representation. The depiction of mortality, which both men and women share, seems to be a new form of unity, but the play of the English language that expresses that unity cannot be easily duplicated in another language. Thus the unity is re-produced (universality) in language, but the multiplicity of languages makes that universality in fact not shareable. Baudelaire expresses this relentless fact about temporality when, in his poem "L'Horloge," he says:

> Horloge! dieu sinistre, effrayant, impassible,
> Dont le doigt nous menace et nous dit: "*Souviens-toi!*
> Les vibrantes Douleurs dans ton coeur plein d'effroi
> Se planteront bientôt comme dans une cible;

> "Le Plaisir vaporeux fuira vers l'horizon
> Ainsi qu'une sylphide au fond de la coulisse;
> Chaque instant te dévore un morceau du délice
> A chaque homme accordé pour toute sa saison.

> "Trois mille six cents fois par heure, la Seconde
> Chuchote: *Souviens-toi!*—Rapide, avec sa voix
> D'insecte, Maintenant dit: Je suis Autrefois,
> Et j'ai pompé ta vie avec ma trompe immonde!

> "Remember! Souviens-toi, prodigue! Esto memor!
> (Mon gosier de métal parle toutes les langues.) . . ."

> [Timepiece! frightful, sinister, impassive god,
> Who points at us threateningly and says: "*Remember!*
> The quivering Sorrows will embed themselves
> In your fearful heart as if it were a target;

"Vanishing Pleasure flees toward the horizon
Like a sylphide disappearing in the wings;
Every instant devours a part of the delight
Accorded to a man to last for his entire season.

"Three thousand six hundred times an hour, the Seconds
Whisper: *Remember!*—Swiftly, with its insect voice,
Each Now says: I am Yesteryear,
And I've sucked your life dry with my filthy trunk!

"Souviens-toi! Remember, prodigal! Esto memor!
(My metal throat speaks every language.) . . ."]

Mortality may speak every language, but it finds a way to do so very differently in each. Here, for example, are some of the puns Shakespeare makes to separate biological mortality from art:

my remains—this remains

thou art—my art

few leaves—must leave

lean penury—that pen

use—usury

still (dead)—still (ongoingly)

stay (stop)—stay (remain)

remains (corpse)—remains (stays)

lie (tell an untruth)—lie (recline, rest)

keep (retain)—keep (prevent)

issue (posterity)—issue (publish)

wear (be dressed in)—wear (be used up)

touch (detail)—touch (feel with hand)

line (wrinkle)—line (verse)

prick (embroider)—prick (penis)

true (faithful)—true (truthful)

rite—write

tongue—tongue

"Tongue" means "language" only for certain expressions in English (like "mother tongue"), but for ordinary use there is another word: "language." In French (and Hebrew), the relation is much closer: *langue* (the same word for "language" and "tongue") and *sapha* (the same word for "language" and "lip") are the literal words for "language." In German, again, we have *Zunge* and *Sprache*. Thus, the French or Hebrew translations might find *more* wordplay, not less, on this point than the original. One of the hardest things to translate is the link between language and the body that the original has made, in part through the linguistic resources of the original. In translation, the body is never in exactly the same place.

The father of modern linguistics, Ferdinand de Saussure, considered language as a system in which every speaker was potentially created equal. But Jacques Lacan took Saussure's diagram of the building block of language—the sign—split Saussure's one into two, and changed the sign's referential function. Where Saussure had represented the sign as shown here,

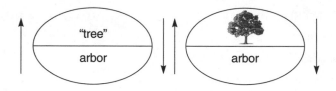

Lacan draws two identical doors and makes them signs of "men" and "women":

LADIES   GENTLEMEN

Thus the signs no longer paint an image of the real, but serve to discipline the reader into sexual difference. Henceforth, the reader is not told what is real; he or she is told where to "go." There are two doors, and every subject has to pick one.

This cultural "translation" of sexual difference means that in all languages that are structured by grammatical gender, gender both is and is not referential. Female entities tend to be feminine and male masculine, but the form of a noun often plays a greater role in its gender than a referential concept of sex. Thus, if abstract nouns are feminine in Latin and the Romance languages derived from it, allegories are female. There are three genders in German, not two; this makes referential sense, but the gender of inanimate objects is masculine or feminine in French. The moon is feminine in French and masculine in German; the sun is masculine in French and feminine in German. Does this have anything to do with French rationalism and German romanticism? In Hebrew, "I love you" has to reveal the genders of the speaker and addressee—no coy hijacking of discourses, therefore, is possible for uses for which they were not intended. Gender is thus somewhat arbitrary in all languages (who would have thought that "girls" were neuter in German?), but that arbitrariness may nevertheless have an unconsciously internalized referential effect.[28]

The concept of sexual difference is fundamental to two of the theories that came out of the late nineteenth century and still have currency today: Marxism and Freudianism. In the post-Mendelian era, when the woman's contribution to biological reproduction could no longer be denied, male dominance had to come up with a new justification for its existence, and it came up with the notion of "separate spheres." The potential competition between the sexes was to be minimized by assigning the woman to the home and the man to the world.

Marx and Freud had to use sexual difference to overcome a different obstacle. The bourgeois revolutions had for the first time theorized equality—political equality for citizens, the absence of inherited privilege, universality, the universal equivalent. "All men are created equal," proclaimed the Declaration of Independence. Coexisting with chattel slavery, such an idea could very well be untrue *in fact,* but its untruth didn't at first inhere in the fact that "all men" didn't stand for "all people." The political problem was NOT inequality—which could go on IN FACT without disrupting the theory, but sexual difference, which was *within* every category of inequality. In France, at least the revolutionaries paid attention to what they were saying and briefly freed slaves, women, Jews—but Napoleon quickly reversed all of that. So if theorists of repression are to represent it as universal—class conflict, civilization as such—they have to find a place for sexual difference that will allow them to get on with it. Marx solved the problem by starting with the sexual division of labor and situating the origin of slavery in the household, but he still acknowledged women's work (women's *labor*) as primarily reproductive. In the workplace, men and women were equivalent. Freud solved the problem by making castration necessary for both sexes—and the concept of castration results directly from the discovery of sexual difference; women thenceforth have to assume it, so that men don't have to.

The placement of sexual difference within a theory of equality is therefore designed to solve a theoretical problem. Then the universality can reappear and remedy something *for everyone*. It was not that sexual difference had not always existed, but that suddenly it became a theoretical *problem*. Given the notions of equality and universality (prerequisites for theory today), where could one put sexual difference? It was a problem that Marx and Freud had to solve before they could go on. One of the things they taught us, in fact, was how to forget sexual difference when they were not thinking about it. Marx forgot quite quickly (and Marxists even more so), but Freud never entirely forgot its effects on the psyche, although those effects could often be described as the same for both sexes. So sexual difference is a problem that must be solved if equality is to work, but because it leaves a residue, it has to be legislated. Marx will see law as preserving bourgeois property and Freud phallic privilege, but both will consider those laws as the source of the damage. Since then, women have won greater and greater legal equality, so that almost all the differences that were maintained by the law have disappeared. At a certain point, sexual difference has stopped mattering legally, which is why gay marriage and sex changes have come to deserve equal rights, and why the Defense of Marriage Act has to reinstitute a legal constraint so that heterosexuality is relegislated. There is no longer a real argument for restricting marriage to one man and one woman, but the defenders of traditional marriage have attempted to invoke God or biology. However, as the example of cloning suggests, science seems to have as its always possible outcome an escaping of sexual difference, not a reinforcement of it, so that what seems like a biological invariant can be gotten around. That, in fact, is one of the aims of science, and perhaps also what makes science seem like a not entirely benign force (Frankenstein: "I thought that I held the corpse of my dead mother in my arms").

What I hope to argue in this book is that the plurality of languages and the plurality of sexes are alike in that they both make the "one" impossible. Two and two thousand are less different than one and two. Rhetorically, though, a certain eloquence depends on one's not thinking about difference. "What does man want?" depends on universality for a rhetorical effect that any qualification curtails ("What does a woman want?" [Freud]; "What does a black man want?" [Fanon]). But at what price do we maintain a rhetoric of universality—with all the appeal that it entails?

TWO

L'Esthétique du Mal

Le Mal—une forme aigüe du Mal—dont elle [la littérature] est
l'expression, a pour nous, je crois, la valeur souveraine.

[Evil—an acute form of Evil—of which literature is the expression, has for
us, I think, the highest value.]

—Georges Bataille, *La Littérature et le Mal*

In 1963, Anne Sexton composed an elegy for Sylvia Plath called
"Sylvia's Death," in which she wrote:

> and I know at the news of your death,
> a terrible taste for it, like salt.[1]

This elegy is unusual in that it expresses not loss but sexual jealousy.
Sylvia's death has awakened an overwhelming appetite and envy, a
terrible taste.

Critics have often accused Anne Sexton of terrible taste, putting
unseemly parts of the female body on display and lusting after death
self-indulgently, even to the point of feeling robbed personally when
someone else commits suicide. But lyric poetry has always been ob-
sessed with death, and I would argue that in seeing Sexton as all
symptom and all body, readers have missed her inventive exploration
of more technical questions of lyric voice. For when she calls Sylvia's
death "an old belonging," something one's mouth opens onto, she
is talking about the way in which death's terrible taste has filled poets' mouths for a long time, like salt.

The fact that the history of lyric poetry is so bound up with the
nature of elegy has created the impression that the lyric was invented
to overcome death, not desire it. Poetry, in this view, acts as a conso-
lation, a monument, a promise of immortality beyond the grave. Yet

even the most traditional elegy contains the guilty secret that desire is not all for life, that poetry offers something other than life as object of desire. From Narcissus in love with an image and Apollo or Petrarch consoling himself with a laurel branch to Keats's "half in love with easeful death," Milton's "Lycidas," or Wordsworth's "Lucy" poems, the mourned person provides an occasion for poetic performance, not just loss. From there to Sexton's "Wanting to Die," the distance is not as great as some would have it.

But the conflation of the desire for writing with the desire for death does not perfectly flow from the fact that both are desires for something other than biological life. It is true that Narcissus dies from loving an image, but the critical theory of the "Death of the Author" was not about literal death but about interpretation and authorial intention. Indeed, it is precisely in the case of an author who has committed suicide that readers who normally restrict their interest to features internal to a text develop a terrible taste for biography as a tool for understanding poetry. Readers are unable to resist asking the poems to tell us why the poet killed herself. The dead author returns to life with a vengeance as the site of an intention to die.

There are two profound taboos threatened when the poet is a woman. There is something monstrous by definition when a woman chooses death over life, because she has so often been the guardian of the life forces, associated with reproduction, comfort, other-directedness, and maternal care. When a woman can in any way be accused of being a "bad mother" (and the grounds for this opinion are not hard to find in Sexton's case), or even of being something other than a counterpart to a man, she is violating the very conditions of her visibility, and is much more likely to be seen as a "bad writer" than to participate in the culturally valued badness that poetry's job is to hold up to the laws of the marketplace—or of reproduction.

The cultural prestige of *le Mal* probably reached its height with Baudelaire's 1857 publication of *Les Fleurs du Mal*. *Le Mal* is notoriously hard to translate into English. Is it "Evil"? "Badness"? "Sickness" ("à Théophile Gautier, je dédie ces fleurs maladives")? "Suffering"? "Melancholy" (spleen)? "Romanticism" *(Mal du siècle)*? But sardonic delight in thumbing one's nose at bourgeois "virtue" was de rigueur for post-revolutionary French poetry. Rimbaud's mother, for example, forbade her son to read the unseemly writings of "M. Hugot" *(sic)*,[2] while parents threatened to withdraw their children from their English class when it was learned that the mild-mannered Monsieur Mallarmé had published poetry.[3] It is perhaps surprising that the Second Empire courts took literally Baudelaire's poetic celebrations of evil and prosecuted him for them. But it is even more surprising how surprised he seemed by this. The rise of the bourgeoisie in France was particularly gender-divided: women stood for virtue, men for badness of every sort. So much so that Baudelaire could exemplify his badness through lesbianism, but could disqualify women completely as readers of his book.

Something of Baudelaire's "badness" is lost, I think, when it is translated by Mallarmé into obscurity alone. Where Baudelaire explained in an unfinished draft of a preface, "Famous poets had long divided up the most flowery realms of poetry. I thought it would be pleasant, and enjoyable precisely to the extent that the task was difficult, to extract *beauty* from *le Mal*." This is a defense of difficulty, too, but not in the same sense as Mallarmé's "I say: a flower! and . . . musically arises . . . that which is absent in all bouquets." Contemporary defenses of difficult writing have gone in the direction of Mallarmé's obscurity rather than Baudelaire's evil. The "death of the author," in fact, is prefigured in Mallarmé's famous statement, "The pure work implies the speaking disappearance of the poet, who yields initiative to words." But this is a death without a corpse, without decay, without worms, without *vers*. Mallarmé makes of death a principle of structure so far-reaching that it has taken the whole twentieth century to understand it. Nevertheless, while making death infiltrate every aspect of signification, Mallarmé is also in some way repressing it, and repressing the badness that no principle can eliminate.

That badness returns, paradoxically, not in the defenses but in the attacks on "bad writing" that have often accompanied obscurity. A sense of such contests at the end of the nineteenth century can be gleaned from Mallarmé's testy defense in his essay "Mystery in Letters":

De pures prérogatives seraient, cette fois, à la merci des bas farceurs.

Tout écrit, extérieurement à son trésor, doit, par égard envers ceux dont il emprunte, après tout, pour un objet autre, le langage, présenter, avec les mots, un sens même indifférent: on gagne de détourner l'oisif, charmé que rien ne l'y concerne, à première vue.

Salut, exact, de part et d'autre—

Si, tout de même, n'inquiétait je ne sais quel miroitement, en dessous, peu séparable de la surface concédée à la rétine—il attire le soupçon: les malins, entre le public, réclamant de couper court, opinent, avec sérieux, que, juste, la teneur est inintelligible.

Malheur ridiculement à qui tombe sous le coup, il est enveloppé dans une plaisanterie immense et médiocre: ainsi toujours—pas tant, peut-être, que ne sévit avec ensemble et excès, maintenant, le fléau.

Il doit y avoir quelque chose d'occulte au fond de tous, je crois décidément à quelque chose d'abscons, signifiant fermé et caché, qui habite le commun: car, sitôt cette masse jetée vers quelque trace que c'est une réalité, existant, par exemple, sur une feuille de papier, dans tel écrit—pas en soi—cela qui est obscur: elle s'agite, ouragan jaloux d'attribuer les ténèbres à quoi que ce soit, profusément, flagramment.

Sa crédulité vis-à-vis de plusieurs qui la soulagent, en faisant affaire, bondit à l'excès: et le suppôt d'Ombre, d'eux désigné, ne placera un mot, dorénavant, qu'avec un secouement que ç'ait été elle, l'énigme, elle ne tranche, par un coup d'éventail de ses jupes: "Comprends pas!"—l'innocent annonçât-il se moucher.[4]

[Pure prerogatives would be, this time, at the mercy of low jokers. / Every piece of writing, outside of its treasure, must, toward those from whom it borrows, after all, for a different object, language, present, with words, a sense even indifferent: one gains by not attracting the idler, charmed that nothing there concerns him, at first sight. / Each side gets exactly what it wants— / If, nevertheless, anxiety is stirred by I don't know what shadowy reflection hardly separable from the surface available to the retina—it attracts suspicion: the pundits among the public, averring that this has to be stopped, opine, with due *gravitas,* that, truly, the tenor is unintelligible. / Ridiculously cursed is he who is caught up in this, enveloped by an immense and mediocre joke: it was ever thus—but perhaps not with the intensity with which the plague now extends its ravages. / There must be something occult deep inside everyone, decidedly I believe in something opaque, a signifier sealed and hidden, that inhabits common man: for, as soon as the masses throw themselves toward some trace that has its reality, for example, on a piece of paper, it's in the writing—not in oneself—that there is something obscure: they stir crazily like a hurricane, jealous to attribute darkness to anything, profusely, flagrantly. / Their credulity, fostered by those who reassure it and market it, is suddenly startled: and the agent of darkness, singled out by them, can't say a single word thenceforth, without, a shrug indicating that it's just that enigma again, being cut off, with a flourish of skirts: "Don't understand!"— the poor author innocently announcing, perhaps, that he needed to blow his nose.]

I have permitted myself this extensive quotation because I think it touches on most of the things that come up when one tries to defend obscurity: the division between the crowd and the writer, the crowd's refusal to think there could be obscurity inside everyone, the scapegoating of anyone who suggests otherwise and the paranoid vigilance about it, the accusation that incomprehensible writing is the cause of incomprehension. But the real mystery is why "I don't understand it" should condemn the *author* rather than the *reader.* Or at least, as Mallarmé goes on to say, should not amount to a suspension of judgment:

> Je sais, de fait, qu'ils se poussent en scène et assument, à la parade, eux, la posture humiliante; puisque arguer d'obscurité—ou, nul ne saisira s'ils ne saisissent et ils ne saisissent pas—implique un renoncement antérieur à juger.[5]
>
> [I know, in fact, that they crowd the stage and expose themselves, actually, in a humiliating posture; since to argue that something is obscure—or, no one will get it if they don't, and they don't—implies a prior suspension of judgment.]

It has become commonplace to allow difficult or transgressive writing to *authors,* but not to *critics.* Poetic badness and critical obscurity seem very different, but the condemnation of any writer for obscurity is itself colored with moral indignation. "Don't understand!"

becomes an accusation. When what was initially condemned enters into the canon, we can smile with superiority at Rimbaud's mother or Baudelaire's and be amazed at their blindness to poetic genius. Yet in the very act of inventing obscure poetry, Mallarmé invented the "poème critique." In other words, it was when he realized that the writer and the reader could no longer be disentangled that Mallarmé became Mallarmé.

The taint of moral unseemliness does not last forever, but literature nevertheless keeps enough of that initial *frisson* to give literary studies a somewhat bad conscience. As Peter Brooks put it:

> We teachers of literature have little hard information to impart, we're not even sure what we teach, and we have something of a bad conscience about the whole business.[6]

Brooks's remarks come in the context of a defense of studying literature as a specific object. It was written for a fascinating compilation of reports and responses published in 1995 as *Comparative Literature in the Age of Multiculturalism,* in which it is suggested that literature be considered "one discursive practice among many others."[7] Comparative literature, it seems, threatens to dissolve into "cultural studies," seen as the triumph of, as Baudelaire would put it, "bonnes actions" over "beau langage." In fact, none of these slippery slopes is unavoidable, but the best way of making sure that literature doesn't dissolve is precisely to keep that "bad conscience."

Comparative literature as a field seems to need to defend itself against the Scylla of "theory" and the Charybdis of "translation." Although many writers recognize the necessary and irreversible changes each has contributed to the field, they lament the day when comparative literature meant reading several languages and literary traditions in the original. Yet their guilt about "elitism" or "Eurocentrism" leads them to overlook some obvious defenses that no one calls up. They mount, with increasing feebleness, what might be called a "Protestant" defense of multiple languages: it is hard to learn a language; therefore students who learn more than one have to make more effort and be more talented. Here is how Harry Levin, author of the first report in 1965, put it:

> If we profess to cover more ground than our sister departments we
> should honestly acknowledge that we must work harder, nor should we
> incur their suspicion by offering short-cuts.[8]

This is true only to the extent that languages can be learned only in
school. The decline of language teaching therefore makes this way of
learning languages even harder. But instead of merely failing to teach
languages, the public school system actually *discourages* the use of
any language other than English. Education consists, then, of *un-
learning* languages, not learning them. Before becoming an elite capable of mastering several languages, children must first pass into the
elite of people who speak only English. The number of languages
spoken in American homes is everything a dream of multiculturalism
could ask for: it is not an idea, it is a reality. If comparative literature
could tap into *that* multiculturalism, however, it would tap into the
true obscurities and insolubilities of a world that cannot be studied
as an object. Every comparatist would already be a part of it.

The "good" object, multiculturalism, would present all the dilem-
mas of the modern world that its idealization—the "It's a small
world after all" refrain—represses. But the "bad" objects, theory and
translation, are actually two versions of the same unrepression. It is
not just that theory involved a mad impetus to translation, but that
the theory that transformed literary studies utterly transformed the
practice of translation. Translating Derrida or Lacan became an art
in itself, and respect for specific effects sometimes became so great
that more and more words were left in the original and glossed.
Thus, more and more French, Greek, or German words began to
have currency in theoretical discourse, which, in turn, increased the
anger of beginning readers frustrated by what felt like unnecessary
impotence to the point that they felt like slamming down the book,
snarling something like, "Take your *Nachträglichkeit* and shove it!"

In 1959, it was still possible to write, as did a translator of Hegel's
Encyclopedia:

> To translate the world's worst stylist literally, sentence by sentence, is
> possible—it has been done—but it is perfectly pointless; the transla-
> tion, then, is every bit as unintelligible as the original. But the world's
> worst stylist is, alas, also one of the world's greatest thinkers, certainly

the most important for us in this twentieth century. In the whole history of philosophy there is no other single work that can hold a candle to his *Logic;* a work incomparable in its range, depth, clarity of thought, and beauty of composition—but it must be decoded.

The attempt must be risked, therefore, to rescue its grandeur from its abstruse linguistic chaos. . . . This is like detective work: what Hegel means, but hides under a dead heap of abstractions, must be guessed at and ferreted out. I have dared to translate—not the ponderous Hegelian jargon, which is as little German as it would be English—but the thought. My "translation," then, is a critical presentation or rendition; it is not a book about Hegel because it faithfully follows the order and sequence of his paragraphs.[9]

After the theory revolution, it is no longer possible so serenely to separate style from thinking, idea from language, thought from jargon. The understanding that thought is not separable from its expression—and in that way sometimes escapes the control of the author himself—is what deconstruction found within the structuralism that claimed a panoptic view of meaning making. "As little German as it would be English" indicates that the original is worth translating precisely because it is foreign to its *own* language. When Mallarmé contributed a series of his "poèmes critiques" without translation to W. H. Henley's journal *The National Observer,* a letter from a reader protested that, while he was ready to accept the anomaly in order to brush up on his French, Mallarmé was writing in a language that was "as little French as it would have been English."[10] Poetry, for Mallarmé, was that which "de plusieurs vocables refait un mot total, neuf, *étranger à la langue*" [out of several syllables remakes a total new word, *foreign to the language*].[11] For Walter Benjamin, too, translation was "only a somewhat provisional way of coming to grips with the foreignness of languages." Only through translation does the work's foreignness to *its own* language become apparent.

If deconstruction is what is often meant by "theory," whether for good or ill, no one could insist more on going back to the original language than Jacques Derrida. His essay on Plato discovers in the word *pharmakon* an undecidability that all translators—and therefore all Platonisms—have assumed was a decidability. The divide between "poison" and "remedy" occurs *in translation*. It is not, however, that such inadequate translations could be avoided if one stayed with the original. It is that an actual history, shaped by a decision that the translators could not choose not to make, makes the original perceptible as resisting it. As Derrida tells his Japanese translator, "The question of deconstruction is also through and through *the* question of translation."[12]

The worry about translation is, of course, always a worry about *bad* translation ("the inaccurate transmission of an inessential content," as Benjamin puts it). But the suspicion is that what is essential about a literary work is precisely what is *always* lost in translation, which is why so many poets have been so intent on *finding* it. That is perhaps why both Baudelaire and Mallarmé wanted to translate the quintessential bad poet of American literature, Edgar Allan Poe. And this takes us back to the badness of literature.

Some time ago, when I came across a reference to one of my colleagues in the *Boston Globe* as a professor of "comparable literature" (October 20, 2000, p. B4), I realized that the field itself is oddly named. Why *isn't* it called "comparable literature," in fact? Doesn't the classic version of the field assume that you can take, say, Romanticism, and compare its French, German, and English versions, which are presumed to be comparable? What does "comparative literature" really mean? That what is studied is comparatively (but not absolutely) literary? Perhaps—but could this have been the original intent? The field that depends on comparison for its very definition somehow at the same time opposes some sort of resistance to comparability. Just enough to echo the irony in the story of Elena Levin explaining to someone why her husband, Harry, author of the 1965 report, was busy working: "The Professors are here to compare the literatures." It is as if the field defined by comparison unconsciously upholds the adage "Comparaison n'est pas raison," or agrees with William Blake when, in his poem *Jerusalem,* he has his hero Los howl:

> I must Create a System, or be enslav'd by another Mans
> I will not Reason & Compare: my business is to Create.[13]

To explore this odd resistance to comparison, I turn to three more texts that each embody some form of "bad writing": popular culture, philosophy, and teaching manuals. My three texts are: the 1995 film *Clueless*,[14] H. Vaihinger's book *The Philosophy of "As If"* (first published in German in 1911),[15] and Andrew Boyd's *Life's Little Deconstruction Book* (1999; billed by the publisher, W. W. Norton, as "Po-Mo to Go").

In the film *Clueless,* the exclamation "As if!" is used by the protagonist, fifteen-year-old Beverly Hills high school student Cher Horowitz, to project the frame of reference of another person into pure fantasy—theirs—and to expel it from herself. For example, when an unprepossessing high school boy approaches Cher in an interested manner, she says, "Ew! get away from me! *As if!*" In other words, "*As if* I would go out with you!" "In your dreams!" "You wish!" When another boy, Elton, reveals that he is interested in *her,* not in the new girl, Tai, with whom she has been trying to fix him up (this is one of the few places where Jane Austen's *Emma* is recognizable as a source), Cher exclaims, "Me? *As if!* Don't you mean Tai?" In other words, "*As if* I had been flirting with you for myself!" "*As if* I had been the object rather than the subject!" Another example: when Cher reports that her teacher has said that her arguments are unresearched, unstructured, and unconvincing, she exclaims, *"As if!"* which I guess means, "Who is *he* to say such a thing?"

The Beverly Hills high school dialect in the film thus makes use of the expression "as if" in an interpersonal sense. It is always an exclamation, and always casts desire or doubt away from the speaker and onto the addressee. I don't have time to do a reading of the film as a rhetorical treatise, but as a study of substitution, transformation (the makeover), and the narcissism of small differences, it would lend itself very well to such treatment.

For Hans Vaihinger, "as if" is an essential mental function enabling people to use fictions *as if* they were true: religions, philosophies, even mathematical constructs. As he writes in the preface to the English edition, "An idea whose theoretical untruth or incorrectness, and therewith its falsity, is admitted, is not for that reason practically valueless and useless; for such an idea, in spite of its theoretical nullity, may have great practical importance" (viii). Kant's *Ding an sich,* for example, which can't be proved, is a necessary part of his philosophical system, just as imaginary numbers operate as a necessary part of a system of calculations, even though, in the end, they don't exist.

Life's Little Deconstruction Book is organized as a series of maxims. There are 365 of them—one for every day of the year (I'm not sure what the reader is supposed to do during a leap year). Maxim 33 reads: "Be as if." I guess that must mean something like, "Ontology is performance" or "Whatever you seem to have in your mind *is* your mind." Or, as Pascal might have put it, "Act *as if* you believe, and belief will follow, or at least you will have gained everything that you would have gained by believing."

Teaching theory, I come up again and again unexpectedly against the problem of belief. In literature I can suspend disbelief, but in theory I feel as if my location with respect to other writers and thinkers is somehow the stuff of the course. Because the writers I am teaching have designs on the most fundamental assumptions I make while I read, I cannot teach them as if they were a subject matter. At the same time, my own relation to the writers has changed over time, and has changed with respect to that of my students. What is different about teaching theory for me now is the sense of my own historicity. Yet if I look at the theory I teach exclusively from the outside, I am not teaching theory, but history. There would certainly be usefulness in teaching the history of theory, but it would not give access to the "Aha!" that ignites an interest in theory in the first place. When Frantz Fanon says about his reaction to Sartre's reading of Aimé Césaire's poetics of Negritude, "I needed *not* to think I was just a minor term in a dialectic," he is saying, in effect, I needed to read *as if* I believed in the Negritude I now take a distance from, in order to get to the next stage in my thinking. *As if* is something that cannot happen right if it happens in the mode of *as if.*

I have found that the way in which students dismiss or take distance from the texts we read in a theory course follows patterns that are quite different from critiques. And that perhaps was true of my own dismissals of their predecessors. But my task is to make sure the students actually *read* whatever is on the syllabus—which may now include some of those predecessors I am reading for the first time. "Bracketing the referent" and "preferring *langue* to *parole*" are important ways of seeing the limitations of Saussure, but they help only in understanding what Saussure *didn't* do, not what he *did* do—not what those limits *enabled* but only what they prevented. Understanding the conceptual breakthrough involved in saying, "In language there are only differences" depends on pausing there long enough (recall Cher's reaction to stop signs—"I totally paused") to see *what Saussure was critiquing himself.* Thought as a *break* is different from thought as a *chain.*

The same is true for elements of a theory—say, female sexuality in Freud—from which one knows one has taken a critical distance, or elements in a theory—say, ethnocentrism in Levi-Strauss—where one may be critical of a framework of which one is nevertheless still a part. What has been called "political correctness" is something I would prefer to call "double consciousness"—the knowledge that one is viewed, not just viewing. W. E. B. Du Bois defined double consciousness, famously, as "the sense of always looking at one's self through the eyes of others, of measuring one's soul by the tape of a world."[16] The strength of those "others" produces double consciousness. But how can white double consciousness or male double consciousness or Eurocentric double consciousness be anything but reactive and defensive, if the power of those "others" is itself what consciousness was defined against? Double consciousness would feel a lot like paranoia. No wonder people might attempt to eradicate it. But in this case, as they say, even paranoids have real enemies. Or perhaps we should say that denying paranoia doesn't make those "real others" go away. What does the necessity of double consciousness have to do with the question of teaching *as if* one believed?

The dangers of representativeness and tokenism are precisely the dangers of losing the "foreignness" of texts to their *own* languages. But to fear such a danger is to forget that what should happen in literature courses is *reading*. Yes, the changes might reflect an unquestioned notion of individualism. And yes, the students will not see that from which a syllabus is departing. But surely the students have imbibed cultural assumptions that will be defamiliarized by some of the texts. Perhaps the use of tokens or of islands of knowledge in a sea of ignorance can homogenize all differences into various versions of the same. But even when something like colonialism attempted to reproduce itself in, say, the Caribbean, it became something quite different from what it started out to be. At the same time, how could a syllabus mark radical change within a culture—and an educational system—that changes much more slowly? If the remedy mirrors the system being questioned rather than the questioning, at least the cognitive dissonance that these contradictory energies embody may correspond to a real conflict in the world rather than the wishful thinking that would seek a more effective critique.

Actually taking seriously the works being read has to become transformative eventually, because what is secondary revision for one generation may become primary process for the next. The very transferential process that tends to absolutize the authority of a text (as if it had always been on the syllabus) will de-absolutize the assumptions that are still operative in the teachers who have put those books on the syllabus. On the one hand, if the map isn't being changed in the primary process of thinking, changing it in a secondary revision is not really *thought*. But on the other hand, acting *as if* the map were changing might actually make it so, in the long run.

How does the structure of the *as if* function, then, allow for a heuristic transference and for a transformative double consciousness at once, even though these two processes draw on the contradictory energies of belief, critique, and defense? Let me end with a quotation from Joan Copjec's book *Read My Desire*, in which a structure she actually designates as "as if" is understood through, and clarifies, the Lacanian notion of "suture":

> Suture, in brief, supplies the logic of a paradoxical function whereby a supplementary element is *added* to the series of signifiers in order to mark the *lack* of a signifier that could close the set. The endless slide of signifiers (hence deferral of sense) is brought to a halt and allowed to function "as if" it were a closed set through the inclusion of an element that acknowledges the impossibility of closure. The very designation of the limit is constitutive of the group, the reality the signifiers come to

represent, though the group, or the reality, can no longer be thought to be entirely representable.[17]

What I want to claim here is that it is precisely comparative literature's role—always risking a certain "badness"—to be this suture. It is the field whose only definition is to be the acknowledgment of the impossibility of the field; to be the "as if" of literary closure. Comparative literature, in other words, is what is *added* to the series of literary signifiers in order to mark the *lack* of a signifier that could close the set. It marks not the *future* of literary studies but the *suture* of literary studies. That is the best way we have of relying on the badness of strangers.

THREE

The Task of the Translator

> For if the sentence is the wall before the language of the original, literalness is the arcade.
>
> —Walter Benjamin, "The Task of the Translator"

I. *"Tableaux Parisiens"*

Why did Walter Benjamin translate Charles Baudelaire? And why did Benjamin begin with just the "Tableaux Parisiens," the section Baudelaire added to *Les Fleurs du Mal* after the courts forced him to remove six poems out of the original hundred? Baudelaire's post-trial (post-traumatic?) poems fit Benjamin's later preoccupation with Paris and with modernity, but they had not at the time begun to inspire the thoughts to which Benjamin would later return. And why has Benjamin's prefatory essay, "The Task of the Translator," become so famous without any discussion—either by Benjamin or by his readers—of the poet to whose work this essay served as an introduction? It seems as though Baudelaire were only a pretext for Benjamin to indulge in—and speculate about—translation itself.

Baudelaire is first mentioned in Benjamin's correspondence in early 1915, between the time of his friend Fritz Heinle's suicide and Benjamin's break with the mentor of his youth, Gustav Wyneken. Both events were occasioned by the First World War, which put an abrupt end to Benjamin's childhood idealism—as well as to the illusions of a whole generation of Europeans. Wanting to establish a relation to literature that would decisively break with the attachments of the past, Benjamin turned his back on the conception of literature most congenial to him, which was identifiably propagated by the circle around Stefan George. For them, the poet was a seer, an aristocrat of the spirit, a voice crying out against the evils of the marketplace and the degradations of modern life. Benjamin seemed to need to renounce the self-satisfactions of such an elite and visionary company in order to grapple *literarily* with what was actually happening.

For Baudelaire, though, translation had come early: about a year after his own suicide attempt and before the revolution of 1848 (and almost ten years before the publication of *Les Fleurs du Mal*), he discovered Edgar Allan Poe with "a strange sort of shock."[1] Baudelaire's Poe translations were the most lucrative of his publications, thus at once calming (a bit) his excruciating debt anxiety, opening up the world of a misunderstood *semblable,* and, perhaps, revealing something that only translation could teach. Stéphane Mallarmé, powerfully affected by Baudelaire, went so far as to learn English in order to read Poe, and ended up enslaved to the profession of high school English teacher for the rest of his life. Along the way, he translated the poems that Baudelaire had not touched. Benjamin, too, when he approached translating Baudelaire, had just broken with his parents and needed to earn a living. The relation between translation and the marketplace deserves further study, especially when the marketplace is being resisted or failed at by modes of writing that remain—intentionally or not—unsalable in their mother tongue.

The most aesthetically successful translation—one of many—of Baudelaire's *Flowers of Evil* into German was already in its sixth edition by the time Benjamin published his "Tableaux Parisiens" in 1922. It was written—of course—by Stefan George. Benjamin had owned George's *Die Blumen des Bösen* since 1918. It seems likely, therefore, that Benjamin first turned to Baudelaire in order to make his break with George on George's own turf. What Benjamin didn't know then was how many times Baudelaire would also occasion his breaks with *himself.* But why was *translation* the ground on which the early battle was fought?[2] Could it have been otherwise?

In a note on Baudelaire written in 1921 or 1922—and thus contemporaneous with his translations—Benjamin differentiates himself from his illustrious precursor:

> *Spleen et idéal.* Because of the abundance of connotations in this title, it is not translatable. Each of the two words on its own contains a double meaning. Both *spleen* and *idéal* are not just spiritual essences but also

an intended effect upon them, as is expressed in [Stefan] George's translation *Trübsinn und Vergeistigung* [Melancholy and Spiritualization]. But they do not express only that intended effect; in particular, the sense of a radiant and triumphant spirituality—such as is evoked in the sonnet "L'Aube spirituelle," among many others—is not rendered adequately by *Vergeistigung. Spleen,* too, even when understood merely as intended effect, not as archetypal image, is more than *Trübsinn.* Or rather, it is *Trübsinn* only in the final analysis: first and foremost, it is that fatally foundering, doomed flight toward the ideal, which ultimately—with the despairing cry of Icarus—comes crashing down into the ocean of its own melancholy. In both the oldest and the most recent foreign word in his language, Baudelaire indicates the share of time and eternity in these two extreme realms of the spirit. And doesn't this ambiguous title also imply that archetypal image and intended effect are mysteriously intertwined? Doesn't the title mean that it is the melancholic above all whose gaze is fixed on the ideal, and that it is the images of melancholy that kindle the spiritual most brightly?[3]

Spleen et idéal is the name of the opening section of *Les Fleurs du Mal,* a section that Benjamin did *not* translate. Later, however, he did translate the introductory poem to the volume "Au lecteur," which George had pointedly excluded from it. Arguing that Baudelaire's fascination with disgusting things was no longer shared by those who took his work seriously, George explained in the foreword to his translation that

> es bedarf heute wohl kaum noch eines hinweises dass nicht die abschreckenden und widrigen bilder die den Meister eine zeit lang verlochten ihm die grosse verehrung des ganzen jüngeren geschlechtes eingetragen haben sondern der eifer mit dem er der dichtung neue gebiete eroberte und die glühende geistigkeit mit der er auch die sprödesten stoffe durchdrang. so ist dem sinne nach "SEGEN" das einleitungsgedicht der BLUMEN DES BÖSEN und nicht das fälschlich "VORREDE" genannte. mit diesem verehrungsbeweis möge weniger eine getreue nachbildung als ein deutsches denkmal geschaffen sein.[4]

"Bénédiction" was a far more appropriate poem to begin the volume than any prefatory poem would be. The elimination of "Au lecteur" and the opening provided by "Bénédiction" place the center of gravity of the volume for George in the realm of transcendental other-worldly poetic justice rather than in a relation to the things of this world. Baudelaire's originality—the appeal of the things that disgust us the most—becomes for George an indictment of the world from which the poet longs to escape, not an indictment of the perversity of the will of the poet. This is why George has no use for images that evoke the specificity of the modern world. Contrasting Benjamin's translation of "Paysage" with George's, Momme Brodersen writes:

> The city, which is the focal point of the "Tableaux Parisiens" cycle, does not appear in George's translations, or is not recognizable as such. He archaizes "Les tuyaux, les clochers, ces mâts de la cité" to become "Den rauchfang den turm und die wolken weit" [The chimney, the tower, and the clouds afar]: the city is simply avoided, so that its specific profile melts into the physiognomy of a rural centre in this German version. How differently this reads in Benjamin's "Auf Turm und Schlot, die Masten von Paris" [To the tower and smokestack, the masts of Paris]![5]

George "translates" into "poetic language" what in Baudelaire breaks out of it. All the things the "poetic" avoids—industry, social unrest, technology—become materials for Baudelaire not *in spite of* their unpoeticness but *because of it*.

But in the act of crisping the edges of Baudelaire's city, Benjamin also solidifies the beings in it. George's soft focus, on the other hand, is sensitive to fleeting images and to the quality of subjective perception per se, not simply to what is perceived. A comparison of the translations of "A une passante" is instructive. This is a poem that will later become so central to Benjamin's reading of Baudelaire that, in the Baudelaire book, he quotes it in its entirety—not once but twice. It is even arguable that the title *Passagen Werk* is a reminiscence of that poem. The word *pas* in French, from which all these words are derived, means "step"—but it also means "not." There is thus a floating negation over "passing" that may or may not have an effect. The description of "love at last sight"[6] in "A une passante" exemplifies for Benjamin Baudelaire's intense but circumscribed capacity for loving and looking. It is somewhat surprising, then, that here Benjamin translates the title as "Einer Dame" [To a Lady], thus missing all the nuances that would later form his theory of modernity. George, in contrast, translates it as "Einer Vorübergehenden" [To a Passing Woman], which preserves the structure of substantivising a feminine noun out of an adjective of fleetingness. The grammatical crystallization duplicates the sudden appearance of the woman in the crowd. She precipitates out from the supersaturated solution of the poet's expectations.

Even a quick glance at George's translation of Baudelaire reveals how anomalous his German is. Instead of the usual punctuation, he scans the poems with floating dots that seem to function like breaths. He does not capitalize nouns the way German usually does; in fact he doesn't capitalize the first word of a sentence, which is not always a sentence. He reserves capitals only for the beginnings of lines of poetry and for special meanings: the word "Master" in his preface or, in "Bénédiction," the words "Gott" [God], "Enterbte" [Disinherited One], "Kräfte" [Strengths], "Mächte" [Powers], "Thronen" [Thrones], "Schmerz" [Pain], "Palmyren" [Palmyra], and "Strahlenherd" [Hearth of Rays]. Most of these words—*but not all*—had been capitalized by Baudelaire. "Strahlenherd," in particular, capitalized and modified by "heiligen" [holy], heightens the sacredness of the poet's consecration. Baudelaire says that the rays are "Puisée au foyer saint des rayons primitifs" [Drawn from the sacred hearth of primal rays]. This is precisely the halo that the prose writer Baudelaire will drop in the mud and then *not* go to look for in the lost and found. At the end of "Some Motifs in Baudelaire," Benjamin quotes almost the whole of the prose poem "Perte d'auréole" to mark how far from his transcendental origins Baudelaire had come.

Benjamin did not at all follow George's lead in idiosyncratic German, but that is far from implying that capitalization was not an issue for him. Because capitalization in French is a traditional sign of allegory, Benjamin was very attentive to Baudelaire's use of capital letters. "One must make one's way through *Les Fleurs du Mal* with a sense for how things are raised to allegory," he writes in his *Arcades Project*. "The use of uppercase lettering should be followed carefully."[7] This is what normally becomes impossible in German: by capitalizing all nouns, German loses the capacity to distinguish between the allegorical and the nonallegorical. It was perhaps an over-sensitivity to such loss that led George to experiment with capitalization. In the poem "Le cygne," where Baudelaire says, "tout pour moi devient allégorie" [everything for me becomes allegory], the word Baudelaire capitalizes is "Travail" [Work]. This is not just any word. Emblazoned on the gates of concentration camps ("Arbeit macht frei"), it was a perversion of the central concept of Marxism ("Workers of the world, unite!"); that is, the most material and least figurative of human activities. The capital letter thus, in a sense, allegorizes the unallegorizable. If Work is awakening ("le Travail s'éveille"), this also has everything to do with the "travaux" of modern Paris—including the construction work that totally transformed the city under the direction of Baron Georges Eugène Haussmann. Haussmann himself, it seems, made liberal use of capitalization. Benjamin quotes from an article of 1882 about Haussmann's *Mémoires:*

> He [Haussmann] demolished some *quartiers*—one might say, entire towns. There were cries that he would bring on the plague; he tolerated such outcries and gave us instead—through his well-considered architectural breakthroughs—air, health, and life. Sometimes it was a Street that he created, sometimes an Avenue or Boulevard; sometimes it was a Square, a Public Garden, a Promenade. He established Hospitals, Schools, Campuses. He gave us a whole river. He dug magnificent sewers. (*Mémoire du Baron Haussmann*, volume 2 [Paris, 1890], pp. x, xi. Extracts from an article by Jules Simon in *Le Gaulois*, May 1882.)

And Benjamin goes on to note: "The numerous capital letters appear to be a characteristic orthographic intervention by Haussmann."[8]

The title Benjamin envisaged for his work on Baudelaire appears to fluctuate between *Charles Baudelaire: A Lyric Poet in the Era of High Capitalism* and *Paris: The Capital of the Nineteenth Century.* Is this double sense of the word "capital" a mere coincidence? Are the two senses of the word related thematically as well as verbally? Are they similar to the two senses of the word "revolution" in the titles of the two leading surrealist journals (*The Surrealist Revolution* and

Surrealism in the Service of the Revolution)? In other words, can these two seemingly unrelated senses of "capital" tell us something about connections we might not otherwise look for?

These two senses of "capital"—the economic basis of capitalism and the main city of a state—are both etymologically related to the Latin word for "head": *caput.* With the French Revolution, the head of the old regime was literally decapitated, but the two senses of "capital" rushed in to fill the void. The city and the market were the seats of power in the modern world. But exactly what does the "head" have to do with it? In some way, Benjamin treated as a genuine unknown the question of where the "head" is in modernity. This is partly a question of where power, control, and centrality are located, but it is also related to the unsettling place of the head in general. A head cannot appear in Benjamin without quickly turning into a skull. The death's head does not result from the event of death alone: mortality grins out in the midst of the liveliest images. In his *Origin of German Tragic Drama*, Benjamin famously sums up the relation between death and meaning:

> Whereas in the symbol destruction is idealized and the transfigured face of nature is fleetingly revealed in the light of redemption, in allegory the observer is confronted with the *facies hippocratica* of history as a petrified, primordial landscape. Everything about history that, from the very beginning, has been untimely, sorrowful, unsuccessful, is expressed in a face—or rather in a death's head. And although such a thing lacks all "symbolic" freedom of expression, all classical proportion, all humanity—nevertheless, this is the form in which man's subjection to nature is most obvious and it significantly gives rise not only to the enigmatic question of the nature of human existence as such, but also of the biographical historicity of the individual. This is the heart of the allegorical way of seeing, of the baroque, secular explanation of history as the Passion of the world; its importance resides solely in the stations of its decline. The greater the significance, the greater the subjection to death, because death digs most deeply the jagged line of demarcation between physical nature and significance.[9]

But what does death have to do with economics and topography? The corpse seems to come from a completely different universe from the workman or the citizen. Perhaps Benjamin's study of Baudelaire was an attempt to link the two. Baudelaire is, after all, the author of "Une charogne."

II. Let There Be Light

> God said: Let there be light! And there was light. God saw the light: that it was good. God separated the light from the darkness. God called the light: Day! and the darkness he called: Night!
>
> —Genesis 1:3–5, The Schocken Bible

It is perhaps time to turn to "The Task of the Translator" in order to shed some light—or perhaps some darkness—upon these questions. The only marked French presence in the preface—which, as we noted, does not mention Baudelaire—is an untranslated sentence by Mallarmé. The fact that the French sentence remains untranslated in a German edition presumably meant for people who don't read French is itself bizarre. In the German edition of the *Collected Works,* there is no footnote. In English, the sentence is translated (in a footnote) as follows:

> The imperfection of languages consists in their plurality; the supreme language is lacking: thinking is writing without accessories or even whispering, the immortal word still remains silent; the diversity of idioms on earth prevents anyone from uttering the words which otherwise, at a single stroke, would materialize as truth.[10]

Benjamin cuts the quotation off here, leaving the reader to desire the supreme, but lacking, language that would be the material truth. The counterfactual conditional—if the diversity of languages didn't prevent it, the supreme language *would be* the truth—establishes the image of a language just out of reach, but therefore *almost grasped.* Mallarmé, however, continues with two important qualifications to this true language: first, if it existed there would be no need for poetry; second, the *lack* of correspondence between sound and sense is what makes us believe in the possibility of their harmony.

> Les langues imparfaites en cela que plusieurs, manque la suprême: penser étant écrire sans accessoires, ni chuchotement mais tacite encore l'immortelle parole, la diversité, sur terre, des idiomes empêche personne de proférer les mots qui, sinon se trouverait, par une frappe

unique, elle-même matériellement la vérité. Cette prohibition sévit ex-
presse, dans la nature (on s'y bute avec un sourire) que ne vaille de raison pour se considérer Dieu; mais, sur l'heure, tourné à de l'esthétique, mon sens regrette que le discours défaille à exprimer les objets
par des touches y répondant en coloris ou en allure, lesquelles existent
dans l'instrument de la voix, parmi les langages et quelquefois chez un.
A côté d'*ombre*, opaque, *ténèbres* se fonce peu; quelle déception, devant
la perversité conférant à *jour* comme à *nuit*, contradictoirement, des
timbres obscur ici, là clair. Le souhait d'un terme de splendeur brillant,
ou qu'il s'éteigne, inverse; quant à des alternatives lumineuses sim-
ples—*Seulement*, sachons *n'existerait pas le vers:* lui, philosophiquement rémunère le défaut des langues, complément supérieur.[11]

[Languages imperfect insofar as they are many, the supreme one is
lacking: thought considered as writing without accessories, not even
whispers, still *stills* immortal speech; the diversity, on earth, of idioms prevents anyone from proffering words that would otherwise be,
struck uniquely, the material truth. This prohibition is explicitly devas-
tating, in nature (one bumps up against it with a smile) where nothing leads one to take oneself for God; but, at times, turned to aesthet-
ics, my own sense regrets that discourse fails to express objects by
touches corresponding to them in shading or bearing, since they do
exist among the many languages and sometimes in one. Beside *ombre*
|shade|, which is opaque, *ténèbres* |shadows| is not very dark; what
a disappointment, in front of the perversity that makes *jour* |day|
and *nuit* |night|, contradictorily, sound dark in the former and light
in the latter. Hope for a resplendent word glowing, or being snuffed,
inversely; so far as simple luminous alternatives are concerned—*Only*,
be aware that *verse would not exist:* |I|it, philosophically makes up
for languages' deficiencies, as a superior supplement.] (Translation
mine)

Mallarmé explicitly equates the missing language with the language of God; or rather, he reminds us that here, on earth, nature
gives us no reason to take ourselves for the Creator. What stands in
the way is a prohibition, not just an impossibility. An angel blocks
the way back. This implies that the original language—both Genesis and John begin with "In the beginning . . ."—*was* the material truth. God's language disappeared with the multiplicity of lan-

guages. The story we tell about that fall into diversity is the story of the Tower of Babel. Diversity itself is a sign of sin. Before the fall, there was unity. Adam named the animals in such a God-language. The animals got names before languages became plural. This implies that the original language was perfectly referential. God was perfect reference. In fact, God created by naming: "Let there be . . ." and "He called." Then he gave the power to name to his creature, Adam, who filled in the rest of the world. Adam named, but he did not create. He brought the animals into language, not into being. But if he brought the animals into language, they must have first existed outside it. The referential world outside of language stilled the creative word—the word that was itself material. The unity of "the word was God" becomes "the word was *with* God." The word could no longer have *been* God if it was *with* God. One only says "with" about two separate things.

In the beginning, therefore, there was no outside to language. God brought the world out of the void in the act of speaking. But for Adam, already, the world and language were two separate things. For him, in fact, naming the animals brought into being *that separation*. What concept of unity, then, would account for the pre-Babelian but noncreative word?

The question we have just asked appears directly related to the "pure language" that translation enables one to glimpse according to "The Task of the Translator." "All suprahistorical kinship between languages consists in this: in every one of them as a whole, one and the same thing is meant. Yet this one thing is achievable not by any single language but only by the totality of their intentions supplementing one another: the pure language" (*Selected Writings*, 1: 257) Where I have somewhat tendentiously translated Mallarmé's "complément" as "supplement," the English translator has Benjamin actually say "supplement" for "ergänzend," about which the dictionary says: "*pr. p.* & *adj.,* supplementary; complementary." Is "supplement" a synonym for "complement" then? If so, all of Jacques Derrida's work on the difference between them is collapsed into nothing, and Jacques Lacan would be wrong to claim of *jouissance féminine:*

It none the less remains that if she is excluded by the nature of things, it is precisely that in being not all, she has, in relation to what the phallic function designates of *jouissance,* a supplementary *jouissance.*

Note that I said *supplementary.* Had I said *complementary,* where would we be! We'd fall right back into the all.[12]

It is thus the status of that "all" that is at stake. *Ergänzend* is a present participle containing the root *ganz,* "whole." The process of completing a whole would seem to dictate the translation of "complement" for both Benjamin and Mallarmé. But there are at least two reasons not to settle for the "all" too soon: if poetry "makes up for the deficiency of languages that is caused by their plurality," then although poetry is an *attempt* to make up for such deficiency once and for all, poetry's very ongoing existence requires that it always fail. And if "the process of trying to make a whole" is a translation of *ergänzend,* then it names not a successfully completed state but a process that stops being ongoing if it succeeds. Thus, what is lacking as a *result* depends on believing that success is just around the corner, but as a process whose ongoingness depends on its failure, the "whole" must never be achieved in *fact.* And that failure to achieve a whole has something to do with sexual difference.

Neither Mallarmé nor Benjamin comes anywhere near asking the question of sexual difference. And yet their ambivalence about the nature of wholeness—ardently desired but somehow taboo if one is to continue to exist—could be connected to it. After all, it is sexual difference that guarantees that every life that exists (at least until cloning) have two parents. Or rather, a sperm cell and an egg cell—not necessarily a father and a mother. Life is thus defined as having a double origin—unlike creation itself, which all comes from God, or Adam and Eve, who are not two separate beings; Eve was produced by budding, like yeast. She is simply made out of Adam.

But what is Adam made out of? Dust, says the Bible. The same dust that the serpent is condemned to eat; the same dust to which mortals who die must return. The book of Genesis itself has two origins: in the first account of creation, God says: "Let us make humankind, in our image, according to our likeness! Let them have dominion over the fish of the sea, the fowl of the heavens, animals, all the earth, and all the crawling things that crawl upon the earth! God created humankind in his image, in the image of God did he create it, male and female did he create them" (Genesis 1:26–27).[13] In the second story, not only did God not create them male and female but also there is no mention of images or likenesses. It is because God is trying to make a companion for Adam that He makes all the other creatures that Adam names. It is because God's creations still haven't given Adam a proper companion ("no helper corresponding to him") that God puts Adam to sleep and performs His rib surgery. Adam's use of language thus occurs at the moment that God is trying and failing to make him a *semblable*. It happens in the place of a sexual difference that, even after the creation of Eve, still has not occurred. In the first story, too, the double origin is in doubt: how can both male and female be in the "image" of God? There are, of course, answers, but they all assume that difference has not really been created, that male and female are really the same.

In an early, unpublished essay entitled "On Language as Such and on the Language of Man," Benjamin, too, considers that, whether or not one believes in it, the creation story in the Bible must "evolve the fundamental linguistic facts":

> The second version of the story of the Creation, which tells of the breathing of God's breath into man, also reports that man was made from earth. This is, in the whole story of the Creation, the only reference to the material in which the Creator expresses his will, which is doubtless otherwise thought of as creation without mediation. In this second story of the Creation, the making of man did not take place through the word: God spoke—and there was. But this man, who is not created from the word, is now invested with the *gift* of language and is elevated above nature. (*Selected Writings*, 1: 67–68)

The "material" out of which God shaped Adam is the earth, not language. Adam *has* language precisely to the extent that he is not *made* by it. In the creative word, the thing *was* the word; in Adam's language, the material thing *is in need* of the word. Adam provides a name to a thing that exists apart from it. "Making something out of material" means that form and content are different.

The problem with our myths of the origin of language is that they don't deal with this crucial difference between creative and uncreative referentiality. We tend to imagine the original language as if it were Adam's language, but Adam's language is not the same as God's. The lost language is considered the language of perfect naming (the sign as perfectly "motivated," to use Saussure's vocabulary), while God's destruction of the Tower of Babel consists precisely in propagating a new diversity of names (the arbitrariness of the sign). In Eden, the "tree" of knowledge was not supposed to be "arb(itrai)re." But how can we imagine a language that is itself materially the truth if it is not creative? Of what "material" could the truth be if it does not immediately *bring into being* what it names? How might a language unmediatedly refer if reference itself is mediation?

The problem, I think, is that we tend to think of Adam's language as *similar* to God's. But God's speech is creative to the extent that it is *not* based on similarity. Not, at least, until the creation of man. A God that tries to make a being similar to himself is already a God that takes himself as an object, a God who is well on his way to the sin of self-consciousness. When Adam names the animals, nothing is said about similarity. In fact, proper names are "proper" because they have no semantic content. To play with the semantic content of a name ("That thou art Peter [Petrus], and upon this rock [petra] I will build my church"; "Pierre qui roule n'amasse pas mousse") is usually disparaged as accidental (and such wordplay, as "the lowest form of humor"), and not seen as a trace of the original language. Yet somehow we retain this image of the one originary language involving a perfect coincidence of sound and sense. Why do we have this fantasy? Why can't we give it up?

It is perhaps not that motivated signs are what we have fallen away from but, rather, what we are trying to climb up to. As Mallarmé puts it, poetry makes up for the imperfections of language caused by its plurality (if there are multiple languages, if they "supplement" each other, no one of them can be "elle-même la vérité"; their very differences reveal that the sign is arbitrary). What makes us long for a perfect correspondence between words and meanings is our perception of its contingent lack in any existing language; that is, of its possibility in general. With a little tweaking, we think, we should surely be able to seize what seems so close! "Mon sens regrette que le discours défaille à exprimer les objets par des touches y répondant en coloris ou en allure, lesquelles existent dans l'instrument de la voix, parmi les langages et parfois chez un. A côté d'*ombre*, opaque, *ténèbres* se fonce peu; quelle déception, devant la perversité conférent à *jour* comme à *nuit*, contradictoirement, des timbres obscur ici, là clair." The closeness that is perceived but somehow "perversely" unaccomplished is not only not achieved in language but, it seems, sometimes willfully contradicted. "Day" and "night" (in French) sound like they mean the opposite of what they do mean. This *jour* and *nuit* are not just examples of language's perversity, however. They happen to be the first two words spoken by God during the creation. If *jour* and *nuit* sound like the opposite of what they mean, then we have fallen very far from the creative word. The arbitrariness of language *is* its perversity. Human language in no way resembles the creative word.

This "light" seems destined to show up again and again to debunk the belief that meaning and reality coincide. When Benjamin, in the same essay, says, "That which in a mental entity is communicable *is* its language," he uses the example of a lamp. "The language of this lamp, for example, communicates not the lamp (for the mental being of the lamp, insofar as it is *communicable*, is by no means the lamp itself) but the language-lamp, the lamp in communication, the lamp in expression." In other words, what is communicated is a certain mode of communicability—the significance of a thing *for* someone and *for* that mode of communicability. By concentrating on "mental being," Benjamin establishes the problem of language in the context of life. "Mental being" can exist only *for* someone. But by including God among such possible beings, Benjamin establishes a structure of addressedness that doesn't presuppose a contingent addressee.

We will shortly turn to Paul de Man's essay on Benjamin's "Task of the Translator," but here I would like to point out that he, too, uses that "light" to demystify the same illusion. "No one in his right mind will try to grow grapes by the luminosity of the word 'day,'" he writes in *The Resistance to Theory*, "but it is very difficult not to conceive the pattern of one's past and future existence as in accordance with spatial and temporal schemes that belong to fictional narratives and not to the world."[14]

Even the "coloris ou . . . allure" of the speaker himself enters into the swirl of floating signifiers for Mallarmé once the possibility of taking oneself for God (that is, for colorless) is eliminated. The patterns of black and white in Mallarmé's work owe much to the "perversity" of their liberation. But he would never have foreseen the use that Aimé Césaire would make of that same passage. In an interview in which Césaire was asked why he continued to write in French and not in the more "authentic" Creole, he replied:

Ah! je ne suis pas prisonnier de la langue française! Seulement, j'essaie, j'ai toujours voulu *infléchir* le français. Ainsi, si j'ai beaucoup lu Mallarmé, c'est parce qu'il m'a montré, parce que j'ai compris à travers lui, que la langue, au fond, est arbitraire. Ce n'est pas un phénomène naturel. Cette phrase prodigieuse que Mallarmé a écrite: "*Mon sens regrette que le discours défaille . . . Seulement,* sachons *n'existerait pas le vers:* lui, philosophiquement rémunère le défaut des langues." Mallarmé a toujours été étonné et frappé de la malencontreuse idée qu'on a eu d'appeler *le jour:* le jour et *la nuit:* la nuit, alors que les sonorités porteraient au contraire. Il serait plus naturel d'appeler la nuit: *le jour,* avec cette voyelle longue, cette chose qui *vous tombe dessus;* c'est cela, la nuit! Tandis que le mot *nuit,* avec cet *i* coloré, conviendrait beaucoup mieux à la clarté du jour.[15]

[Ah! I am *not* a prisoner of the French language! Nevertheless, I try, I've always wanted to *inflect* French. Thus, if I've read a lot of Mallarmé, it is because he showed me, because I understood through him, that language, finally, is arbitrary. It's not a natural phenomenon. That prodigious sentence that Mallarmé wrote: "*My own sense regrets that discourse fails . . . Only,* be aware that *verse would not exist:* |l|it, philosophically makes up for languages' deficiencies." Mallarmé was always surprised and struck by the infelicitous idea that you could call *day:* day, and *night:* night, whereas the sonorities would rather suggest that it should be the other way around. It would be more natural to call night: *day* |jour|, with that long vowel, that thing that *falls:* that's what

night is! While the word *night* |nuit| with that colorful *i*, would corre-
spond much more closely to the clarity of day.]

In the hands of the foremost poet of Negritude, it is the bright *i* that
is "colored." Day and night, light and dark, the first things created,
are not fixed: it depends on who is viewing them. The "gift" of language must be "inflected," but it carries the inertia of ideology (is no
longer ex nihilo) and therefore cannot be created entirely anew.

III. Pain

> And as they were eating, Jesus took bread, and blessed it, and brake it, and
> gave it to his disciples, and said, Take, eat; this is my body.
> —Matthew 26:26, King James Bible

Among the moments in Benjamin's "Task of the Translator" that
Paul de Man lingers upon in his own analysis of Benjamin's essay,
none is more significant than Benjamin's example of the difficulty
of translating both the denotation and the network of associations
called up by every sign. Benjamin writes:

> In the words *Brot* and *pain*, what is meant is the same, but the way of
> meaning it is not. This difference in the way of meaning permits the
> word *Brot* to mean something other to a German than what the word
> *pain* means to a Frenchman, so that these words are not interchange-
> able for them; in fact, they strive to exclude each other. (*Selected Writ-
> ings*, 1: 257)

"What is meant is the same." Does this mean, "What is named is the
same thing"?[16] Is the sameness something outside of language or inside it? If what is meant is the same *object*, then that sameness exists
to the extent that "what is meant" is equivalent to "what is referred
to": the sameness *in the world*. The role of all languages would be to
point noisily toward the same "thing," the thing that would silence
them, the thing whose reality doesn't depend in any way on language. Translation would thus liberate the "thing" from language
altogether, and one would approach a form of communication that
would be "matériellement la vérité."

But if the "thing" *is* liberated from language altogether, then we no longer have to do with translation. Translation is a relation between two languages, not a relation between words and things. What is the sameness that all languages share if it isn't the language of things? What is the sameness that French and German share if it is something entirely *within* language? What do French and German share if their referential meanings are *mutually exclusive?* The object remains the same and the words compete for the same space, yet they are not interchangeable because *one is French and the other German*. The sameness they share is their linguisticness itself, and they necessarily imply the rest of a language, the rest of a world that is specifically German or French. "Language communicates the linguistic being of things," writes Benjamin in "On Language as Such and on the Language of Man" (*Selected Writings*, 1: 63). "Translation attains its full meaning in the realization that every evolved language (with the exception of the word of God) can be considered a translation of all the others" (69–70). "The German language, for example, is by no means the expression of everything we could—theoretically—express *through* it, but is the direct expression of that which communicates *itself* in it" (63). These are not national characteristics of *persons* but linguistic characteristics of the *language*.

After mentioning that *Brot* and *pain* strive to exclude each other, Benjamin goes on:

> As to what is meant, however, the two words signify the very same thing. Even though the way of meaning in these two words is in such conflict, it supplements itself in each of the two languages from which the words are derived; to be more specific, the way of meaning in them in relation to what is meant. In the individual, unsupplemented languages, what is meant is never found in relative independence, as in individual words of sentences; rather, it is in a constant state of flux—until it is able to emerge as the pure language from the harmony of all the various ways of meaning. (257)

Until there is more than one language, then—until there is translation—language is absolute in relation to things. The language of an original is compared only to the world. But the moment a comparison is set up that requires one language to be seen in terms of another, both languages are seen in their systematicity, their linguisticness. "Language communicates the linguistic being of things" (63). This, however, is not exactly the same as "mental being": "Mental being is identical to linguistic being only insofar as it is capable of communication" (63). This means that there is such a thing as mental being that is not capable of being communicated. Translation, confronting the difference between what is linguistic and what is untranslatable, makes possible a glimpse of the mental being of mankind that is not linguistic. But in that it is not linguistic, it is incapable of being communicated. "No poem is intended for the reader, no picture for the beholder, no symphony for the audience" (253). In the original is glimpsed that incommunicable mental being that no translation can capture, yet until what *is* communicable has been collected, the incommunicable is not glimpsed as such. It is at the moment of translation that the original gives off fleetingly its glow of incommunicability. It is a "love at last sight" seen at the moment it disappears, like Baudelaire's "Passante": "Ô toi que j'eusse aimée! ô toi qui le savais!" [O you I would have loved! o you who knew it!]. Its temporality is the imperfect subjunctive. "Just as a tangent touches a circle lightly and at but one point—establishing, with this touch rather than with the point, the law according to which it is to continue on its straight path to infinity—a translation touches the original lightly and only at the infinitely small point of the sense, thereupon pursuing its own course according to the laws of fidelity in the freedom of linguistic flux" (261). The German word here translated (twice) as "lightly" is "flüchtig," "fleeting(ly)." Transitoriness, not imperceptibleness, is what is emphasized. The fact that "light" is the first thing God created must be an accident, mustn't it? We have no way of talking about these creations ex nihilo of translation.

If the creative word was "elle-même matériellement la vérité," then the miracle of transubstantiation is an attempt to return to it: "Take, eat; this *is* my body." In the *Brot* and *pain* example, Benjamin may well have consciously or unconsciously brought up a figure that refers to the Eucharist—to the separation between Judaism and

Christianity, as well as to that between Catholics and Protestants (a rift created, after all, *by translation*), over its nature. Does the bread *become* Christ's body or *represent* it? For whom? The gap between God's language and Adam's is replayed as soon as translation is admitted. And the question of whether the Messianic wait can end in *this* world or not is an argument that Benjamin will never renounce. But in fact it is not Benjamin but rather Paul de Man who turns Benjamin's "bread" into Hölderlin's "bread and wine":

> If you hear *Brot* in this context of Hölderlin, who is so often mentioned in this text, I hear *Brot und Wein* necessarily, which is the great Hölderlin text that is very much present in this—which in French becomes *pain et vin.* "Pain et vin" is what you get for free in a restaurant, in a cheap restaurant where it is still included, so *pain et vin* has very different connotations from *Brot und Wein.*[17]

As we move from German to French, we move from a great poem to a cheap restaurant. We also move from transubstantiation to digestion. The "presence" of Hölderlin behind all this is asserted with a lot of authority, but the phrase "so often mentioned in this text" indicates that such a "presence" needs some justification as an association. In other words, this "necessary" association is far from automatic, even if the excess of assertiveness is meant to silence any doubts. "Hölderlin" and "Brot und Wein" may well be "present," but it is that fluctuating subject (sometimes "you" and sometimes "I") who "hears" the association. If there is any doubt about who is free-associating and what is necessarily present, de Man goes on to make clear just how arbitrary and individual some associations can be:

> *Pain et vin* has very different connotations from *Brot und Wein.* It brings to mind *pain français, baguette, ficelle, bâtard,* all those things— I now hear in *Brot* "bastard." This upsets the stability of the quotidian. I was very happy with the word *Brot,* which I hear as a native because my native language is Flemish and you say *brood,* just like in German, but if I have to think that *Brot* [*brood*][18] and *pain* are the same thing, I get very upset. It is all right in English because "bread" is close enough to *Brot* [*brood*], despite the idiom "bread" for money, which has its

problems. But the stability of my quotidian, of my daily bread, the re-assuring quotidian aspects of the word "bread," daily bread, is upset by the French word *pain*. What I mean is upset by the way in which I mean—the way in which it is *pain*, the phoneme, the term *pain*, which has its set of connotations which take you in a completely different direction. (87)

In this set of associations, de Man seems to offer some very revealing things: "bastards," mother tongues, daily bread, and being upset. These seem all the more revealing in that later, in the question period following his lecture, de Man seems to feel guilty about them and to disavow their importance:

> Well, you're quite right. I was indulging myself, you know, it was long, and I was very aware of potential boredom, felt the need for an anecdote, for some relief, and Benjamin gives the example of *pain* and *Brot,* and perhaps shouldn't . . . whenever you give an example you, as you know, lose what you want to say; and Benjamin, by giving the example of *pain* and *Brot*—which comes from him—and which I've banalized, for the sake of a cheap laugh . . . (95–96)

This set of associations could at first be read as an unusual admission of personal pain and autobiographical precision. To demonstrate the power of the signifier, de Man speaks about his native language, illegitimacy, perhaps his mother. His attempts to take the whole thing back later serve only to reinforce the impression that something has slipped out. The comment is similar to what Freud says while analyzing the Irma dream: peering down a woman's throat, he cuts off his analysis by saying, "Frankly, I had no desire to penetrate more deeply at this point."[19] The sexual desire and repression seem so obvious that the comment is read as a simple denial of Freud's wish. And both in de Man's case and in Freud's, the moment *may* be truly revealing. Whatever psychoanalytic paydirt one would hit, however, the very intense interest of the revelation would obscure the theoretical point. By treating the play of a signifier or the text of a dream as signifying only something about individual psychology, the two texts are distracted away from making a general point. Whatever is true of the individuals Paul de Man and Sigmund Freud, the point is that *everyone* has a set of associations for every signifier, and everyone dreams. The writers are trying to talk about *that*. In both cases it is the power and communicativeness of something unconscious and unmeant that is in question. Individual psychology is an effect, not a cause, of something that happens independently of any intention. The very fact that the two men unwillingly say revealing things is the only way to make their point, but it is at their own expense.

De Man's analysis of Benjamin's essay on translation begins with the somewhat banal but often overlooked problems that arise when the essay itself is translated:

> If I say stay close to the text, since it is a text on translation, I will need—and that is why I have all these books—translations of this text, because if you have a text which says it is impossible to translate, it is very nice to see what happens when that text gets translated. And the translations confirm, brilliantly, beyond any expectations which I may have had, that it is impossible to translate, as you will see in a moment. (74)

He goes on to show that "translatable" and "untranslatable," "human" and "inhuman," which seem diametrically opposed, are in fact close enough to have induced the translators into French (Gandillac) and English (Zohn) to mistake them for each other. The expression he singles out for particular comment is "Wehen," which both the English and the French translator have rendered "birth pangs." The scenario of suffering designed to lead to new life is everywhere suggested by Benjamin's text, but here he says merely "die Wehen des eigenen"—"the suffering of the self-identical." Thus, de Man notes, the proper translation of "Wehen" would be neither "birth pangs" nor "death pangs" but, rather, "pains." But Ah! says the alert reader, welcoming a presence that has been lingering on the edge of consciousness for an English speaker all this time. "Pain" is the English pronunciation of that *pain* whose Frenchness was so emphasized before. What was untranslatable—but nevertheless a gold mine of associations—in the French *pain* becomes, in English, the correct translation of the German original, but by a path that is completely "illegitimate": the word the translators have missed here is not a

translation but the mispronunciation of a word that shows up elsewhere. Trying not to hear it is itself part of the process for an English
speaker.

The task of the translator suddenly becomes even more complicated if he has to edit out a swarm of associations that are not func-
tional in order to stick to "what is meant." Clearly those associations
form no part of "what is meant," and their presence is purely irrele-
vant. Yet the linguistic "noise" of the act of translating, in *not* being
meant or intended, comes close to the pure linguisticness of language itself. The very obstacles to translation, then, may point toward the "pure language" that translation enables one to glimpse.

IV. *The Breaking of the Vessel*

> Fragments of a vessel that are to be glued together must match one another in
> the smallest details, although they need not be like one another. In the same
> way a translation, instead of imitating the sense of the original, must lovingly
> and in detail incorporate the original's way of meaning, thus making both the
> original and the translation recognizable as fragments of a greater lan-
> guage, just as fragments are part of a vessel.
>
> —Benjamin, "The Task of the Translator"

When Benjamin compares translation to archeology, he refers to two
entirely different notions of the wholeness that has to be pieced together. The wholeness of the original is an illusion that can be maintained only so long as the original is not translated. "Whereas content and language form a certain unity in the original, like a fruit and
its skin, the language of the translation envelops its content like a
royal robe with ample folds" (*Selected Writings*, 1: 258). Wholeness
itself is an illusion; the vessel seems whole in the original language
only because the skin and the fruit have been produced together.
Any translation immediately has to separate them. The appearance of
wholeness is fragmented the moment the signifier and the signified
are linked by the "folds" of a different system of differences. Blinded
by the mirage of wholeness in the original language, the translator
nevertheless has no choice but to fragment the vessel. The original
reveals its illusion of wholeness to have already drawn on resources

that were, at bottom, arbitrary. The work of art has simply found a way to make that arbitrariness work *for* it. The precarious appearance of unity was achieved by using the fortuitousness of the original language, but in any other language, such luck falls apart. In the process, though, the *two* languages are "recognized" as fragments of a larger vessel. Behind the diversity of languages shimmers a "pure" vessel whose unity no one will ever piece together. And yet, only translation can make it visible at all. Humpty Dumpty's great fall creates the desire to put an egg back together again. But the wholeness translation reveals is not a restoration. The completion it points to is still—and perhaps forever, in human time—deferred.

Even if one resists believing that there is a divine creator at the beginning and the end, the structure of what comes in between is shaped by the notions of the Fall and the Telos. An unreachable something and an unreachable nothing are less different than any assertion of the nature of that something—or of that nothing. Thus, even if I don't believe that the ultimate wholeness really exists, the piecing together of the fragments made visible by translation is structured as if it could. Benjamin's "Messianism" needs to be understood as asserting nothing more than that. Whenever the shape of what exists can only be accounted for by positing a God, Benjamin defines God as that which would explain it. Thus, *by definition,* God exceeds any presence or knowledge one could have without Him. He exists in the shape of what is lacking. The image of a missing piece would occur to almost anyone here *except* Benjamin—God would exist as something that would make the world coherent. But Benjamin insists that God can take the shape of something lacking *without* positing the coherence of the world. The wholeness of the vessel can be a different fantasy each time any two pieces happen to fit together. But the fantasy of wholeness can have a structural effect even if it has no validity. Even the assertion that wholeness is *always* a fantasy testifies to the ubiquity of such a fantasy.

At this point in my argument it was clear to me that I needed to know something about Kabbalah, the scholarly specialty of Gershom Scholem, who was Benjamin's close friend and correspondent for all of Benjamin's life. Always deferring a move to Palestine that he kept describing to Scholem (who had moved there in 1923) as imminent, Benjamin showed great interest in what Scholem was investigating, requesting copies of Scholem's research on Kabbalah while sending to Jerusalem copies of everything he (Benjamin) was writing. What Scholem says about the image of "the breaking of the vessels" is, however, less unambiguous than I had expected. Loaded with scholarly meticulousness and nowhere asserted as true, Scholem writes:

> Isaac Luria's main preoccupation, it would appear, was to trace the further development of the vessels that received the light of emanation which shone into primordial space after the act of *zimzum* ["contraction"].[20]

The moment of creation is slowed down, therefore, into successive moments: into primordial space shone the light of the emanation of a God whose existence was attested by that very light. But "in the beginning was a contraction"? Surely it's only in English that the allusion to the end of pregnancy is readable! Following the progress of that ray, Scholem goes on:

> In the actual emergence of these vessels a part was played both by the lights that were located in the *tehiru* [primordial space] after the *zimzum* and by the new lights that entered with the ray. The purpose of this process was the elimination *(berur)* of the forces of *Din* [judgment] that had collected, a catharsis that could have been attained either by eliminating these forces from the system entirely or else by integrating them within it by first "softening" and purifying them—two conflicting approaches which we frequently encounter side by side. (136)

Encountering conflicting forces side by side seems to be the *aim* and not the infelicity of Luria's creation story. What needs to be explained is not unity but plurality. Thus, there are two ways primordial space can be filled:

> Practically speaking, a point can expand evenly in one of two ways, circularly or linearly, and herein is expressed a basic duality that runs through the process of creation. (136)

We recognize here, whether the connection was present to his mind or not, Benjamin's tangent:

> Just as a tangent touches a circle lightly and at but one point, . . . a translation touches the original lightly and only at the infinitely small point of the sense, thereupon pursuing its own course according to the laws of fidelity in the freedom of linguistic flux. (*Selected Writings*, 1: 261)

Translation, then, combines the contradictory resources of these two forces. But what of the kabbalistic "breaking of the vessels"? After describing the disagreements over the nature and sources of the primordial rays, Scholem writes:

> At this point, however, there occurred what is known in Lurianic Kabbalah as "the breaking of the vessels" or "the death of the kings." The vessels assigned to the upper three *Sefirot* managed to contain the light that flowed into them, but the light struck the six *Sefirot* from *Hesed* to *Yesod* all at once and was too strong to be held by the individual vessels; one after another they broke, the pieces scattering and falling. (138)

From this quotation, one begins to understand Benjamin's unusual tolerance for elaborate stories whose surface absurdity is no obstacle to his taking them seriously. (Blanqui's *L'Eternité des astres* comes immediately to mind.) The story of the contraction does not at all point toward a mysterious, mystic unity, but rather *away from it*. Introducing Lurianic doctrine, Scholem writes:

> The main originality of this Lurianic doctrine lay in the notion that the first act of the *Ein-Sof* [the infinite, literally "without end"] was not one of revelation and emanation, but, on the contrary, was one of concealment and limitation. (129)

The vessel exists, one might say, only in order to break. Unity may well have existed in the beginning, but it is not a unity we are progressing *toward*. In fact, every effort to patch the vessel together only breaks it further. And *that* ends up being the thankless but necessary task of the translator.

FOUR

The Poet's Mother

Mother, you are the one mouth
I would be tongue to. Mother of otherness
Eat me.

—Sylvia Plath, "Poem for a Birthday"

I. The Mother's Address

Que tout dise: "Ils ont aimé."

[So that everything will say: "They once loved."]

—Alphonse de Lamartine, "Le Lac"

Charles Baudelaire and Sylvia Plath are both important writers of lyric poetry, but the nineteenth-century man and the twentieth-century woman seem at first sight to have little in common. Therefore, it is surprising to see to what extent the critics of the two poets are united on one point: they participate unrestrainedly in the poets' anger and hostility toward their mothers. Baudelaire and Plath may be anomalous in the pressures their lives brought to bear on their mothers, but the unanimity of the critics against the mother's effect on the child indicates that something more universal is at stake. What, if anything, does the mother have to do with the lyric?

In an essay called "Apostrophe, Animation, and Abortion," I studied the animating force of direct address, and concluded with the following remarks inspired by the psychoanalytic work of Jacques Lacan:

> The verbal development of the infant, according to Lacan, begins as a demand addressed to the mother, out of which the entire verbal universe is spun. Yet the mother is somehow a personification, not a person—a personification of presence or absence, of Otherness itself. "Demand in itself bears on something other than the satisfactions it calls for. It is demand of a presence or of an absence—which is what is mani-

fested in the primordial relation to the mother, pregnant[1] with that Other to be situated *within* the needs that it can satisfy. . . . Insofar as [man's] needs are subjected to demand, they return to him alienated. This is not the effect of his real dependence . . . , but rather the turning into signifying form as such, from the fact that it is from the locus of the Other that its message is emitted."[2] If demand is the originary vocative, which assures life even as it inaugurates alienation, then it is not surprising that questions of animation inhere in the rhetorical figure of apostrophe. The reversal of apostrophe we noted in the Shelley poem[3] ("animate me") would be no reversal at all, but a reinstatement of the primal apostrophe in which, despite Lacan's disclaimer, there is precisely a link between demand and animation, between apostrophe and life-and-death dependency. If apostrophe is structured like demand, and if demand articulates the primal relation to the mother as a relation to the Other, then lyric poetry itself—summed up in the figure of apostrophe—comes to look like the fantastically intricate history of endless elaborations and displacements of the single cry, "Mama!"[4]

This may be valid for the poet, but it does not take into account *the mother's address to the child.* The mother tongue is the child's first language; it is a language taught by the mother. If, as theorists of the pre-Oedipal mother insist, the mother represents pure bodily closeness and nonverbal communication, she should not be so invested in getting the child to speak. As Freud says about dreams of unpleasure, her fundamental role in language learning "astonishes people far too little."[5] A child beginning to speak does not always address anyone. But a mother teaching language to a child consistently speaks to that child even when teaching the child the names of things. Names, in other words, are addressed to the child by the mother-teacher. "What's that?" she says, constantly checking the lesson. A child comes into language through the mother's address. It is her job to transform a little animal into a little human being. The fact that she does this by teaching the child to speak indicates that, however dependent on her the child may be in fact, her most important lesson will be to turn "into signifying form" everything that unites them. Might poetry be an attempt not to address the mother but to *hear her voice*? Is poetry perhaps a way of *being addressed*?

II. *The Maternal Voice*

Hélas! le poison et le glaive
M'ont pris en dédain et m'ont dit:
"Tu n'es pas digne qu'on t'enlève
A ton esclavage maudit,

Imbécile!—de son empire
Si nos efforts te délivraient,
Tes baisers ressusciteraient
Le cadavre de ton vampire!"

[Alas! the poison and the blade
Have answered with disdain:
"You are not worth saving
From your slavery and damnation,

Imbecile!—even if we tried
To free you from its empire,
Your kisses would resuscitate
The body of your vampire!"]

—Charles Baudelaire, "Le Vampire"

At first sight, it would seem that both Plath and Baudelaire, far from wanting to hear the mother's voice, would like on the contrary to shut it up. In a 1962 poem entitled "Medusa," Plath snarls to her mother:

Green as eunuchs, your wishes
Hiss at my sins.
Off, off, eely tentacle!
There is nothing between us.[6]

The French pun on "méduse" (both jellyfish and Medusa; in English, too, a medusa is the adult stage of a jellyfish) allows the mythological figure to appear as a sea creature. While the mythological Medusa was a woman who had snakes for hair and was capable of turning viewers to stone, jellyfish have snakelike tentacles, and those tentacles often sting and paralyze. In addition, the Latin name for the common Moon jellyfish is *Aurelia aurita;* Plath's mother's name was Aurelia (a pun on which Plath was undoubtedly playing). And the body shape of a jellyfish is maintained by a transparent structure called a bell (did Plath know this when she called her novel *The Bell Jar*?). The "nothing" that is proclaimed as what is "between us" is also a sea creature: the transatlantic telephone cable that connected England (where Plath was) and the United States (where Aurelia was), and that was mentioned earlier in the poem. By cutting the cable that had allowed the telephone to substitute for the letters Plath once addressed to her mother, Plath disconnects the stinging tentacles of the mother-daughter relationship as if for good. The poem "Medusa" seems to carry out the disconnection implicit in Plath's attempts to put into practice her Boston therapist's liberating words: "I give you permission to hate your mother."[7]

Baudelaire's case is equally stinging. In his opening poem to *Les Fleurs du Mal,* entitled "Benediction," he describes a mother's horror at having given birth to a poet:

Lorsque, par un décret des puissances suprêmes,
Le Poète apparaît en ce monde ennuyé,
Sa mère épouvantée et pleine de blasphèmes
Crispe ses poings vers Dieu, qui la prend en pitié:

—"Ah! que n'ai-je mis bas tout un noeud de vipères,
Plutôt que de nourrir cette dérision!
Maudite soit la nuit aux plaisirs éphémères
Où mon ventre a conçu mon expiation!

"Puisque tu m'as choisie entre toutes les femmes
Pour être le dégout de mon triste mari,
Et que je ne puis pas rejeter dans les flammes,
Comme un billet d'amour, ce monstre rabougri,

"Je ferai rejaillir ta haine qui m'accable
Sur l'instrument maudit de tes méchancetés,
Et je tordrai si bien cet arbre misérable,
Qu'il ne pourra pousser ses boutons empestés!"

Elle ravale ainsi l'écume de sa haine,
Et, ne comprenant pas les desseins éternels,
Elle-même prépare au fond de la Géhenne
Les bûchers consacrés aux crimes maternels.

[When, by decree from the forces above,
The Poet is born into the boredom of this world,
His horrified mother, cursing a sympathetic God,
And shaking her fists, cries out:

"Ah! why couldn't I have given birth to a nest of vipers
Rather than nourish this derision!
Damned be that night with its fleeting pleasures
During which I conceived my expiation!

"Since you have chosen me alone of all my sex
To be the disgust of my long-suffering husband,
And since I can't just throw into the fire,
Like a love letter, this deformed monster,

"I will turn the hate with which you have afflicted me
Upon the cursed instrument of your spite,
And I will twist this miserable tree so violently
That it will produce only infected life!"

She thus swallows the bitterness of her hate,
And, not understanding the eternal designs,
Prepares to journey to Hell herself
To stoke the fires of maternal crimes.]

In a thinly disguised version of an immaculate conception and an annunciation, Baudelaire has the mother experience a thoroughly maculate conception and a denunciation. Surprised like the Virgin Mary by the unpredictable turn of events, she, in contrast, takes the occasion to curse rather than to bless a maternal relation she did not expect.

But even in these stinging words, things are not as simple as they seem. "There is nothing between us" could be a description of perfect fusion and not a description of lack of relation. If there is nothing between the self and the other, there is no space of separation, no difference, perfect oneness. As Plath will later say about her relationship with her husband, Ted Hughes, "*Between us* there are no barriers—it is rather as if neither of us—or especially myself—had any skin, or one skin *between us* & kept bumping into and abrading each other" (emphasis added).[8] The desire to have "nothing between us" may be a deep wish as well as a disconnection. Even the image of Medusa is as fascinating as it is fearsome: "The ghost of the unborn novel is a Medusa-head," Plath writes in her journal on July 7, 1958.

So, too, with Baudelaire's desire to be Christ. If the Poet were not martyred and misunderstood by his flesh and blood, he would not seek his salvation in the transcendental realm of Poetry. The mother's curse is thus necessary for the son's apotheosis. The son's ascension is in fact dependent on the mother's abjection.

The telephone cable figures in Plath explicitly as an umbilical cord in the poem "Medusa." But it is astonishing how many other telephones there are in Plath's work: the voices in the poem "Daddy" that "can't worm through," the telephone number of Grammy Schober that Plath uses as the title of her late memoir: "Ocean 1212-W," and of course the "Words heard, by accident, over the phone" that confirmed, for Plath, the affair between Ted and Assia and provoked the crisis that disrupted Plath's marriage. And one of the contributing factors in Plath's suicide was doubtless her inability, that cold English winter, to obtain a telephone.

Even in the poem "Lady Lazarus," the performance of death, said to be an art, a vocation, is described as *a call:*

> I do it so it feels like hell.
> I do it so it feels real.
> I guess you could say I've a call.[9]

"Having a call" obviously precedes the telephone by many centuries, but the relation between art and *calling* deserves some attention. In French, the translation of "my name is . . ." is "je m'appelle" (I call myself). I make a call to myself? In the French expression, the function of naming is composed of an address from the subject to himself. It is when he can become both the subject and the object of language that he gets a name. If the mother's voice is the primal caller, the subject can perhaps inhabit his place in language as soon as he can take over the calling function for himself.

Plath's rumination about calling extends to plays on the word itself. The exclamation "a miracle!" at Lady Lazarus's resurrection is meant to rhyme with the word "call." And the word "caul" seems to be a synonym for "bell jar": a transparent shell that both protects and imprisons:

> What inner decision, what inner murder or prison-break must I commit if I want to speak from my true deep voice in writing . . . and not feel this jam up of feeling behind a glass-dam fancy-façade of numb dumb wordage. . . . Most heartening, the feeling I were breaking out of my glass caul.[10]

III. Addressing the Mother

> How we cling to these days of July: August is a September mother month (there, I've got so used to writing "mother" in the last days that it nips out to usurp all words beginning with "m").
>
> —Sylvia Plath, journal entry for July 25, 1957, while writing an unfinished story called "The Trouble-Making Mother"

Because of the vagaries of survival and publication, we have access to huge quantities of Plath's letters to her mother. We also have a large number of letters written by Baudelaire to *his* mother, by far the most frequent addressee in his two-volume correspondence. The relation between these two poets and the structure of address found in their correspondence suggests that the mother functions as a default setting for the formulating of the I-you relationship in general. Their lives were structured by that address, and their poetry explores the complexities of it. The fact that, in Plath's poems, the I-you relationship is often supplemented by a "him" indicates that, no matter how deeply in love Sylvia was, she was still addressing the person to whom she often said, "Picture me!"

Aurelia Plath begins her introduction of *Letters Home* by saying that she had long had the intention of giving Sylvia back her own letters as "material" for her stories and poems. Instead, she was forced to edit the letters herself after her beloved daughter had committed suicide, leaving behind a novel, *The Bell Jar*, in which the portrait of Esther Greenwood's mother is merciless. Plath may never have gotten up the courage to tell her mother she hated her, but her failed attempts to do so inflicted inexpressible hurt.

Rather than telling the mother, "I hate you," Charles Baudelaire tells her, over and over again, "You kill me." Most of their correspondence is about money. He has crippling debts; she does not alleviate them. He needs money; she withholds it. To get it, he has to seduce it out of her. Hence, his letters are always the expression of a double bind: to get money, he must play on her maternal sympathies in order to get her to violate the system her maternal sympathies have put in place to safeguard what remains of an inheritance from his father. Baudelaire's biological father died in early 1827, when the future poet was five years old; in late 1828, Caroline Baudelaire married a second—and fairly comfortable—husband, the army officer Jacques Aupick. The double bind in Baudelaire's letters has everything to do with his mother's relation to these two fathers. In effect, he has to play the living father off against the dead father and force his mother to make a choice between her son and her husband. The structure she has put in place to mediate her relation to her son's money is the imposition of a *conseil judiciaire,* a job designed to guard the funds and mete out an allowance. But the result is to maintain Baudelaire in a state of permanent infantilization. By withholding his own money from him, his mother has not made him independent of her husband; she has made a state of necessity into a state of demand. The man appointed to the job of *conseil judiciaire,* the family lawyer, was named, appropriately enough, Narcisse Ancelle. If Baudelaire was in need of money, he thenceforth was supposed to address himself to Narcissus.

Plath's father, too, died while she was a child. But she immediately made her mother sign a promise that she would never marry again. And her mother never did. When Plath later asked her mother whether that document had really *kept* her from remarrying, her mother assured her that it had not.

The death of the father in both cases has to be seen as an integral part of the perception—both theirs and their critics'—of the mother. Whereas Plath's mother stepped into the role of breadwinner and economic provider, however, Baudelaire's mother, whose professional and economic options were in any case much more limited, did not. Although her education and her prospects had prepared her for the possibility that she might have to earn a living, she never did: her fortunes rose and fell with her marital situation. When Baudelaire's father died in 1827, she found her means drastically reduced. When Aupick died (just months before the publication of *Les Fleurs du Mal*), her income was still somewhat reduced, but, with her widow's pension (Aupick had become a senator during the Second Empire), she remained comfortable. Baudelaire oversaw the sale of some of her property and made sure that her pension was in order. He had won the battle of survivorship with Jacques Aupick, but he could not enjoy it. No sooner had he finally published his life's work than *Les Fleurs du Mal* was prosecuted by the court for immorality and blasphemy. The role of judge and censor that Jacques Aupick had recently vacated was simply taken up by the court.

Let us go back now to some crucial scenes that structure the poets' relations to their mothers. On the day that the *conseil judiciaire* became official, Baudelaire wrote to his mother, changing from the intimate *tu* to the more formal *vous* form that he would use with her off and on until Aupick's death:

> M. Ancelle m'a donné hier les derniers sacrements. Ainsi je n'ai plus rien à faire qu'à me retourner à moi tout seul, et qu'à me creuser le cerveau.
>
> Ayez la bonté de venir m'assister aujourd'hui après votre déjeuner, ne fût-ce que par quelques heures de conversation.[11]

> [Yesterday, M. Ancelle gave me the last rites. Thus I have only to return alone to myself and blow my brains out.
>
> Be good enough to come keep me company today after your lunch, if only to give me several hours of conversation.]

The double bind of Baudelaire's address to his mother is starkly delineated: "You are killing me; come keep me company."

For Plath, it is her mother who sets the terms by which the father's death is to be survived. In her introduction to *Letters Home*, she writes:

> At the request of Dr. Loder, I permitted an autopsy to be performed when he assured me that Otto [the father] could still be given the "normal" funeral that he had once stated was his wish. When I viewed Otto at the funeral parlor, he bore no resemblance to the husband I

knew, but looked like a fashionable store manikin. The children would never recognize their father, I felt, so I did not take them to the funeral, but placed them in the kind, understanding care of Marion Freeman for that afternoon. What I had intended as an exercise in courage for the sake of my children was interpreted years later by my daughter as indifference. "My mother never had time to mourn my father's death." I had vividly remembered a time when I was a little child, seeing my mother weep in my presence and feeling that my whole personal world was collapsing. *Mother,* the tower of strength, my one refuge, *crying!* It was this recollection that compelled me to withhold my tears until I was alone in bed at night. (*Letters Home,* 29)

There is something about this self-defense that resembles Freud's analysis of kettle logic in dreams: any one of several arguments would be convincing in itself, but they can't all be true simultaneously. Why does Aurelia Plath's determination to present motherhood as a tower of strength depend on her reminiscences as a daughter? One daughter (Aurelia) wants tears withheld; the other (Sylvia) reproaches the withholder of tears for her indifference. But did Aurelia keep her children away because she didn't want them to see her cry, or because Daddy, as presented by the funeral parlor, looked like a store mannequin? Was she crying because of the unrecognizable artifice, or because of the loss? Sylvia Plath's late poem entitled "The Munich Mannequins" picks up on the image of the mannequin, and seems to comment on what is going on around the father's corpse. It begins:

> Perfection is terrible, it cannot have children.

Is this somehow a response to the mother's arguments in her own defense?

The critics have been quick to see these mothers from the point of view of their children. I will cite Janet Malcolm in the case of Plath. In Malcolm's extraordinary study of the Plath biographies entitled *The Silent Woman,* we find the following account of Aurelia Plath as commentator and editor:

> When *The Bell Jar* was finally scheduled for publication in America, in 1971, Aurelia Plath was beside herself. In a letter to the publisher she

wrote: "Practically every character in *The Bell Jar* represents some-one—often in caricature—whom Sylvia loved; each person had given freely of time, thought, affection, and, in one case, financial help dur-ing those agonizing six months of breakdown in 1953. . . . As this book stands by itself, it represents the basest ingratitude." The shade of Plath must have read these words with a mocking and rather satisfied smile. Mrs. Plath giving freely of time is indistinguishable from Mrs. Greenwood [the mother in *The Bell Jar*] reasoning sweetly.[12]

For Janet Malcolm, then, Aurelia Plath's protests against the novel only bear out its truth. The mocking smile of Plath's shade as she reads these words can only be Malcolm's own. Malcolm goes on:

> However, Mrs. Plath didn't end matters there. In 1975, to make good her claim that the not-nice persona of *Ariel* and *The Bell Jar* was Plath's sick "false self," and that her healthy "real self" was a kindly, "service-oriented" good girl, she asked for and received permission from Ted Hughes, Plath's literary executor, to publish a book of Plath's letters to her written between 1950 and 1963. (Malcolm, 33)

The expressions "false self" and "real self" are not quotations from Mrs. Plath, however, but quotations from Ted Hughes's introduc-tion to his edition of Plath's journals. The war over Plath's real and false selves is more complicated—even in Malcolm's book—than the simple irony of this passage would lead one to believe. In a symp-tomatic moment in the middle of Plath's journals (as edited by Ted Hughes and Frances McCullough), Aurelia Plath's protests can be heard again when they break into the text. At the moment Dr. Ruth Beuscher is giving Plath permission to hate her mother, Aurelia in-serts the following paragraph:

> Much of the material in these pages relating to Sylvia Plath's therapy is of course very painful to me, and coming to the decision to approve its release has been difficult. I have no doubt that many readers will accept whatever negative thoughts she reveals here as the whole and absolute truth, despite their cancellation on other, more positive pages. In any case, the importance of this material to Sylvia Plath's work is certain, and in the interest of furthering understanding of her emotional situa-

tion, I have given my consent to the release of this material.—Aurelia
Plath[13]

In using the word "cancellation" ("some readers will believe the
negative despite its 'cancellation' by the positive"), Aurelia Plath reveals that for her the positive and the negative are mutually exclusive.
What she seems unable to admit is the possibility that the two things
might coexist. The effort to eliminate the negative, then, might have
been entailed by the "tower of strength" a mother had to present.

Aurelia Plath's consent to the release of material hurtful to herself
was doubled by Ted Hughes's decision to destroy Plath's last journal
for the sake of her children. "The last of these contained entries for
several months, and I destroyed it because I did not want her children to have to read it" (*Journals,* xv). Hughes's gesture of destroying the journals is very similar to Aurelia Plath's decision not to let
the children attend their father's funeral. Protection of children from
trauma is the explanation both give for their actions. It may also be a
cover for their *own* horror of recognition.

Malcolm describes Aurelia Plath's decision to publish her daughter's letters as follows:

> The idea was to show that Plath was not the hateful, hating ingrate, the
> changeling of *Ariel* or *The Bell Jar,* but a loving, obedient daughter.
> The shade's smile of satisfaction must have faded when the letters ap-
> peared, in a volume called *Letters Home.* "Mother, *how could you?*"
> would be any daughter's anguished response to an act of treachery like
> the publication of these letters. . . . Instead of showing that Sylvia
> wasn't "like that," the letters caused the reader to consider for the first
> time that her sick relationship with her mother was the reason she *was*
> like that. (Malcolm, 33–34)

From the shade's fading smile to "any daughter's anguished response" to the reader's considered opinion that Plath's relationship
with her mother was "sick," Malcolm lays her cards on the table.
People should think twice before exposing their not-for-publication
selves to their mothers. Of course, Aurelia Plath says that she had
kept the letters with the intention of one day giving them back to her
daughter as raw material for publication. So which is the public self,
here, and which the private? Malcolm seems to believe that Plath

would simply have resisted appearing "in her bathrobe." But perhaps what is exposed is not just a failure to comb one's hair for the camera. Perhaps combing one's hair for the camera was itself the problem. "One cannot blame the poor woman for her innocence," Malcolm writes. "When a child commits suicide, the parents may be forgiven anything they do to dull the pain, even (or especially) acts of unconscious aggression" (34). As if the act of committing suicide itself didn't seem to the survivors like an act of unconscious aggression.

IV. Violence and Motherhood

> Il me semble parfois que mon sang coule à flots,
> Ainsi qu'une fontaine aux rythmiques sanglots.
> Je l'entends bien qui coule avec un long murmure,
> Mais je me tâte en vain pour trouver la blessure.
>
> [Sometimes it seems to me that my blood gushes out,
> Like a fountain with its rhythmic sobs.
> I hear it flowing with a long murmur,
> But I check myself in vain to locate the wound.]
> —Charles Baudelaire, "La Fontaine de sang"

> The blood jet is poetry,
> There is no stopping it.
> —Sylvia Plath, "Kindness"

The cultural construction of ideal motherhood suggests that, when asked for a topic involving violence, the chances are very great that motherhood is one of the *last* things most people will think of. Motherhood seems in our culture to connote the very opposite of violence—a recourse against it and a refuge from it. And yet we know that that ideal conflicts with a world in which maternal child abuse is very real. There may be something inherent in the ideal that makes it violent in itself. As Simone de Beauvoir writes about the ideal of the Eternal Feminine:

> As against the dispersed, contingent, and multiple existences of actual women, mythical thought opposes the Eternal Feminine, unique and changeless. If the definition provided for this concept is contradicted

by the behavior of flesh-and-blood women, it is the latter who are
wrong; we are told not that Femininity is a false entity, but that the
women concerned are not feminine.[14]

The very exclusion of violence is itself violent. If a person is trying to
live up to a role that prohibits violence, selfishness, or even indifference, the prohibition itself may involve a form of violence to oneself.

Psychoanalysts tend to idealize the mother as the first object of desire and to locate all violence and rivalry in the father. The perception of infantile sexual life and the functioning of the Oedipus complex constitute, indeed, the birth of psychoanalysis. It was when
Freud "abandoned the seduction theory" in favor of psychic, and
not necessarily factual, reality that he was able to open up the world
of unconscious desire. But in changing from abuse to desire, Freud
also changed the sex of the typical analytic subject. Before, the father
had been guilty of abusing his daughter. Now, the son is (unconsciously) guilty of desiring his mother. The father has gone from being a lawbreaker to being a lawgiver. Women are either victims of
abuse or objects of desire. The "reality" of women's desire is invisible either way.

This is even more true of women's aggression. Even in a book that
aims to critique the Oedipus complex as Freud defined it, the attempt to consider the little girl normative breaks down when the
topic is rivalry:

> The child (I refer to the young girl for economy of exposition and also
> to stress important elements of the Oedipus complex that are experi-
> enced similarly by both sexes) between approximately the ages of three
> and six indicates, in more or less verbalized fantasies, that she is in-
> volved in a new and striking way with her parents. She talks with in-
> creasing conviction of being a grown-up someday. When she gets big-
> ger, she will replace her mother and marry her father, or she will marry
> somebody unmistakeably (from the adults' perspective) like him. Plans
> for having babies of her own are discussed. . . .
>
> Triangulation is interesting and important because it heralds the
> child's more complex, textured experience of her life. . . .
>
> Interpersonal factors determine oedipal dangers more directly than
> they affect oedipal wishes. The clearest example is the boy's fear of
> physical retaliation by his rivalrous father.[15]

We never stop being a child. Only mothers are supposed to subordinate themselves entirely to the needs of someone else. The fantasy of being fully responded to is a fantasy we all have. That is why we remain so angry at the mother for frustrating that desire—or perhaps even more for fulfilling it. Besides, have we learned nothing from fairy tales? "Mirror, mirror, on the wall / Who's the fairest one of all?" The rivalry between mother and daughter is thinly disguised by calling all bad mothers stepmothers. In her analyses of the split between good breasts and bad breasts, between cannibalism and the fear of being devoured, Melanie Klein opens up a space for maternal violence, but she then situates that split within the fantasies and fears of the developing *child,* not within the attitudes of the mother.[16] As Susan Suleiman puts it:

> Melanie Klein speaks with great sympathy and understanding about the murderous impulses that every child feels toward its beloved mother; she does not speak about the murderous impulses that a mother may feel toward her beloved child.[17]

Analyses like Serge Leclaire's *On tue un enfant,* too, focus on the disturbing effects *on the child* of the parents' wish to get rid of the child.[18] Oedipus, for example, before killing his father and marrying his mother, had been put out to die by those very same parents. The parents, of course, had been warned by an oracle to beware of their son. But what were they thinking? Is the parental desire to get rid of the child simply unspeakable?

Psychoanalytic theories allow for violence toward or from the father, but the taboo on thinking about violence emanating from or performed by the mother is very strong. That taboo underlies the opposition to legal abortion in the United States. I have been approaching the topic of violence *within* the mother indirectly, by looking at the spectacular way in which the critics have no hesitation in participating in the violent feelings of Charles Baudelaire and Sylvia Plath. When floods of violence are unleashed *toward* the mother, there seems to be no taboo against participating in it. And yet what the critics in both cases hold against the mother is her attempt to live up to an ideal of responsible maternal behavior—which those same critics would claim they value. How are we to understand the critics' willingness—often eagerness—to participate in the scorn and belit-tlement of Aurelia Plath and Caroline Aupick?

V. *Violence toward the Mother*

Better than shock treatment: "I give you permission to hate your mother."
. . . In a smarmy matriarchy of togetherness it is hard to get a sanction to hate one's mother especially a sanction one believes in.
—Sylvia Plath, December 12, 1958, *Unabridged Journals*

It had become a commonplace among Baudelaire critics to lament that "he didn't have the life he deserved" until Jean-Paul Sartre came along to reverse the refrain. "He didn't deserve, certainly, that mother," Sartre summarizes the litany, "that perpetual scramble for money, that *conseil de famille,* that avaricious mistress [Jeanne Duval], that syphilis—and what could be more unjust than his pre-mature death?"[19] But Sartre protests: didn't get what he deserved? Hogwash! He got *exactly* what he deserved, including the appear-ance of having wanted something else. His small-minded mother, his uncomprehending stepfather, his debts, his *conseil judiciaire,* his in-capacity to travel—all were exactly what he needed in order to go on thinking he really wished he could be free of it all. His rage against all that was an act of bad faith—he wouldn't have known what to do with a freedom he could have seized at any time. His rage is propor-tional to his dependency. If he were truly free, he would not need to say so.

Although Sartre accuses Baudelaire of wanting the things he says he doesn't want and of not wanting the things he says he does, he nevertheless doesn't change his opinion of Baudelaire's mother. Hated or needed, she remains the small-minded bourgeoise that she had always been. In a revisionary essay entitled "(S)(m)othering Baudelaire," Margaret Miner uses the image of Baudelaire's mother to open up many of his poems, yet the title of the essay perpetuates the ambivalence it also questions.[20]

The logic of motherhood implicit in the condemnation of both mothers is as follows: "If only she hadn't tried so hard, her child would not have been unhealthy in such-and-such a way." Or, "If only she had given more, her child would have avoided such-and-such a situation." Of course, both Baudelaire and Plath would never have become the poets that they became, but if the mothers have *both* failed the children *and* been unable to understand them, the mothers can still be blamed for creating the poetic genius unintentionally, and for not seeing the value everyone else takes for granted in what their children accomplished. Baudelaire's mother refused to give; Plath's mother refused to lack. And that made all the difference.

Refused to give. She could have offered relief, and she refused. She was rich; he remained poor. He asked; she did not answer. She sometimes said "no." He suffered; she didn't do anything to alleviate that suffering. When she did give him money, it was always too little, too late, and too conditional. He beseeched, went without heat or food or shirts, and what did she do? She accompanied Jacques Aupick to Constantinople. After Aupick's death and after Baudelaire's trial, he finally used the *tu* form to reestablish intimacy with his mother, but quoted his own intense thoughts about her in the third person:

> Je ne veux pas qu'en me lisant tu croies que l'égoïsme seul me dirige. Une grosse partie de ma pensée est ceci: *Ma mère ne me connaît pas, elle m'a à peine connu; Nous n'avons pas eu le temps de vivre ensemble. Il faut pourtant que nous trouvions en commun quelques années de bonheur.* (*Correspondance,* 1: 452)

> [I don't want you to think, upon reading me, that all this is motivated by egoism. A large part of my thought is this: *My mother does not know me, she has barely known me; we have not had time to live together. We must nevertheless together find some years of happiness.*]

To whom is Baudelaire speaking here? He is not speaking *to* his mother directly, but to the great stereotype in the sky. Being known by the mother—wanting to be known by the mother—having no patience with the mother's failures to know perfectly—all belong to an ideal of motherhood Baudelaire does not question. In the letter he wrote to her right after Aupick's death, he had said:

Vous m'avez, il y a peu de temps, adressé un compliment très outrageux sur le changement de mes manières à votre égard, ce qui prouve que, quoique mère, vous me connaissez imparfaitement. (1: 403)

[A little while ago you gave me an outrageous compliment about my change of manners toward you, which proves that, even though you are a mother, you know me imperfectly.]

"Quoique mère, vous me connaissez imparfaitement." Caroline Aupick's imperfect knowledge of her son never ceases to amaze him. Mothers are expected to know perfectly. They are even supposed to share perfectly the child's nostalgia for the lost paradise or former life the child once had with the mother. Baudelaire indeed wrote movingly about those lost paradises and those former lives in many of his poems. And he even wrote undisguisedly to his mother about his nostalgia for their lost intimacy. In an astonishing letter of May 6, 1861, he confides:

Il y a eu dans mon enfance une époque d'amour passionné pour toi; écoute et lis sans peur. Je ne t'en ai jamais tant dit. Je me souviens d'une promenade en fiacre; tu sortais d'une maison de santé où tu avais été reléguée, et tu me montras, pour me prouver que tu avais pensé à ton fils, des dessins à la plume que tu avais faits pour moi. (2: 153)

[There was in my childhood a period of passionate love for you; listen and read without fear. I have never told you so much about it. I remember one outing we took in a carriage; you were just coming out of a sanatarium in which you had been confined, and you showed me, in order to prove that you had thought about your son, some pen-and-ink drawings that you had made for me.]

His father's death, while painful for his mother, left him in sole possession of her.

Ah! ça été pour moi le bon temps des tendresses maternelles. Je te demande pardon d'appeler *bon temps* celui qui a été sans doute mauvais pour toi. Mais j'étais toujours vivant en toi; tu étais uniquement à moi. (2: 153)

[Ah! those were the good times of maternal tenderness for me! I beg your pardon for calling *good times* what must have been bad times for you. But I was always living in you; you were uniquely mine.]

To be the good times remembered by the son, this period *had* to be the period during which the fresh loss of the father defined the intensity with which the mourning mother turned toward the son. In other words, there were not two people in this new intimacy, as Baudelaire remembers, but necessarily three: the mother, the son, and the dead father. Perfect reciprocity is a fantasy—and a deadly one, as Baudelaire had earlier in the same letter suggested:

> Nous sommes évidemment destinés à nous aimer, à vivre l'un pour l'autre, à finir notre vie le plus honnêtement et le plus doucement qu'il sera possible. Et cependant, dans les circonstances terribles où je suis placé, je suis convaincu que l'un de nous deux tuera l'autre, et que finalement nous nous tuerons réciproquement. (2: 150–151)

> [We are evidently destined to love each other, to live for each other, to end our days as honestly and as peacefully as possible. And yet, in the terrible circumstances in which I am placed, I am convinced that one of us will kill the other, and that finally we will kill each other reciprocally.]

This is quite a request for money. Even if Baudelaire is here pulling out all the stops just to persuade his mother to come to his financial rescue, he is quite right about the deadliness of perfect reciprocity.

But let us go back to that blissful carriage ride. There is something funny about Baudelaire's memory here. His mother might have spent several periods in a sanatorium, but the most dramatic one was surely the one that immediately followed her hasty second marriage, not the death of her first husband. Why was her second marriage hasty? Because she was pregnant. In November, she married the father of the child she was carrying, but in December she gave birth to a stillborn girl. Did Baudelaire know what was happening? Did he know how quickly his new rival had entered his mother's life? Did he know anything about her relationship with a dashing young army officer, which must have begun about a year after his father's death? François Baudelaire had left a widow seriously hard up for funds—as hard up, perhaps, as her son would later be. Jacques Aupick was at the start of a promising career. But whatever might have impelled her, like her son, to conflate financial need with passion, the ghost of the dead child suggests that her relation to Aupick quickly became sexual, and that despite her piety and propriety, she shared her son's openness to transgression. But back to that carriage ride. Couldn't Baudelaire have confused two moments here: the moment of his mother's loss of her first husband, and the moment when, having married a second time to render legitimate the child she was carrying, she was recovering from a different kind of health crisis, and had different reasons to think about her remaining child? What Baudelaire remembered as pure possession might in fact have felt to her like pure loss. And not the loss of a father, which only confirms the son's possession, but the loss of a child, which signifies for the son not one rival but two.

What the ideal of perfect motherhood excludes for the mother, in any case, is—her life. That is, a mother who adapts too well or too long to a child's needs and doesn't agree to "fail" at mothering may not be perceived as a separate person, but as part of the self. This was the reason that D. W. Winnicott put forward the notion of the "good enough mother" in place of the "good mother":

> The good-enough 'mother' (not necessarily the infant's own mother) is one who makes active adaptation to the infant's needs, an active adaptation that gradually lessens, according to the infant's growing ability to account for failure of adaptation and to tolerate the results of frustration. Naturally, the infant's own mother is more likely to be good enough than some other person, since this active adaptation demands an easy and unresented preoccupation with the one infant; in fact, success in infant care depends on the fact of devotion, not on cleverness or intellectual attainment.
>
> The good-enough mother, as I have stated, starts off with an almost complete adaptation to her infant's needs, and as time proceeds she adapts less and less completely, gradually, according to the infant's growing ability to deal with her failure. . . .
>
> *If all goes well* the infant can actually come to gain from the experience of frustration, since incomplete adaptation to need makes objects real, that is to say hated as well as loved. The consequence of this is that *if all goes well* the infant can be disturbed by a close adaptation to need that is continued too long, not allowed its natural decrease, since exact adaptation resembles magic and the object that behaves perfectly becomes no better than a hallucination.[21]

Although the "good-enough" mother began as a critique of the rigidity of the ideal of the "good" mother, it, in turn, comes to stand as a new ideal. The dire consequences that await the mother who does not adapt to the child or who adapts to the child too long are suggested by the twice-repeated, italicized phrase, *"If all goes well."* The "good-enough mother" is the new "good mother"; the former "good mother" has now become "bad."

It is not only in the first phases of development that the mother must adapt to the child, however. She has to consent to fail, and to be felt as failing, *for the good of the child.* She has to suspend her own pride in doing the job of mothering well—and do it less well. It is likely that, in the ordinary course of life, other things will call for the mother's attention, and that her failures will be part of attending to those things. But if a particularly talented mother cannot tolerate failure, and cannot allow the child any justification to feel that the mother is failing, then the mother's perfection will eventually take precedence over the needs of the child. From then on the child is expected to give the mother *the mother's own perfection.*

In accusing her of not giving enough, the child implicitly believes that money is like milk, which is construed as abundant and free. The fact that children who were breast-fed often feel that their mothers failed to give them enough milk is a sign of the same unforgiving attitude toward the mother's actual life, needs, and limitations. The mother's limitations cannot be forgiven: they can only be a source of deprivation for the child. The child thus gets to believe in the possibility that deprivation is not necessary but contingent, a function of the sins of this particular mother and not of the process of becoming human itself. As a result, the more the mother is blamed, the more the ideal of motherhood is maintained—often by the mother herself. In other words, to maintain an ideal of motherhood, the mother is even willing to shoulder the blame herself for what has malfunctioned. And for critics, children, and psychoanalysts, the most efficient way to maintain the structure is to blame the mother.

This puts the child in an impossible bind if she tries to become a mother herself. This was not a problem Baudelaire faced; he could afford to think of himself as a child for his whole life. But how does one go from being the object of the mother's attentions to being the giver of them to someone else? Sylvia Plath relied on her mother to type, notarize, and send out her manuscripts; when she married Hughes, Plath did the same for him. But she went on asking her mother to get applications and find things out, to adopt her cat and to send her checks, well past the moment when the daughter had children of her own. What does a former child feel about becoming a mother? How can the transformation be accomplished without ambivalence?

The mother must continue to fail to live up to an ideal based on infantile need long past any physical dependency on the part of an adult child. The mother can even be blamed for the damage caused by her own failure to force the child to separate from her. This puts her in a bind from which she cannot extricate herself: she must optimally respond to the child and then optimally assure the frustration that enables him to separate. But she can't oversee that separation herself, otherwise the child will only say, "My mother won't allow me to separate." Baudelaire in effect sometimes suggests that he would have been better off if his mother had let him squander all his patrimony and then face the consequences. The mother *cannot* give permission to the child to separate. This would be a form of the classic double bind: "Disobey me." Separation can occur only when the child risks becoming independent of what the mother allows or prohibits. And at that point another destructive ideal kicks in: the ideal of the autonomous subject. It is as if the adult subject has no relation to dependency, no relation to the mother, which reinforces the notion that, as that from which the adult subject must be completely separate, mothers can be defined only in terms of their ability to satisfy someone else's needs.

VI. Primal Scenes

Psychoanalytic theory calls the nostalgic ideal of the perfect mother the *phallic mother*, not because she is a mother with a phallus, but because she is a mother prior to the discovery, by the male child, of sexual difference. She is the mother as *all* and as *me*. For the female child, the encounter with difference on the mother's body cannot itself immediately be perceived as the discovery that the mother lacks what the girl may still be ignorant of. For this reason, separation occurs less traumatically for the girl, but less cleanly. But *that* the mother lacks—that the mother is not all for the child—may simply be the discovery that there are other people in the mother's life. The paradise lost brought into being by the fall never existed, except in retrospect in the mind of the child. The perfect fusion of mother and child never existed even in the womb, but the discovery that the mother *has a life* is called, by Freud and Lacan, castration. The phallic mother is thus the ideal everyone wants the mother to live up to, the ideal of perfect reciprocity, perfect knowledge, total response. It is not that people *know* that that is what they want, but that they suddenly notice they have lost something, and that if "castration" is the name for that loss, the phallic mother must have once existed.

Here let me cite what for me function as the "primal scenes" for each poet. In Plath's case the scenario involves the loss of the mother. In Baudelaire's case the scenario involves the mother's loss. These scenes present almost too perfectly the classic male and female responses to the mother's "castration."

The first few letters in Baudelaire's correspondence are addressed to his older half-brother from his father's first marriage, Alphonse. A married man who felt it his obligation to see to the welfare of his younger brother, he has asked little Charles to write to him on the first of every month. On February 1, 1832, Jacques Aupick is ordered to quell the workers' riots in Lyon, where he is dispatched. His wife and child soon follow in a coach from Paris to Lyon. This *fiacre* ride may very well call up for Baudelaire the memory of their earlier intimacy. The connection between vehicular locomotion and sexual emotion ("transport" can be used for both) seems already well established, and only grows stronger with the technological development of public transportation, as Benjamin notes in his study of the nineteenth century. In Flaubert, the famous erotic cab ride in *Madame Bovary* taken by Emma and Leon was the first scene to be cut from the *Revue de Paris* serial publication in an (unsuccessful) attempt to escape the censors.[22] A flavor of eroticism and illicitness, at

least at that time, thus comes to suffuse all cab rides. Eleven-year-old
Charles describes his hasty departure from Paris with his mother:

> Première étourderie de maman: en faisant charger les effets sur l'impé-
> riale, elle s'aperçoit qu'elle n'a plus son manchon et s'écrie en faisant
> un coup de théâtre: "Et mon manchon!" Et moi de lui répondre tran-
> quillement: "Je sais où il est et je vais le chercher." Elle l'avait laissé
> dans le bureau sur une banquette. (*Correspondance*, 1: 3–4)

> [Maman's first scatterbrained action: as the things are being loaded
> onto the coach, she notices that she has lost her muff and shouts in
> high drama: "My muff!" And I respond calmly: "I know where it is
> and I'll go get it." She had left it in the office on a bench.]

The mother's theatrical if not hysterical reaction to noticing something missing is calmed by the knowledgeable actions of the unflap-
pable son, who knows where the missing thing is and brings it back
to her. The mother's loss is the son's potency. Calmly, he finds and
restores what she lacks.

In the next letter to Alphonse, Charles proudly tells his brother
about wandering away from the same coach later on in the journey.
He is delighted to hear the other passengers refer to his independent
self as *Monsieur*. But already as of the third letter, Baudelaire begins
apologizing, and in the first letter we have addressed to his mother,
he apologizes for his disappointing behavior and promises to *change
completely;* a promise he will repeat in almost every letter. He is particularly embarrassed by his grades, and he pledges to give his
brother, as a New Year's present, his own achievement of a first
place. In the earlier carriage scenes—and they *must* have some connection with the one he remembers—he enjoys a brief *fantasy* of
omniscience (knowing where the muff is) and an even more brief
fantasy of autonomy (a momentary independence from his mother)
that take place within, and are a brief forgetting of, dependency. He
begins to require himself to live up to a perfection he cannot achieve,
but it is as if that perfection were the desire of someone else. (Even if
the ideal to be lived up to initially *did* come from the other, of all the
things that Alphonse wants for New Year's, Charles's first probably
isn't high on the list.)

But as a result, only imperfection is "mine"; all perfections are gifts for the other. Thus, when Plath realized that her mother expected and appropriated everything she wrote, so that in a sense only something the mother *didn't* want would be the daughter's, she wrote *The Bell Jar.*

Second scene. Sylvia Plath's mother is breast-feeding Plath's recently born younger brother, but Sylvia wants to climb into her lap at the same time. Her mother needs to find an acceptable substitute for her own body that will provide some of the satisfaction she can no longer provide for the older child. The following description of the scene is, again, from Aurelia Plath's introduction to *Letters Home:*

> When we were reunited as a family, the one difficult period was when I nursed the baby; it was always then that Sylvia wanted to get into my lap. Fortunately, around this time she discovered the alphabet from the capital letters on packaged goods on the pantry shelves. With great rapidity she learned the names of the letters and I taught her the separate sounds of each. From then on, each time I nursed Warren, she would get a newspaper, sit on the floor in front of me and pick out all the capital letters to "read." In her baby book, I found the note that it was in July (at the age of two years and nine months), as we waited to cross the street to enter the Arboretum with Warren in the carriage, that Sylvia stared at the big STOP sign with fascination. "Look, Mummy," she cried, pointing to the sign, "Look! P-O-T-S. It says 'pots,' Mummy; it says 'pots!'"[23]

The place of poetry is henceforth established. For Baudelaire, it is a prize, an object lost by the mother and brought to her in triumph to restore wholeness. For Plath, it is a substitute for the mother's body. All letters—the very letters of the alphabet—are "letters home."

VII. Addressing the (M)other

When Plath first arrives at Smith College in 1950, she writes to her mother:

The food here is fabulous. I've had two helpings of everything since I got here and should gain a lot. I love everybody. If only I can unobtrusively do well in all my courses and get enough sleep, I should be tops. (*Letters Home*, 48)

Plath assures her mother that she intends to be well fed and well rested. But the problem of competition (rivalry over the breast with the brother) is not entirely solved. How do "unobtrusive" and "tops" go together? How does one win without appearing to compete? Her poem "Mushrooms" has an answer: if unobtrusive things are determined and numerous and self-effacing enough, they shall inherit the earth. "Our foot's in the door," say the mushrooms (*Collected Poems*, 140). "Tops" of course is also spelled P-O-T-S.

The problem of competition is often figured by Plath in her journals as an inability to decide whether there are two or one in a relationship. In 1952, she writes about her current boyfriend, Dick Norton (the Buddy Willard of *The Bell Jar*):

So [Dick] accuses me of "struggling for dominance"? Sorry, wrong number. Sure, I'm a little scared of being dominated. . . . But that doesn't mean I, ipso facto, want to *dominate*. No, it is not a black-and-white choice or alternative like: "Either I'm victorious on top or you are." It is only *balance* that I ask for. (*Unabridged Journals*, 43)

In the domination scenario, there is always only one. In the balance scenario, there are two. When later she writes over and over again, "I'm so glad Ted is first" (*Letters Home*, 297; *Unabridged Journals*, 154) and on the next page suffers from "some paralysis of the head" (*Unabridged Journals*, 155) the problem is still unresolved. Perhaps it is unresolvable. This is a problem that can be expected in any relation perceived as equal. But the problem of whether her relation with her mother involves one or two is perhaps less expected, more fully explored in her poetry, and ultimately at the heart of her relation with her husband, Ted, I would argue, as well. In her poem "In Plaster," Plath combines an image of a cast on a healing broken leg, a relationship with a perfect thing, and marriage into one complicated and ironic structure. Here are the last two stanzas:

I wasn't in any position to get rid of her.
She'd supported me for so long I was quite limp—
I had even forgotten how to walk or sit,
So I was careful not to upset her in any way
Or brag ahead of time how I'd avenge myself.
Living with her was like living with my own coffin:
Yet I still depended on her, though I did it regretfully.

I used to think we might make a go of it together—
After all, it was a kind of marriage, being so close.
Now I see it must be one or the other of us.
She may be a saint, and I may be ugly and hairy,
But she'll soon find out that that doesn't matter a bit.
I'm collecting my strength; one day I shall manage without her,
And she'll perish with emptiness then, and begin to miss me.
      (*Collected Poems*, 159–160)

For Baudelaire, the question of two versus one takes a different, more grammatical form. In his poem "L'Héautontimorouménos," he begins:

Je te frapperai sans colère
Et sans haine . . .

[I will strike you without anger
And without hate . . .]

But later in the same poem the I-thou relationship becomes a relationship within the self:

Je suis la plaie et le couteau!
Je suis le soufflet et la joue!
Je suis les membres et la roue,
Et la victime et le bourreau!

[I am the wound and the knife!
I am the slap and the cheek!
I am the limbs and the rack,
The victim and the torturer!]

Interestingly, in a letter to his mother Baudelaire speaks about "your happiness and yours," to which an editor's note explains that this must be a lapsus for "your happiness and mine." But it is clear that the "mistake" makes the same grammatical move as the poem.

The difficulty of telling the difference between "I" and "thou" can never be resolved. What if, in the child's mind, it is the *mother*, finally, who is the solipsist, and the child just an image that she created? As Plath put it, the mother can always take the child's existence away, because

> I
> Know you appear
> Vivid at my side,
> Denying you sprang out of my head,
> Claiming you feel
> Love fiery enough to prove flesh real,
> Though it's quite clear
> All your beauty, all your wit, is a gift, my dear,
> From me.[24]

Both Sylvia Plath's mother and Charles Baudelaire's mother ended up outliving their children. Baudelaire's was by his side during his final illness, when Caroline Aupick tried over and over to teach the aphasic poet to speak again. Aurelia Plath learned of her daughter's suicide a continent away. Outliving one's child is also something mothers are not expected to do.

Rather than question the tyranny of the ideal, then, both the mothers and the children continue to negotiate its frustrations. The deaths of the fathers merely allow the ideal to be exposed more sharply: if the fathers had lived, they would have absorbed the permissible ambivalence the children would have had an outlet for. Ambivalence toward the father would have allowed the mother to function as a lost paradise without difficulty. But with the father dead, the children are left with an ambivalence they can't find an appropriate object for, if they are to maintain their ideal of motherhood.

The regulating prohibition on *all* violence in the mother or *any* considerations that compete with the needs of the child suggests that the child cannot benefit from recognizing considerations that might put him or her second. This seems to me self-defeating, unnecessary, and unrealistic. The attempts the mothers of our two poets made to be who they thought they were supposed to be were much more damaging to their children than any mere imperfection. We have to renounce the irresistible attractions of blaming Caroline Aupick and Aurelia Plath for falling short of an ideal that they thereby allow us to continue to uphold. Such a renunciation is very hard to accomplish. But perhaps by freeing them from being the cause of everything, we can free ourselves from the constraints of the ideal, too. We are holding against them the wielding of a power that they do not really possess. In the final analysis, we are just as likely to resemble *them* as to resemble their genius children. We have met the enemy and, whether we like it or not, she is us.

FIVE

Passage Work

Baudelaire's unique importance consists in having been the first one, and the most unswerving, to have apprehended, in both senses of the word, the productive energy of the individual alienated from himself— agnosticized and heightened through concretization.

—Walter Benjamin to Max Horkheimer, April 16, 1938

Ah! êtes-vous encore bien disposé à me gronder; si tu l'es encore, cela prouve que tu m'aimes davantage.

[Ah! are you still well-disposed toward yelling at me; if you are, that goes to prove all the more that you love me.]

—Charles Baudelaire to his half-brother, Alphonse, November 2, 1837

Consumed with that which it was nourished by.

—William Shakespeare, Sonnet 73

I. Consumption

Charles Baudelaire was a part of Walter Benjamin's life from as early as 1915 until September 25, 1940, when Benjamin took his own life while fleeing the Nazis.[1] Baudelaire thus encompasses the two poles of Benjamin's thought that have traditionally been called Messianism and Marxism, or—using the names of Benjamin's two most important correspondents—Gershom Scholem (who followed Zionism to Palestine) and Theodor Adorno (who followed the Institute for Social Research to the United States).[2] And indeed Benjamin does seem torn between addressing Scholem and addressing Adorno, but, although his vocabulary changes between *Origins of German Tragic Drama* (1928) and *Charles Baudelaire: A Lyric Poet in the Era of High Capitalism* (1938), something prevents one from seeing in this a simple progression from one to the other—if only because it was Adorno who first saw the importance of the *Trauerspiel* book.[3]

Benjamin's aim, as he put it in the recently translated *Arcades Project* (*Passagen-Werk*, a monumental collection of quotations and commentaries that comes without an instruction manual), was to use Baudelaire as a passageway into the whole nineteenth century, and particularly into the development of industrial capitalism after the French Revolution. But the figure Benjamin uses to describe Baudelaire's importance is interesting:

> What I propose is to show how Baudelaire lies embedded in the nine-teenth century. The imprint he has left behind there must stand clear and intact, like that of a stone which, having lain in the ground for decades, is one day rolled from its place.[4]

We will come back to this rolling stone later, but for the moment, let us follow the traces of Benjamin's Marxism.

There are curious slippages in reports of Baudelaire's importance for Benjamin's attempts at a historical materialist analysis, complicated by problems in translation. On the back cover of the French edition of Benjamin's book on Baudelaire, Baudelaire's importance is advertised as follows: "Baudelaire—le premier à avoir appréhendé la force productive de l'homme réifié" (Baudelaire—the first to have apprehended the productive force of reified man). The importance of this notion for the editors of the book is reinforced by its slightly lengthened—but still truncated—occurrence in Jean Lacoste's preface: "La signification tout à fait exceptionnelle de Baudelaire tient en ceci que, le premier (. . .), il a appréhendé (. . .) la force productive de l'homme aliéné: il l'a reconnue et, par la réification, lui a donné plus de force" (Baudelaire's exceptional significance lies in the fact he was the first [. . .] to have apprehended [. . .] the productive force of alienated man: he recognized it and, through reification, gave it even more force [ellipses in the French]).[5] We are told that the quotation is from a letter Benjamin wrote to Max Horkheimer on April 16, 1938, explaining his new plans for his Baudelaire project (to be rejected by Adorno six months later). The full sentence from the letter, which I have already cited as one of my epigraphs, reads, in English: "Baudelaire's unique importance consists in having been the first one, and the most unswerving, to have apprehended, in both senses of the word, the productive energy of the individual alienated from himself—agnosticized and heightened through concretization."[6] The German text reads: "Die einzigartige Bedeutung Baudelaires besteht darin, als erster und am unbeirrbarsten die Produktivkraft des sich selbst entfremdeten Menschen im doppelten Sinne des Wortes dingfest gemacht—agnosziert und durch die Verdinglichung gesteigert—zu haben."

The *Arcades Project* is indeed filled with sentences from Benjamin and others beginning, "Baudelaire was the first. . . ." Here is another one, very close to the passage from the letter:

> The unique importance of Baudelaire resides in his being the first and the most unflinching to have taken the measure of the self-estranged human being, in the double sense of acknowledging this being and fortifying it with armor against the reified world.[7]

A footnote to this passage indicates that the German plays on the expressions *ding-fest gemacht* and *gegen die verdinglichte Welt*. What becomes clear from all these quotations is that the self-estranged human being becomes "dingfest" (arrested? made into a thing?) while the reified world becomes "verdinglicht" (solidified? made into a thing?). But what exactly is a self-estranged human being? And what is its productivity?

The larger question raised by this fluctuating quotation could be formulated, "What is the relation between reification and alienation?" On the one hand, they can be seen to be the same. Private property, on the one side, and the private name, on the other, both involve appropriations as if they constituted essences. One's "own" name and one's "own" property constitute illusory possessions that economics and psychoanalysis will put in question. But on the other hand, they pose a question about the relation between inner reality and outer circumstances that cannot be so simple. If "alienation" can be produced when anything considered natural or transparent is displaced, then the economic and the psychological experiences of the human being are analogous, but somehow the *discrepancy* between inner and outer reality in part defines what it means to be human. It is as if the economic and the psychological should reflect each other, but yet the sense of one's own existence inheres in the ways in which one escapes determination by that reflection. How can this gap be understood?

The analogy takes on a characteristic form with the development of capitalism. Both kinds of alienation have the structure of a commodity—that is, both the human being and the thing are worth only what they will sell for. Benjamin was very aware of the conflation of those two structures—as, for example, in the whore, who was both seller and commodity in one. But the "double sense" on which Benjamin insists indicates that they are not quite the same, and that Baudelaire's importance lies in exploring the productivity of their relation. The poet and the whore are all too much alike when art has to compete in the marketplace (as Baudelaire himself proclaimed by comparing art to prostitution), but what is the relation between resembling a whore and resembling an old boudoir?

Jean-Paul Sartre, theorist of alienation in an existential sense, revolutionized Baudelaire studies by suggesting—after years of critics' lamenting that Baudelaire did not have the life he deserved—that in fact Baudelaire had *exactly* the life he wanted.[8] This was alienation with a capital *A*, but only in a psychological sense. In fact, Sartre could take on all the geniuses of the nineteenth century and express his anger at the simple fact that they *had* a psychology. Modern psychology takes precisely the form of getting what you say you don't want, and no one fleshed out this notion better than Baudelaire, Flaubert, and Mallarmé. As Baudelaire puts it in a letter to his mother dated March 26, 1853:

> Je suis coupable envers moi-même;—cette disproportion entre la volonté et la faculté est pour moi quelque chose d'inintelligible.—Pourquoi, ayant une idée si juste, si nette du devoir et de l'utile, fais-je toujours le contraire?[9]

> [I am guilty toward myself;—this disproportion between the will and the ability is for me something unintelligible.—Why, if I have such a clearly defined sense of duty and utility, do I always do exactly the opposite?]

All the stages and rages of life, which Sartre documents so mercilessly, are in fact not the exception but the rule. The immense productivity of Baudelaire consists of creating a psychology that doesn't have health and well-being as its end, but is rather alienated *irremediably*. Instead of claiming, as Adorno did of Benjamin while editing Benjamin's correspondence, that he was productive *"in spite of self-alienation,"*[10] Benjamin would claim that Baudelaire (and indeed Benjamin) was productive *because of it*. Or rather—that it was that alienation itself that became productive, often against the express wishes of the author.

Because hope and illusion had kept the image of imminent health and happiness constantly before workers' eyes, previous psychologies had been able to cover over the fact that the alienation of labor was structural, not contingent. But the experience of the workplace is tied to the fact that the fruits of one's labor do not belong to oneself but to those who pay for them. Baudelaire renounces any illusions of happiness and explores what human psychology would be like if it didn't imagine a remedy. Or rather—he imagines a remedy but knows he will never reach it. As Benjamin puts it, "'Spleen et idéal'—. . . For Baudelaire, there is no contradiction between these two concepts. He recognizes in spleen the latest transfiguration of the ideal; the ideal seems to him the first expression of spleen" (*Arcades*, 24). Baudelaire does not recommend such a state of affairs, but neither does he turn away from it in favor of a more desirable outcome. He describes the diminishing returns—and the perverse liberation—of such a structure in many ways: as autophagy, as irony, as the resuscitation of one's own vampire. Self-estranged man takes himself as an object of consumption because the production of objects of consumption is always for the benefit of someone else. "Je fais bouillir et je mange mon coeur" [I boil up and eat my own heart] is assuming ownership of one's own labor, even at the expense of eating oneself up.[11] The addictive nature of this self-defeat is what is genuinely unbearable. We do not want to admit that modern desire comes into being as desire for what is not good for us. But everything else can too easily be appropriated by the forces of control. As Michel Foucault has exhaustively demonstrated, the law creates

more of whatever it forbids. What Sartre calls "bad faith" can otherwise be called "life." To the extent that there is a desiring subject at
all, it cannot coincide with its own use value for the other.

But if "free" labor is free only to alienate its labor, then labor
power enters into the circuit of commodities, and the difference between persons and things takes on a new form. A person's "worth"
becomes inseparable from the marketplace. It was in an attempt to
deny this reduction of all value to a universal equivalent that nineteenth-century artists *and* nineteenth-century moralists clung desperately to maintaining a difference between "my value" and "my
values." As Baudelaire says in his projects of self-defense (between
his indictment and his trial), "Je sais que l'amant passionné du beau
style s'expose à la haine des multitudes. Mais aucun respect humain,
aucune fausse pudeur, aucune coalition, aucun suffrage universel ne
me contraindront à parler le patois incomparable de ce siècle, ni à
confondre[12] l'encre avec la vertu." [I know that the passionate lover
of beautiful style opens himself up to the majority's hatred. But no
human respect, no false modesty, no coalition, no universal suffrage
will constrain me to speak the incomparable dialect of this century,
nor to conflate ink with virtue.][13] In an economy run more and
more by the marketplace, all values are eventually converted into exchange values.[14] But as a result, the commodity acquires what both
Marx and Freud call "fetishism."

It seems curious that both Marx and Freud should have recourse
to the same word to describe what seem like totally different phenomena. For Marx, the "fetishism of the commodity" is the way in
which value seems to inhere in the object rather than in the labor
that produced it. For Freud, sexual fetishism is the election of an
(often inorganic) sexual substitute so as to deny the sexual lack
that would otherwise have been discovered in the mother. Benjamin
speaks more than once in *The Arcades Project* of "the sex appeal of
the inorganic," which brings Marx and Freud together in a surprising new way. Of course, Marx and Freud lived during the golden age
of imperialism, during which cross-cultural exchange underpinned
invisibly all forms of metropolitan prosperity. Could imperialism
have underpinned its most visible alienations as well? Nothing could

suit our postcolonial moment better than a rectification of the proper meaning of the fetish. But, as William Pietz has written, it is precisely the absence of such a proper meaning that has called the fetish into existence in the first place:

> My thesis is that the fetish, as an idea and a problem, and as a novel object not proper to any prior discrete society, originated in the cross-cultural spaces of the coast of West Africa during the sixteenth and seventeenth centuries.[15]

By speaking of the sex appeal of the inorganic, Benjamin could combine the eroticism of the prosthesis (the prosthesis of the Mother's phallus, according to Freud) with the mystic attraction of the commodity. Marx was intent on combating precisely that attraction: it is the gleam of the commodity that blinds the buyer to the human labor that produced it.

It is therefore surprising to read in one of Marx's early texts that the sensuous enjoyment that is lost in alienated labor is similar to the relation between a fetishist and his object—surrounded by the gleam of its spiritual value as the gleam of a commodity that gets itself to market without human labor: "The nations which are still dazzled by the sensuous splendour of precious metals, and are therefore still fetish-worshippers of metal money, are not yet fully developed money-nations."[16] Marx therefore has to document the stripping away of such sensual enjoyment by the money form (the universal equivalent) before being able to demystify the subsequent enjoyment of the commodity (the "fetishism of the commodity") as a refusal to see the human labor that produced it.

Here is how Baudelaire's poetry gives voice to what Marx tries to repress, as described in Benjamin's book on Baudelaire:

> If the soul of the commodity which Marx occasionally mentions in jest existed, it would be the most empathetic ever encountered in the realm of souls, for it would have to see in everyone the buyer in whose hand and house it wants to nestle. Empathy is the nature of the intoxication to which the *flâneur* abandons himself in the crowd. "The poet enjoys the incomparable privilege of being himself and someone else as he sees fit. Like a roving soul in search of a body, he enters another person

whenever he wishes. For him alone, all is open; if certain places seem closed to him, it is because in his view they are not worth inspecting" ("Les Foules"). The commodity itself is the speaker here. Yes, the last words give a rather accurate idea of what the commodity whispers to a poor wretch who passes a shop-window containing beautiful and expensive things. These objects are not interested in this person; they do not empathize with him. In the sentences of the significant prose poem "Les Foules" there speaks, with other words, the fetish itself with which Baudelaire's sensitive nature resonated so powerfully; that empathy with inorganic things which was one of his sources of inspiration.[17]

If Baudelaire was indeed a poet who understood the immense productivity of alienated or reified man, it was thus because, far from taking the route of the healing, lucidity, or health that *both* Marx and Freud imply lies behind the distortions of the fetish, he was capable of going in the opposite direction and making the distance itself into poetry. In a note appended to the paragraph quoted above, Benjamin writes:

> The second "Spleen" poem is the most important addition to the documentation for this that was assembled in the first part of this essay. Hardly any poet before Baudelaire wrote a verse that is anything like "Je suis un vieux boudoir plein de roses fanées" (I, 86) ["I am an old boudoir full of faded roses"]. The poem is entirely based on empathy with material that is dead in a dual sense. It is inorganic matter, matter that has been eliminated from the circulation process.[18]

Thus, on the one hand, there is no difference between reification and alienation; on the other, the history of conflict between Marxism and psychoanalysis suggests that things cannot be so simple.

These two realms of discourse begin, in fact, with a gesture that sweeps away either inner or outer reality. Marx becomes Marx by renouncing his youthful relation to poetry and emotion; Freud becomes Freud when he realizes that the truths his hysterical patients tell him are psychic truths not necessarily borne out by historical reality.[19] The relation between inner and outer realities is severed, and that severing brings with it powerful insights. Each side is able to concentrate on and analyze its differences from itself. Henceforth, economics and psychology become radically distinct studies. But language fits neatly into neither side—it is the network that articulates the difference and the passage between them. There would be no inside and outside if it weren't for language, but once there is, the two cannot be told apart. Value, sexuality, and cross-cultural contact continue to run on a necessary misprision: the fiction that what is wrong can be rectified.

"Commodities" appears to be an odd translation of "goods" (another odd word)—a strange rendition of what in German is simply "wares" [*Waren*]. Why was this word chosen in English? I thought it must be a distortion of a simpler concept, but was surprised to find that such a "simpler concept" was—at least in English—itself a distortion. The word "commodity" originates in the production of things that have a reference to the needs and desires of man. "Commodity" is the ease which the commodity is supposed to produce. The relation between psychological well-being and material objects is present in the word from the beginning. Therefore, it is not possible to distinguish desire from need in humans, between use value and exchange value. Marx wants to strip off all exchange value (all mimetic desire produced because of someone else's desire; all price, a fiction that corresponds to no properties of the object) from things and get back to use value. But the fetishism of the commodity he rails against is contained in the word "commodity" itself. At least in English.

What about French? Baudelaire has no thought of Marxism in his preface to *Petits poèmes en prose*, but something of that archaic sense comes through when the new genre is advertised as catering to everyone's *commodité:* "Mon cher ami, je vous envoie un petit ouvrage dont on ne pourrait dire, sans injustice, qu'il n'a ni queue ni tête, puisque tout, au contraire, y est à la fois tête et queue, alternativement et réciproquement. Considérez, je vous prie, quelles admirables *commodités* cette combinaison nous offre à tous, à vous, à moi et au lecteur"[20] [My dear friend, I'm sending you a little work about which people can't say, without injustice, that they can't make heads or tails of it, because everything, on the contrary, is at once head and tail, alternatively and reciprocally. Just think, I beg you, of what perfect *convenience* that combination offers everyone—you, me, and the reader; *Oeuvres complètes,* 1: 275, emphasis mine]. In other words, the philological transformation of facility into marketability is itself a process of making something *dingfest.* The same process is at work in a passage from Wladimir Weidlé that Benjamin quotes (*Arcades,* 225):

> Etymology of the word "comfort." "In English, it is used to mean *consolation* ('Comforter' is the epithet applied to the Holy Spirit). Then the sense became, instead, *well-being.* Today, in all languages of the world, the word designates nothing more than rational convenience."

Benjamin could have added: "In English, the word stands for an item of bedding," and the concretization of "comforter" would be complete.

Hence the double meaning of *dingfest*—made into a thing, on the one hand, and arrested or made subject to the law, on the other. The word "apprehend," surprisingly, has these two senses as well, plus one more: understand, arrest, and *fear.* Here, the psychological sense of "apprehend" comes like a parasite along with the senses of "fix" and "arrest." The psychological dimension is thus an unwanted third sense entirely created by translation. But in a sense it is the possibility of such accidental productivity that Baudelaire seeks out by making things *dingfest. Agnosziert* means something like "entirely material" and *durch die Verdinglichung* means "through concretization, reification," which are indeed the same words Marx chose, for the same reasons.

But the unidentified dread—which comes out of translation and thus has no proper origin—deserves to be followed further. Perhaps that sense was what led Freud to study the "uncanny": the uncanny that comes from making things prematurely *dingfest*—burying them alive. This is exactly what happens to the "comforter." Or to the "afghan." The commodity is produced as a search for "ease." Benjamin indeed remarks on the fate of the word "souvenir" in a similar sense:

> The things sold in the arcades are souvenirs [*Andenken*]. The "souvenir" is the form of the commodity in the arcades. One always buys only mementos of the commodity and of the arcade. Rise of the souvenir industry. (*Arcades,* 864)

From being the stuff of history, the souvenir becomes *dingfest* into the kitchiest of reminders. What then becomes of the past that continues to haunt us?

II. *Correspondences*

One could say that the decline of bourgeois life is presented here through the decline of the art of correspondence.

—Theodor Adorno to Walter Benjamin, November 7, 1936

The magic columns of these palaces
Show to the amateur on all sides,
In the objects their porticos display,
That industry is the rival of the arts.

—Epigraph to the opening section of Benjamin's exposés of 1935 and 1939 of *The Arcades Project*, from *Nouveaux Tableaux de Paris* (Paris, 1828)

Tout va bien au Sonnet, la bouffonnerie, la galanterie, la passion, la rêverie, la méditation philosophique. Il y a là la beauté du métal et du minéral bien travaillés. Avez-vous observé qu'un morceau de ciel, aperçu par un soupirail, ou entre deux cheminées, deux rochers, ou *par une arcade*, etc., donnait une idée plus profonde de l'infini que le grand panorama vu du haut d'une montagne?

[Everything looks good as a Sonnet—foolishness, gallantry, passion, reverie, philosophical meditation. It has the beauty of metal or stone that has been well cut. Have you noticed that a view of the sky, glimpsed through a basement window, or between two chimneys, two rocks, or *through an arcade*, etc., could give a more profound sense of the infinite than the grand panorama seen from the top of a mountain?]

—Charles Baudelaire to Armand Fraisse, February 18, 1860 (emphasis added)

Eager to earn the support of the Institute for Social Research for his work on *The Arcades*, Benjamin sent Adorno his first "Exposé" of the whole project, and responded eagerly to Adorno's comments on it. On June 10, 1935, he wrote:

Amongst all the things in your letter, none struck me more forcibly than the position you seem to take up with regard to the question of the "mediation" between society and psychology. Here we are both pulling at the *same* rope, although I was unaware of the fact in this particular form—though it is hardly an ideal situation to find Fromm and Reich are both pulling hard at the other end. I shall be looking at Freud soon. Incidentally, can you recall whether there is any psycho-analytic study of waking, or studies to that effect, in Freud or his school?[21]

Three years later, an even more financially desperate Benjamin sent a longer essay to be published in the institute's journal, and again it was Adorno who tried to explain the institute's rejection of Benjamin's text for its lack of "mediation":

> Unless I am very much mistaken, your dialectic is lacking in one thing: mediation. You show a prevailing tendency to relate the pragmatic contents of Baudelaire's work directly and immediately to adjacent fea-tures in the social history, and, whenever possible, the economic fea-tures, of the time.[22]

This question of "mediation" between economic features and so-cial history implies that the two domains are distinct and that there is a middle ground between them. But this was precisely what Benja-min's model of historical materialism denied. Rejecting all "develop-ment" that implies a gradual process, Benjamin likened his dialecti-cal process to the shock of awakening. There is no middle ground between dreams and awakening. "The compelling—the drastic—ex-perience, which refutes everything 'gradual' about becoming and shows all seeming 'development' to be dialectical reversal, eminently and thoroughly composed, is the awakening from dream" (*Arcades*, 389). The formative role for modernity played by Marcel Proust re-sided for Benjamin partly in the fact that his seven-volume novel be-gins with a scene of awakening. Elsewhere, Benjamin writes: "Ar-cades are houses or passages having no outside—like the dream" (*Arcades*, 406).

Another model for Benjamin's "lack" of mediation can be found in the trace of that Baudelaire-stone rolled from its place in the nine-teenth century. The hollow left by such a stone does not relate to it as the material fact does to the total social process but rather as a photographic negative relates to a print. Studying Baudelaire is like studying art in the age of its mechanical reproduction, like studying its lost aura when its halo has already fallen in the mud. Confirmation of the photographic metaphor for Baudelaire's relation to the nineteenth century comes from one of Benjamin's earliest remarks about the poet:

> An image to characterize Baudelaire's way of looking at the world. Let us compare time to a photographer—earthly time to a photographer who photographs the essence of things. But because of the nature of earthly time and its apparatus, the photographer manages only to register the negative of that essence on his photographic plates. No one can read these plates; no one can deduce from the negative, on which time records the objects, the true essence of things as they really are. Moreover, the elixir that might act as a developing agent is unknown. And there is Baudelaire: he doesn't possess the vital fluid either—the fluid in which these plates would have to be immersed so as to obtain the true picture. But he, he alone, is able to read the plates, thanks to infinite mental efforts. He alone is able to extract from the negatives of essence a presentiment of its real picture. And from this presentiment speaks the negative of essence in all his poems.[23]

What is striking in this depiction of history is the absolute dependence of the essence of things on technological invention. Fluids and negatives were precise enough to capture the true picture even when they hadn't quite been invented yet. Indeed, they *were* the true picture, of which a talented poet could have a presentiment. It was not really a matter of the mechanical reproduction *of art* that had changed in the nineteenth century, but the speed at which technology was developing mechanical *representation* itself. Involuntary memory and unconscious traces enabled a new kind of detection of a history that had never been conscious. Photography was first put to use in criminology. And the detective novel could have been invented only when the reading of traces was a meaningful and possible intellectual challenge.

In other words, what Benjamin discovered as he pored over the engravings and photographs in the Cabinet des estampes was *the historicity of the means of representation*—the relation between the increasing tempo of technological change and the precise dating of the representation of the world that each change entailed. His fascination—and ours—is not only with a vanished world but also with the grain and techniques of representation itself. All the short-lived technological experiments had a different valence to those who did not know which technological inventions would survive. At the time of gaslights, daguerrotypes, and wax cylinders, people had no idea that electricity, photography, and phonograph records would render them roads not taken. The arcades came and went with a speed that makes them a snapshot of a moment in the development of marketing and city planning. Some Métro stations still preserve the traces of Art Nouveau (Benjamin analyzes it as *Jugendstil*) that, contemporary with discoveries in mass transportation, appeared 100 years later as a quaint and old-fashioned style having nothing to do with technology itself. But the organic forms after which Art Nouveau strove are displayed at the precise moment that the organic was being definitively overtaken by the mechanical. This changed the very notion of *what was real*. Benjamin quotes from Félix Nadar's description of photographic work in the Paris catacombs:

With each new camera setup, we had to test our exposure time empirically; certain of the plates were found to require up to eighteen minutes.—Remember, we were still, at that time, using collodion emulsion on glass negatives. . . . I had judged it advisable to animate some of these scenes by the use of a human figure—less from considerations of picturesqueness than in order to give a sense of scale, a precaution too often neglected by explorers in this medium and with sometimes disconcerting consequences. For these eighteen minutes of exposure time, I found it difficult to obtain from a human being the absolute, inorganic immobility I required. I tried to get around this difficulty by means of mannequins, which I dressed in workman's clothes and positioned in the scene with as little awkwardness as possible; this business did nothing to complicate our task. . . . This nasty ordeal of photographing in sewers and catacombs, it must be said, lasted no less than three consecutive months. . . . Altogether, I brought back a hundred negatives. . . . I made haste to offer the first hundred prints to the collections of the City of Paris put together by the eminent engineer of our subterranean constructions, M. Belgrand. (Nadar, *Quand j'étais photographe* [Paris, 1900], quoted in *Arcades*, 673–674)

Like Proust's *mémoire involontaire,* memory is a prisoner of material objects—which might very well correspond to no original. "That is the reason," writes Benjamin, "old photographs—but not old drawings—have a ghostly effect" (*Arcades,* 393). Whatever the truth-value of an involuntary memory, therefore, it cannot help being historical. It belongs to its time all the more for never having been conscious.

Excavations in the Paris underworld play a crucial role in the analysis of the arcades for Benjamin. It is as though the arcades themselves were the aboveground version of the underground. Below the streets of Paris, a whole second world opened up when Haussmann's modernization projects began. Benjamin writes many times out of his fascination for that world:

> But another system of galleries runs underground through Paris: the Métro, where at dusk glowing red lights point the way into the underworld of names. Combat, Elysée, Georges V, Etienne Marcel, Solférino, Invalides, Vaugirard—they have all thrown off the humiliating fetters of street or square, and here in the lightning-scored, whistle-resounding darkness are transformed into misshapen sewer gods, catacomb fairies. This labyrinth harbors in its interior not one but a dozen blind raging bulls, into whose jaws not one Theban virgin once a year but thousands of anemic young dressmakers and drowsy clerks every morning must hurl themselves. □ Street Names □ Here, underground, nothing more of the collision, the intersection, of names—that which aboveground forms the linguistic network of the city. Here each name dwells alone; hell is its demesne. Amer, Picon, Dubonnet[24] are guardians of the threshold. (*Arcades,* 84)

Benjamin's Barthesian system of thematic cross-references constitutes yet another parallel "linguistic network." Here are some more quotations from Benjamin's *Arcades* about the Métro as an underground roadmap of Paris:

> "Paris is built over a system of caverns from which the din of Métro and railroad mounts to the surface, and in which every passing omnibus or truck sets up a profound echo. And this great technological system of tunnels and thoroughfares interconnects with the ancient vaults, the limestone quarries, the grottoes and catacombs which, since the Middle Ages, have time and again been reentered and traversed.

Even today, for the price of two francs, one can buy a ticket of admission to this most nocturnal Paris, so much less expensive and less hazardous than the Paris of the upper world." Benjamin, Convolute C [Ancient Paris, Catacombs, Demolitions, Decline of Paris] (*Arcades*, 85)

In 1899, during work on the Métro, foundations of a tower of the Bastille were discovered on the Rue Saint-Antoine. Cabinet des Estampes. (91)

"The prisoners gave all the passages the names of Paris streets, and whenever they met one another, they exchanged addresses." (Engländer, quoted by Benjamin, 89)

"The Paris stone quarries are all interconnected. . . . In several places pillars have been set up so that the roof does not cave in. In other places the walls have been reinforced. These walls form long passages under the earth, like narrow streets." (Benzenberg, quoted by Benjamin, 89)

The modern transportation system requires the traveler to pay *only* when passing from one world to the other. "One is reminded," writes Paul de Man, "that, in the French-speaking cities of our century, 'correspondance' meant, on the trolley-cars, the equivalence of what is called in English a 'transfer'—the privilege, automatically granted on the Paris Métro, of connecting from one line to another without having to buy a new ticket."[25] De Man makes this remark in the course of an analysis designed to deflate the mystical pretensions while elevating the rhetorical achievements of Baudelaire's most famous poem, entitled, precisely, "Correspondances." But Benjamin shows that the poem's mystical aims cannot be so easily dismissed. The poem "Correspondances" seems to promote the coherence of the natural world, a coherence among the five senses that points to an underlying spiritual coherence. Benjamin does not discount the seduction of natural coherence:

La Nature est un temple où de vivants piliers
Laissent parfois sortir de confuses paroles;
L'homme y passe à travers des forêts de symboles
Qui l'observent avec des regards familiers.

Comme de longs échos qui de loin se confondent
Dans une ténébreuse et profonde unité,
Vaste comme la nuit et comme la clarté,
Les parfums, les couleurs, et les sons se répondent.

Il est des parfums frais comme des chairs d'enfants,
Doux come les hautbois, verts comme les prairies,
—Et d'autres, corrompus, riches et triumphants,

Ayant l'expansion des choses infinis
Comme l'ambre, le musc, le benjoin et l'encens,
Qui chantent les transports de l'esprit et des sens.

[Nature is a temple, where the living pillars
Sometimes murmur indistinguishable words;
Man passes through these forests of symbols
Which regard him with familiar looks.

Like long echoes conflated in the distance
Into a unity obscure and profound,
Vast as the night and as the light,
The perfumes, colors, and sounds correspond.

There are some perfumes fresh as a baby's skin,
Mellow as oboes, verdant as prairies,
—And others, corrupt, rich, and triumphant,

With all the expansiveness of infinite things,
Like ambergris, musk, benjamin, incense,
That sing the transports of spirit and sense.]

De Man writes—and Benjamin would agree—that "the prosaic transposition of ecstasy to the economic codes of public transportation is entirely in the spirit of Baudelaire and is not by itself disruptive with regard to the claim for transcendental unity. For the transfer indeed merges two different displacements into one single system of motion and circulation, with corresponding economic and metaphysical profits" (de Man, 251). As Benjamin put it in a letter to Max Horkheimer in April 1938, "The fundamental paradox of his theory of art—the contradiction between the theory of natural correspondences and the rejection of nature—should become transparent" (*Correspondence*, 557). But just when Benjamin might have demystified the natural symbol in favor of historical allegory and considered the poem a perfect example of the "myth" of the coherence of the natural world, he writes:

> The important thing is that the *correspondances* record a concept of experience which includes ritual elements. Only by appropriating these elements was Baudelaire able to fathom the full meaning of the breakdown which he, as a modern man, was witnessing. . . . The cycle of poems that opens the volume probably is devoted to something irretrievably lost. . . . What Baudelaire meant by *correspondances* may be described as an experience which seeks to establish itself in crisis-proof form.[26]

The mystical, mythical elements—however deluded—can never be eliminated. In the nineteenth century they were simply transferred from the forest of nature to the cathedral of industry: "On Baudelaire's 'religious intoxication of great cities': the department stores are temples consecrated to this intoxication" (*Arcades*, 61).

III. Postal Survival

The delay in writing this letter threatens to indict me and all of us.
—Theodor Adorno to Walter Benjamin, November 10, 1938

You were surely not surprised to see that I did not compose a response to your letter of Nov. 10 from one minute to the next. Your letter gave me a shock, even if the long time it took you to respond made it possible for me to surmise its contents.
—Walter Benjamin to Theodor Adorno, December 9, 1938

N'oublie pas ton adresse.

[Don't forget your address.]
—Charles Baudelaire to his half-brother, Alphonse, April 1, 1832

Ma chère mère, je me suis toujours défié de la poste d'Honfleur. Cependant, je ne sais pas si l'insuffisance est constatée à Paris ou à Honfleur.

[My dear mother, I've never trusted the Honfleur post office. But I don't know whether the postage due was noted in Paris or Honfleur.]
—Charles Baudelaire to Caroline Aupick, January 15, 1862[27]

I would like now to take another look at a moment in Adorno's letter critiquing Benjamin's Baudelaire that to me identifies very precisely the incompatibility between traditional Marxism and what Benjamin was trying to do: "I have a sense of such artificiality whenever you put things metaphorically rather than categorically. This is particularly the case in the passage about the transformation of the city into an interior for the flâneur. I think that one of the most powerful conceptions in your study is here presented as a mere 'as if'" (*Correspondence*, 581).

A mere "as if." The logic of your argument, he implies, is metaphorical rather than categorical. Adorno, of course, was no stranger to the metaphor that takes over the category. He wrote, for example, to Benjamin on January 3, 1937:

> The image of the dive has often been a source of consolation to me in my work. For with the latter I am rather like someone who, in a den of ill repute, comes upon the stricken body of a sad old acquaintance from earlier and better times; and the unfortunate man expresses his dying wish to be buried in a mountain cemetery; getting the body up there is no easy task; and we can only hope that the funeral attendants enjoy the splendid view to be had from the top. (*Adorno Correspondence*, 169)

Yet in this letter to Benjamin he disallows such writing. Metaphor is a mere "as if"; to be taken seriously, a statement has to be categorical. Artifice is out of place here: the statement has to be a new truth. But perhaps it is the difference between metaphorical and categorical that for Benjamin has changed. "As if" got a bad name from Browning's "Last Duchess," who is described by her murderer as "looking as if she were alive." Perhaps it is all too easy to see the killing, the crime against life, that art is. But is there no "as if" in life? Does "as if" imply that something else is the real thing? Isn't what constitutes the "real thing" the fundamental question here?

Some light may be shed on the fallacy of "as if" by Benjamin's comment on child's play and toys:

> An adult relieves his heart from its terrors and doubles happiness by turning it into a story. A child creates the entire event anew and starts

again right from the beginning. Here, perhaps, is the deepest explanation for the two meanings of the German word *Spielen:* the element of
repetition is what is actually common to them. Not a 'doing as if' but a
'doing the same thing over and over again,' the transformation of a
shattering experience into habit—that is the essence of play.[28]

For Adorno, then, "as if" is not uncanny—not the premonition of
a shift in *the literal* itself. For Benjamin, "as if" *is* the uncanny.

The biggest difference between Adorno and Benjamin involves
the status of Marxism itself. For Adorno—perhaps speaking for the
institute—it is a metadiscourse designed to explain the unfolding of
history; for Benjamin, it is itself historical.

> This research—which deals fundamentally with the expressive charac-
> ter of the earliest industrial products, the earliest industrial architec-
> ture, the earliest machines, but also the earliest department stores,
> advertisements, and so on—thus becomes important for Marxism in
> two ways. First, it will demonstrate how the milieu in which Marx's
> doctrine arose affected that doctrine through its expressive character
> (which is to say, not only through causal connections); but, second, it
> will also show in what respects Marxism, too, shares the expressive
> character of the material products contemporary with it. (*Arcades,*
> 460)

Benjamin has often been described as interpreting nineteenth-century "reality" directly: the "wide-eyed presentation of mere facts," as
Adorno put it (*Correspondence,* 283). Such an aim led Susan Buck-
Morss to call her study of *The Arcades Project, The Dialectics of Seeing,* saying it was designed "to illuminate the world that Benjamin
experienced and described" and only to add "captions" to that
world.[29] In philosophy, the "fallacy of misplaced concreteness" concerns treating abstractions *as if* they were in the world. This, too, is
called "fetishism."[30] But Benjamin's radical approach to historical
materialism is precisely to treat *the world itself* as a fallacy of misplaced concreteness.

Of course, Benjamin encourages this conflation of world and text
by saying, "The expression 'the book of nature' indicates that one
can read the real like a text. And that is how the reality of the nine-

teenth century will be treated here" (*Arcades*, 464). Because *The Arcades Project* consists in a huge collection of quotations and comments without an overriding synthesis, it is often compared, by Benjamin himself as well as by his commentators, with a great montage:

> For Benjamin, the technique of montage had "special, even total rights" as a progressive form because it "interrupts the context into which it is inserted" and thus "counteracts illusion" and he intended it to be the principle governing the construction of the *Passagen-Werk*: "This work must develop to the highest point the art of citing without quotation marks. Its theory connects most closely with that of montage." (Buck-Morss, 67; the quotations are from Benjamin)

> Method of this project: literary montage. I needn't *say* anything. Merely show. I shall purloin no valuables, appropriate no ingenious formulations. But the rags, the refuse—these I will not inventory but allow, in the only way possible, to come into their own: by making use of them. (Convolute N: "On the Theory of Knowledge, Theory of Progress," *Arcades*, 460)

> Notes on montage in my journal. Perhaps, in this same context, there should be some indication of the intimate *connection* that exists between the intention making for nearest nearness and the intensive utilization of refuse—a connection in fact exhibited in montage. (*Arcades*, 861)

Heterogeneous fragments are simply juxtaposed; "I needn't *say* anything." Benjamin tried to "show" not "tell," but he underlines the use of throwaway items (old newspapers, fish bones, ticket stubs) in montage. "By their waste shall you know them." "Showing" involves displaying that which never constituted the valuable or interesting spectacle, but rather its unconscious backdrop.

It quickly becomes apparent to his best interpreters—sometimes as if against their own intentions—that, far from adding mere "captions" to realities, Benjamin is transforming what counts as "real." Even captions become allegorical texts, and the question of reading reality "like a text" becomes a question of what reading a text is like.

Benjamin spent years in the Bibliothèque Nationale and the Cabinet des estampes collecting, gathering, taking notes. When, at the end of 1939, he was advised to get out of Paris, he instead renewed his library card. Susan Buck-Morss reports:

> From May to September 1935, and again in January 1936, he worked in the archives of the Cabinet des estampes in the Bibliothèque Nationale. If such research in iconographic documentation was "still rare" among historians, it was unheard of among philosophers. Benjamin had copies made of relevant illustrations which he found there, keeping them in his Paris apartment as "a kind of album."
>
> The album appears to have been lost. It makes little difference, however. (71)

On the contrary, if we are to take seriously Benjamin's distinction between "image" and "text," this album would have been invaluable. Not as "illustration" or "documentation" but as the thing itself. In other words, not *meta-*, not a supplement to a reality known otherwise. Benjamin writes:

> It is said that the dialectical method consists in doing justice each time to the concrete historical situation of its object. But that is not enough. For it is just as much a matter of doing justice to the concrete historical situation of the *interest* taken in the object. ("Dream City and Dream House, Dreams of the Future," *Arcades*, 391)

Historical concreteness is thus always misplaced if it is considered to reside in the object alone. Dialectical history is a history of the interaction between objects and subjects.

The expression "the book of nature" belongs to the metaphysical realm. If the world is a book, God is its author. Is this still in some way true for Benjamin? Not in any obvious sense, certainly—at least as an origin or end. Yet how are we to understand the role theology plays with respect to dialectical materialism? In Benjamin's first thesis on history, written right after the Institute for Social Research rejected his essay on Baudelaire, he describes the historical materialist as a puppet who always wins at chess—but only because a wizened theologian hidden under the table pulls the puppet's strings. Perhaps it is after all Marxism that seeks to attain a God's-eye view of phenomena—and indeed, any *meta*discourse that aspires to stand outside the phenomenon it describes. Historical materialism can always win, but only because of a hidden theological framework. The two discourses that seem to promise a clear-cut opposition between the world and what lies beyond or beneath it—theology and philology— are in fact the only ones capable of taking the measure of both the desire for, and the impossibility of, that separation.

In *The Arcades Project* itself, Benjamin warns, "Bear in mind that commentary on a reality (for it is a question here of commentary, of interpretation in detail) calls for a method completely different from that required by commentary on a text. In one case, the scientific mainstay is theology; in the other case, philology" (*Arcades*, 460). At another point, he adds, "To prove by example that only Marxism can practice great philology, where the literature of the previous century is concerned" (*Arcades*, 476).

The Arcades Project develops the way all scholarship develops: through notetaking, quotation, and commentary. But it seems to stop there, and thus is always considered "unfinished." And indeed, Benjamin's death did bring the work to a halt. But how do we know what "finished" means any more, if there could be no overriding thesis or synthesis?

The word "passages" describes the collection of quotations of other books—but not in German. The *Passagen-Werk* is as if awaiting its translation into English or French. The idea that there is some truth behind the displacements drives the displacements, but again and again one discovers only the NOTHING that is there. Yet that "nothing" can be discovered only when one is looking for something else. Mallarmé:

> Nous savons, captifs d'une formule absolue que, certes, n'est que ce qui est. Incontinent écarter cependant, sous un prétexte, le leurre, accuserait notre inconséquence, niant le plaisir que nous voulons prendre: car cet *au-delà* en est l'agent, et le moteur dirais-je si je ne répugnais à opérer, en public, le démontage impie de la fiction et conséquemment du méchanisme littéraire, pour étaler la pièce principale ou rien.[31]
>
> [We know perfectly well, prisoners of an absolute formula, that there exists nothing but what is. However, precipitously to set aside illusions, on this account, would point up our inconsistency, denying the plea-

sure we aim to take: for that very *beyond* is its agent, its motor I would even say if I were not reluctant to take fiction apart, in public, unbelievingly, and thus expose the whole literary mechanism, in order to display its principal part or nothing.]

Impie has the same significance as *agnoziert.*

The central nothing is the navel of the dream of representing the world. Going back to it is the only way to keep discovering that nothing, that world, that language. It is not that the world does not exist. It can fall down on your head at any time. But it is that the closer you get to it, the more it dissolves into the technologies of representation, which both enable and produce what can be seen. There is a difference between the image and the word, but both are profoundly historical, and both fail to be the "wide-eyed presentation of mere facts" they pretend to be. "The circumstances of this failure are multifarious. One is tempted to say: once he was certain of eventual failure, everything worked out for him *en route* as in a dream."[32]

This is why Benjamin writes to Adorno "on est philologue ou on ne l'est pas" ["either one is a philologist or one isn't"] about the rejection of *The Arcades Project.* In other words, unless the process of becoming *dingfest* is understood as something that also happens in language and in representation and not just in the world, then the very concept of "world" is inadequate. Souvenir, comforter, logo.

Is there any relation, then, between the writing of scholarship and the writing of letters? Does the existence of an addressee—and an address—change the nature of writing and its relation to history? What are the *correspondances* in correspondence?

The search for material and psychological ease is very apparent in the letters of both Baudelaire and Benjamin, but in different ways. Both lived in miserable material conditions most of their lives, and they wrote in part to earn money. Sons of the bourgeoisie unreconciled to not being supported by it, they scraped together an inadequate existence through literary commissions and translations. Some perverse sense of honor prevented them from making life easy. They sold but did not violate themselves. But whereas Baudelaire's correspondence reads like one long financial lament mainly addressed to the mother, Benjamin's is itself a place of thinking addressed to the friend. Benjamin was very lucky in having the misfortune of having to keep in touch with friends at a distance. One has the impression that if they hadn't moved away, he would have treated them as if they had. Benjamin always sounds both utterly alone and utterly collaborative. His thought was dialectical in the truest sense—it needed the response of the other. Adorno sometimes found it more dialectical than he could handle—it made too many demands on the reader. Benjamin tended to write dialectical questions, not answers. He wrote as if he could take for granted that the other wanted his thought—that the other wanted nothing more than his every thought (which he was sometimes reluctant to reciprocate). But Baudelaire wrote as if the other wanted not his thought but only his success.

In his first letters to his brother and mother, he constantly apologizes for not being able to deliver the prize he has promised. His letters are promises to reform, not thought. In fact, he was probably right—Baudelaire's thought would no doubt *not* have been welcome. Everyone he wrote to would probably have been appalled at it. If the court considered his poems intolerable, this was no accident: they were probably written with everything he left out of his letters. Which did not mean that his poems did not also address the figure of the lost mother. Benjamin, on the other hand, was amazingly fortunate in the number of people who wanted him to think. When he was forced to write to friends with requests for money, he was very aware of the danger of losing that freedom (Benjamin to Adorno, *Adorno Correspondence*, 49).

Even before his financial debts, in other words, Baudelaire had the task of explaining to the other why he had fallen short. The other is treated as someone who wants only his success from him, but also as someone who really wants it. Baudelaire writes to his brother that he wants to give him a first in school as a New Year's gift. His ensuing guilt over falling short of his promise was the proof that Baudelaire *had* a place in his brother's, mother's, and stepfather's lives. But in fact nothing is less certain. The elicitation of the promise in the first place was, unbeknownst to the young Baudelaire, already the gift of something to live up to. I am worth only what living up to what I promised satisfies in you, he seems to say, but to satisfy you would enable you to turn your attention away from me. If I want to keep your attention, I will have to keep failing. For in fact, you actually want NOTHING from me: your life would be simpler if I didn't exist. This is another part of the Oedipal structure: the parents who leave their son out to die. At his own expense, Baudelaire was able to make that ever-unfulfilled promise—and the ever-renewed address—into poetry. "Baudelaire's unique importance consists in having been the first one, and the most unswerving, to have apprehended, in both senses of the word, the productive energy of the individual alienated from himself—agnosticized and heightened through concretization." Reading the intolerable struggles and the intolerable wisdom of both Baudelaire and Benjamin with helpless hindsight, one can only wish it would have been possible *then* to fulfill a fantasy of Nadar's: "As if an enchanter or a stage manager, at the first peal of the whistle from the first locomotive, gave a signal to all things to awake and take flight."[33]

Construction Work

Just now, as I was crossing the boulevard, and hopping in the mud, in quite a hurry, through the shifting chaos where death comes galloping from all sides at once, my halo slipped off my head, in one abrupt movement, into the mire of the macadam.

—Charles Baudelaire, "Loss of Halo"

Milton's allegory of Sin and Death is undoubtedly faulty. . . . That Sin and Death should have shown the way to hell, might have been allowed; but they cannot facilitate the passage by building a bridge, because the difficulty of Satan's passage is described as real and sensible, and the bridge ought to be only figurative. . . . Sin and Death worked up a *mole* of *aggravated soil*, cemented with *asphaltus;* a work too bulky for ideal architects.

—Samuel Johnson, *Lives of the English Poets*

I. Ode on a Public Thing

Robert Lowell's poem "For the Union Dead" has become one of the most canonical poems in the English language.[1] The occasion for the poem seems to be a stroll on the Boston Common, during which the poet notices that the ground has been dug up for an underground parking garage. But both the title ("For the Union Dead") and the epigraph ("Relinquunt Omnia Servare Rem Publicam") of Lowell's poem lead the reader to expect that the poem will be an elegy with political ramifications. The epigraph is a variant on the motto of the Saint-Gaudens monument, located on the Common, which commemorates Colonel Robert Gould Shaw's all-Negro regiment that fought to the death in the Civil War. Lowell's change in the Saint-Gaudens monument's inscription from the original "Relinquit" [he leaves] of the motto of the Society of Cincinnati to the plural "Relinquunt" [they leave] appears to make a simple but powerful point: that the black soldiers who enlisted in Colonel Shaw's Fifty-fourth Massachusetts Regiment were as heroic and self-sacrificing as their leader. In keeping with the structure of loss one might expect from an elegy, the poem indeed begins with a contrast between "now" and "once." But that contrast is not about the Civil War or about American race relations. It is about fish. The first lost thing in the poem is the old South Boston Aquarium. What do fish have to do with the Union dead?

The poem lists an astonishingly disparate collection of things and moments while drawing everything together through the language in which they are described. For instance, the word "nose" unites the poet, the fish, and the cars at the end of the poem: "Once my *nose* crawled like a snail on the glass," "my hand tingled to burst the bubbles drifting from the *noses* of the cowed, compliant fish," and "Everywhere, giant finned cars *nose* forward like fish; a savage servility slides by on grease." "Cowed, compliant" also echoes "savage servility." And servility seems to mock the *servare* from the epigraph. The poem is filled with such uncanny echoes: "parking *spaces* luxuriate" and "*space* is nearer." "Space is *nearer*" and "the ditch is *nearer.*" The colonel "lean as a compass-needle" echoes the "bronze weathervane cod." A "girdle" of "girders." "One morning last *March*" and "Two months after *marching*[2] through Boston." Colonel Shaw is riding on a bubble. Negro schoolchildren's faces rise like balloons. Bubbles came from the noses of the fish. My hand tingled to burst the bubbles. Colonel Shaw waits for the blessed break. The poem quickly reveals itself to be a network of echoes. But what does it all mean?

The poem is seductive in its skill in seeing a dinosaur in a steam shovel, Colonel Shaw in a bubble like the fish. But the poem also cites the promiscuous use of images out of context for commercial purposes: Hiroshima and the hymn "Rock of Ages" combine to advertise a Mosler safe. Does the poem give us any means by which to distinguish between its own figurative promiscuity and that of the commercial? Its own fishy images and those of 1960 model cars? Is there any difference between poetry and advertising?

Here we might go back to Lowell's second modification of the motto on the monument. Like many modern Latin coinages, the motto of the Society of Cincinnati, "Omnia relinquit servare rempublicam," is of dubious grammatical exactitude. *Relinquo,* I am told, does not usually take the infinitive alone to express purpose.[3] *Servare* does not mean "to serve" but rather "to save." It is *servire* that means "to serve." What, then, does Lowell's revision of *rempublicam* to *rem publicam* mean? Given the echo in the poem between *servare* and "servility," and between the subjacent *servire* and the question of slavery, could it be legitimate to conflate *servare* and *servire* as the *Norton Anthology*'s translation of the original motto ("He leaves all else to serve the republic") appears to do? This would give the somewhat fanciful translation of Lowell's epigraph as "They leave all else to serve (as) a public thing."

A monument is a public thing. The Fifty-fourth Regiment has relinquished life to become a monument, a thing. The poem mentions other statues of Union soldiers, other graves. Yet, in contrast, Shaw's father wanted no monument except the ditch where his son's body was thrown and lost with his "niggers." There are no statues for the last war here. Does the poem think a monument is a good thing? Was Shaw's father wrong? Should there be a statue for the last war? What, exactly, is a monument?

In this poem a monument is very much a thing. It is vulnerable to the construction work going on around it. The abstract Union soldier is growing slimmer each year. The boarded-up aquarium, too, stands like a monument, almost like Ozymandias in the desert—here, a Sahara of snow. The city is full of stuff. How can we tell a monument from a fish bone?

A monument may be a thing, but things have a curious capacity to become animate. William James could almost hear the bronze Negroes breathe. The State House tingles. The dinosaur steam shovels grunt and crop. The colonel seems to wince and suffocate. The stone statues doze and muse. The statues and monuments seem more alive than anything else in the poem. Even the city becomes animate when the poem says, "Their monument sticks like a fishbone in the city's throat." Yet the moment when Colonel Shaw comes alive most fully is when the poem says, "He rejoices in man's lovely, peculiar power to choose life and die." To choose life and die. Is this the same as to become a thing and live? The idealization the poem conveys if not endorses is an idealization that sees the highest of human capacities in choosing life and dying. This is what gets monumentalized. "They leave all else to serve as a public thing." Without that, what would a republic be? But there is perhaps something rigid about this structure—"When he leads his black soldiers to death, he cannot bend his back." This may be a simple description of Shaw's posture in the monument. Or it may have something to do with the absolute nature of what is monumentalized.

The poem seems to admire Shaw's stance of choosing life and dying, but to see it as unavailable in the present. "He is out of bounds now." When the poem says, "the ditch is nearer," it refers at least in part to the excavation next to the monument, the encroachment of urban modernization not only on the monument of the past but on the values of the past. But is it possible to choose life and live? Has New England culture gone from a heroism of and for the slaves to a savage, servile present? Has there been no compensating progress? Perhaps white New Englanders have learned not to say "niggers," but technological progress that has brought space nearer (a literal translation of the word "television") nevertheless places the white New England poet in front of his television screen watching the faces of Negro schoolchildren in the early civil rights period as if they were a mere spectacle, separated from him by a wall of glass, in a bubble, like the fish in the old aquarium. William James may have been able to hear the bronze Negroes breathe at the dedication ceremony, but Negroes remain trapped in the plane of representation in this poem. The television screen that brings the vision nearer also places it in a domain of unreachability because the people on the screen are in the plane of representation, under glass.

The poem therefore ultimately asks about its own participation in this structure of representation. The poem itself is one of the series of objects it interrogates. Each has its rigid but fragile outline—the Saint-Gaudens relief, the statue of the Union soldier, the fish tanks, the television. Only the Mosler safe seems invulnerable. Does this mean that the poem is lamenting the fact that commercial values are driving out heroic values? That the only thing safe is what can be put in a safe? That technological progress that gives us televisions, space exploration, and the atom bomb does not yield any corresponding moral progress? Yes, in part, but that doesn't quite explain the role of the aquarium. While the lament for the lost capacity to choose life and die seems to express mourning for the loss of the heroic, what exactly is being mourned in the loss of the aquarium? Let us look at what the poem says:

> Once my nose crawled like a snail on the glass;
> my hand tingled
> to burst the bubbles
> drifting from the noses of the cowed, compliant fish.
>
> My hand draws back. I often sigh still
> for the dark downward and vegetating kingdom
> of the fish and reptile.

The scene is one of desiring to burst the plane of representation, to break through the glass separating the spectator from the spectacle. If the fish are cowed and compliant, the boy's desired gesture of violence is both transgressive and a protest designed to provoke them out of their compliance, perhaps even liberate them. The gesture prefigures and parodies one the poet may be tempted to repeat as he crouches before his television or looks at Shaw in his bubble. Between the second stanza and the third, which I have just quoted, the tense of the poem goes from past to present. "My hand draws back" is in the present. If the poet's hand draws back in the present, it has a pen in it. The piercing of the plane of representation through to the thing itself has been enacted in reverse. The hand that was in the memory draws back into the writing present. "I often sigh still for the dark downward and vegetating kingdom of the fish and reptile." If the poem mourns for the heroic, it also sighs over the prehuman, the premoral universe. But in the last stanza, everywhere, giant finned cars nose forward like fish. It is as though we are presently *in* the aquarium. The small boy has his wish. But at the same time *things* have taken the place of everything, fulfilling the mandate of the monumentalizing process.

The poem laments, then, two things—access to the premoral universe and access to the monumental universe—which it recognizes as having been nightmarishly combined and brought back in the form of an entirely commercial, urban, modernized universe. This unidealizable fulfillment is not only a decline from past to present: it puts in question the clarity of the values of the past. While everything in the poem is organized as though there is a clear then-versus-now division, its own creation of networks of similarities among all its elements erases the possibility of maintaining the clarity of that structure. It is as though you cannot have *both* seductive metaphors *and* moral clarity. The structure of loss still functions, but the difference between heroic and commercial, natural and technological, aesthetic and moral, monument and urban debris, is no longer clear. Perhaps what the poem is really lamenting is the possibility of writing a then/now elegy that would not become drowned in its own self-irony. But since that irony is created by the poem's aesthetic success, by the tightness of its system of transferred properties, even *that* lament is double-faced. Which is why, I think, this poem has become so canonical. There is nothing like a good thick description of ambivalence toward monumentality to promote a poem to the status of monument in the literary canon.

II. My Dearest Memories Are Heavier Than Rocks

The analyst has neither experienced nor repressed any of the material under consideration; his task cannot be to remember anything. His task is to make out what has been forgotten from the traces which it has left behind or, more correctly, to *construct* it.
—Sigmund Freud, "Constructions in Analysis" (1937)

About a hundred years earlier, another poet was strolling past another construction site, and another elegy was written. Paris was being redesigned by Baron Haussmann into the neoclassical city it is today, simply by bulldozing whole neighborhoods. Charles Baudelaire, passing the new Caroussel monument, sighs that "The form of a city changes, alas, faster than a human heart." He thinks of Andromache, the widow of the Trojan hero Hector, who had to descend to becoming the wife of the defeated Trojan Helenus, after having been the wife of the Greek Pyrrus. Every second-year French student conjures up Racine's Andromache, but Baudelaire is referring to Virgil's. Regretting the lost river of Troy, she simulates it with the Simois, a far smaller stream. Is there something about poets and construction sites that brings these poems together?

Two years before reading a first version of "To the Union Dead" to a Boston Arts Festival celebration in June 1960, Robert Lowell published a book of translations entitled *Imitations*. These were no ordinary translations but poems that just happened to closely resemble the originals. He writes in his introduction, "My Baudelaires were begun as exercises in couplets and quatrains and to get away from the longer, less concentrated problems of translating Racine's *Phèdre*" (the translation of which was also published in 1960). Baudelaire began as an exercise, then, in form.

One of the poems Lowell translated was Baudelaire's "The Swan," which contains the line in the subhead above and the line "Tout pour moi devient allégorie" [Everything for me becomes an allegory], which for Walter Benjamin defined modern man's relation to the city. In the poem, a poet crosses a public square and notes that it has become a construction site, leading the poet to lament, "My dearest memories are heavier than rocks."

Baudelaire's "Le Cygne" has become as canonical in French as "For the Union Dead" is in English. One begins to suspect that what is canonized is precisely the "becoming-thing" of the subject and the animation of the inanimate world around him. Baudelaire's poem derives its irony from the supposed falsity of the statement "The form of a city changes, alas, faster than a human heart." Who wouldn't see the notorious mutability of human feelings as giving rise to faster change than rocks? Yet perhaps the statement is ironic, alas, because it is all too true. The failure of Reconstruction after the American Civil War suggests that it *is* easier to change cities than to change hearts. That both Baudelaire and Lowell would perceive this in a construction site testifies to the rapidity of urban change that has only accelerated since the midnineteenth century. (As I write this, Lowell's Boston is still torn up by the ever-unfinished, everoverbudget Big Dig, the most expensive construction project in history.) The fragility of all structures becomes perceptible at the moment it is clear that nothing material can ever be a "Rock of Ages."

Freud, imagining that the human heart could precisely transcend urban change and represent as simultaneous what in the real world would have to be successive, makes the famous analogy, in *Civilization and Its Discontents*, between the psyche and an urban setting in which nothing disappears when new forms are added:

> Now let us, by a flight of imagination, suppose that Rome is not a human habitation but a psychical entity with a similarly long and copious past—an entity, that is to say, in which nothing that has once come into existence will have passed away and all the earlier phases of development continue to exist alongside the latest one.[4]

In Freud's model of the mind, the "indestructibility" of unconscious desire dictates that the "phases" of human development do not so much succeed each other as supplement each other: lower impulses continue to exist alongside higher developments. Freudian theory in fact makes no sense without this idea: that the top layers of the personality must be stripped away so that the sedimentation of more archaic desires can be readjusted. But what invalidates the analogy for him is not only the impossibility of representing *pictorially* more than one thing in one place but also the damage and reconstruction that even the most peaceful city undergoes. For him, the norm of mental life is a perfect unconscious memory; if memory is transformed, it must have been traumatized, and the goal of analysis would be to root out the disturbance that has caused disease and restore everything to its proper place. "Destructive influences which can be compared to causes of illness like these are never lacking in a city," he writes.

> The question may be raised why we chose precisely the past of a *city* to compare with the past of the mind. The assumption that everything past is preserved holds good even in mental life only on condition that the organ of the mind has remained intact and that its tissues have not been damaged by trauma or inflammation. But destructive influences which can be compared to causes of illness like these are never lacking

in the history of a city, even if it has had a less chequered past than Rome, and even if, like London, it has hardly ever suffered from the visitations of an enemy.[5] Demolitions and replacements of buildings occur in the course of the most peaceful development of a city. A city is thus *a priori* unsuited for a comparison of this sort with a mental organism. (Freud, 71)

Now, if Baudelaire and Lowell implicitly disagree with this last assessment, exactly what is the nature of their disagreement?

The sign of materiality, paradoxically, is the capacity to be destroyed. Only immaterial agents are completely indestructible. For Freud, then, the psyche *was* an immaterial agent. Nothing that ever existed could be erased. But while the *effort* to erase could always fail, involuntary transformation could always happen. Both Baudelaire and Lowell, then, faced with a construction site, suddenly see that everything material could become different. And therefore anything's continued existence in the mind might separate from the material facts: "Everything for me becomes allegory." But, for that very reason, things that are no longer highlighted do not simply disappear—from the mind any more than from the city. Baudelaire and Lowell separate from Freud to the extent that, for them, the mind *is* material. The opposition between mental and material is really an opposition between mental *contents* and material *facts*. The mental can be imagined as immaterial, but to imagine the mental as immaterial is one of the most persistent fantasies of the human mind. The two poems are precisely about the melancholy discovery that the immateriality of the mind is just a tenacious idealization. By seeing the rubble of supposedly solid rocks, they recognize that the analogy between the city and the mind is actually an attempt to repress that very analogy. The ruins that seem to invalidate the analogy in fact confirm it. Their Rome is more like Hawthorne's:

> You pass through the grand breadth and height of a squalid entrance-way, and perhaps see a range of dusty pillars, forming a sort of cloister around the court; and in the intervals, from pillar to pillar, are strewn fragments of antique statues, headless and legless torsoes, and busts that have invariably lost—what it might be well if living men could lay aside, in that unfragrant atmosphere—the nose. Bas-reliefs, the spoil of

some far elder palace, are set in the surrounding walls, every stone of which has been ravished from the Coliseum, or any other imperial ruin which earlier barbarism had not levelled with the earth. Between two of the pillars, moreover, stands an old sarcophagus without its lid, and with all its more prominently projecting sculptures broken off; perhaps it once held famous dust, and the bony frame-work of some historic man, although now only a receptacle for the rubbish of the courtyard and a half-worn broom.[6]

This is about as good a description of the unconscious as any I know.

III. Empire

> Là, tout n'est qu'ordre et beauté,
> Luxe, calme et volupté.
>
> —Charles Baudelaire, "L'Invitation au voyage"

I would like to end this essay by focusing on three of Lowell's most revealing "infidelities" in his Baudelaire translations. The first is the common one I have already mentioned: to take the Andromache Baudelaire mentions as Racine's, not Virgil's. Students who have successfully made their way through Racine's *Andromaque* can be forgiven, but why does Lowell explicitly have Baudelaire say:

> Andromache, I think of you. Here men
> move on, diminished, from those grander years,
> when Racine's tirades scourged our greasy Seine,
> this lying trickle swollen with your tears!

Of course, it is always possible that Lowell made a mere mistake, but if he did it intentionally, what might he have gained? The lost heroic past for Lowell, in fact, might be no longer the Greek and Latin epics but the world of French classicism. For Baudelaire, perhaps, Racine was still alive: to be truly lost, Andromache had to be Latin, which already stood for the fall from Greek. But for Lowell—who, let us not forget, was interrupting his own translation of Racine's *Phèdre* to play with Baudelaire—the felt loss was less that of the classics than that of classicism. If Andromache was doubly a widow, trying to content herself with a diminished and mocking substitute in the modern city, then her loss had to still be alive for it to be mourned, not simply footnoted. Thus, if Baudelaire is to Virgil as Lowell is to Racine, then Lowell's translation is in fact correct. In the "greasy" Seine, one also hears the rumbling of those modern automobiles that, for the Lowell of "For the Union Dead," "slide by on grease."

Lowell's second notable infidelity is not found this time in the translation of "Le Cygne," but rather in that of "Au lecteur," the introductory poem to *Les Fleurs du Mal,* which, as we recall, Stefan George had refused to translate in his celebrated edition of the *Blumen des Bösen.* In the original, the poem ends by personifying the boredom that the poet and the reader are presumed to share. Baudelaire writes:

Il rêve d'échafauds en fumant son houka.
Tu le connais, lecteur, ce monstre délicat,
—Hypocrite lecteur,—mon semblable,—mon frère!

Lowell translates:

You know it well, my Reader. This obscene
beast chain-smokes yawning for the guillotine—
you—hypocrite Reader—my double—my brother!

The yawn is in the last line of the previous stanza, so it technically does not constitute an infidelity. But changing "échafauds" [scaffolds] to "guillotine," "semblable" [fellow man] to "double," and, especially, "fumant son houka" [smoking its hookah] to "chain-smokes" is more than a verbal translation. From the generic "échafauds" on which people are hanged in any country, we have the particularly French, particularly French-revolutionary way of death evoked in the word "guillotine"—one of the first, but certainly not the last, technological inventions designed to produce death faster. The guillotine's "Frenchness," however, may be more perceptible outside France than inside it (sort of like "French toast," "French fries," and the "French kiss"). So that Lowell's poem says "French" in a way that French cannot.

By substituting "double" for "fellow man," Lowell calls upon

Freud rather than God. While God created man in his image and then prevented man from doing likewise by prohibiting graven images, to find that that unpleasant person in the mirror is oneself is not a reassuring or creative feeling. The "hypocrite" is already double, so the double of a double is more likely to be an involuntary proliferation than a form of companionship—like those endless old men or old women that keep multiplying in front of Baudelaire on a Paris street ("Les Sept Vieillards," "Les Petites Vieilles"). And— most subtle of all—the vocabulary of "fraternité" promoted by the search for freedom and equality precisely during the French Revolution becomes uncanny with this multiplying "semblable" and this unaffectionate embrace of "mon frère." With his guillotine, Lowell brings out the political subtext that was present, but less obvious, in the original.

But the real *trouvaille* for me in this translation is in the depiction of boredom as a chain-smoker. The concept of chain-smoking would not have been contemporaneous with Baudelaire (in whose texts, according to Richard Klein, the word "cigarette" makes one of its first appearances in writing, although cigarette smoking was already taking Paris by storm as early as the 1840s).[7] While the French actually *do* it (look at all the pictures in Klein's book!), the expression "to chain-smoke" expresses a certain ambivalence about the enslavement that a nicotine addiction can cause. It has to have had currency mainly in the United States, the land of ambivalence toward all pleasures that one is not giving up. Baudelaire was, however, no stranger to the splendors and miseries of addiction, which he rather equated with poetry. "Il faut être toujours ivre . . . De vin, de poésie, ou de vertu, à votre guise" [You just have to be constantly high . . . On wine, on poetry, or on virtue, as you wish].[8] His book *Les Paradis artificiels* (Artificial Paradises) was an analysis of what one might seek—or find—in a mind-altering substance.

Boredom is the flip side of intoxication: the more you take a drug, the more of it you have to take to get the same effect; the mere repetition and routinization of an addiction becomes more and more necessary as it becomes less and less effective. The quest for stimulation becomes the incapacity to feel. Baudelaire's poem details the self-torturing attempts to feel something, and then calls "boredom" something like a permanent hangover. Chain-smoking is exactly an image of this, whereas the more exotic and more obscure reference to an Oriental pipe in the original suggests that stimulation can still come from elsewhere. If there is one thing Baudelaire's poetry says over and over again, it is that manic hopes always have depressive results, and that the nostalgia or hope for a desirable elsewhere only has the effect of rendering the "here" all the more intolerable.

The final "infidelity" in "The Swan" was the only one that struck me, at first, as completely wrong. Baudelaire writes:

Je pense à la négresse, amaigrie et phthisique,
Piétinant dans la boue, et cherchant, l'oeil hagard,
Les cocotiers absents de la superbe Afrique
Derrière la muraille immense du brouillard.

But instead of this generic image of the lost paradise, Lowell forces us to see this:

I think of you, tubercular and sick,
blindly stamping through puddles, Jeanne Duval,
peering into the Paris fog's thick wall
for the lost coco-palms of Mozambique.

My first reaction was that Lowell, in substituting the name of the only real black woman known to have been in Baudelaire's life, was simply replacing a generic image with a particular one. But then I realized that a change of myth was thereby rendered inescapable. The generic image of the exile mourning the lost homeland is one with which a good many Parisians could identify. But what that identification made invisible was the nature of the displacement that had brought the Negress to Paris in the first place. The slave labor, colonial exploitation, and metropolitan prosperity on which the Parisian implicitly stands have rendered his relation to her one of conflict, not identification. Furthermore, the Parisian is dependent on the colony; it is not simply that the Negress is out of place in a Paris with which she has nothing to do. Nostalgia for Africa is nostalgia for a natural, pretechnological harmony that exists only in the mind of the metro-politan citizen, who benefits from colonial labor but feels loss, and renames the lost thing a possession of those who, were it not for his exploitation, would, in his mind, have gone on in their blissful, premodern state forever. By adding the "Negress" to his list of ex-iles, Baudelaire might well have been subscribing to this myth.

But Lowell does not let him get away with it. Using known ele-ments from Baudelaire's life, Lowell gives us the name of Baude-laire's mulatto mistress, her tuberculosis, her blindness, her lame-ness, and her role as streetwalker trapped on a foggy Paris street. What if the exiled Negress is not just an image seen but a person see-ing? What is a beautiful young woman hoping to find by moving from Santo Domingo with her mother to Paris? How soon is it be-fore she falls into prostitution and disease and dependency, living by her wits and becoming the poet's reviled companion? By using the proper name that has accrued a certain negative judgment around the poet, Lowell makes it impossible not to see the fallen and pitiful state of the Negress in Paris. We no longer see the idealized Africa in her head; we see *her* as we have seen Jeanne Duval. Unvarnished and unidealized attitudes about colonialism lie in the attitudes of genera-tions of readers whose only known metropolitan exile from the colo-nies is Baudelaire's much-scorned mistress. By calling Baudelaire's "négresse" by the proper name "Jeanne Duval," Lowell turns the reader from an idealized identification—which in fact could not have existed outside the metropolitan reader's imagination—to the atti-tudes the reader has *already* formed about a person whom the reader has never connected with colonialism. The Negress's exile is in fact her separation from any real non-Parisian story.

IV. The Streets of Paris

It would be profitable to discover certain definite features leading toward the physiognomy of the city dweller. Example: the sidewalk, which is reserved for the pedestrian, runs along the roadway. Thus, the city dweller in the course of his most ordinary affairs, if he is on foot, has constantly before his

eyes the image of the competitor who overtakes him in a vehicle.—Certainly
the sidewalks were laid down in the interests of those who go by car or
horse. When?

—Walter Benjamin, *The Arcades Project* (Convolute M, "The Flâneur")

"Tell me, what is that awful stew which smells so bad and is warming in that
great pot?" says a provincial sort to an old porter. "That, my dear sir, is a
batch of paving stones that are being baked to pave our poor boulevard! . . .
As if strolling wasn't nicer when you walked on the soil, the way you do in a
garden!"

—Walter Benjamin, *The Arcades Project*, quoting from an article titled "Le Bitume"

The material that seems impossible to integrate into an ongoing
story is, for Samuel Johnson (in our first epigraph to this chapter), as
well as for the biblical author (in the epigraph to this book), the material used to pave streets. Bitumen, asphalt, and macadam are sure
signs that halos are falling thick and fast. But why is street paving the
sign of a Fall?

This question does not seem to have been what motivated Walter
Benjamin to study the Paris arcades, but it could have been. It is uncanny how often he touches upon paving materials in the course of
his rambles. Benjamin, of course, also had much to say about allegory in his earlier study of German baroque drama, so that Johnson's remark about Milton's "work too bulky for ideal architects"
would have struck a resonant chord for him as he investigated a city
where, according to Baudelaire, anything can turn to allegory at any
moment.

In taking up the image of a woman from the colonies stamping
through puddles, we have not yet sufficiently explored exactly what
she is doing there. That this foggy, wet condition is meant to evoke
modern Paris as opposed to the eternally sunny and rainless paradise left behind seems obvious. But apart from the value of contrast,
what is actually being said? It should be recalled that young Charles
Baudelaire was sent by his stepfather, Jacques Aupick, on his one
exotic journey precisely to get him away from "those slippery streets
of Paris." The tropical paradise may thus have been a foil for Paris all
along.

If the Negress is stamping through puddles, then three things must be true: she is outdoors, it has rained, and she is on foot. Let us begin with the rain. Rain pervades Baudelaire's "Spleen" poems:

Pluviôse, irrité contre la ville entière,

[Pluviose (a revolutionary month named for the rainy season),
irritated against the whole city . . .] ("Spleen LXXV")

Je suis comme le roi d'un pays pluvieux

[I am like the king of a rainy country . . .] ("Spleen LXXVII")

Quand la pluie étalant ses immenses traînées

[when the rain spreading out its vast traces . . .] ("Spleen LXXVII")

In the land of Baudelaire's spleen, then, it is always raining. But what the swan that has given the poem its name is suffering from is, on the contrary, too great a *lack* of rain. He fruitlessly stabs his beak into a dry, dusty gutter, and says reproachfully to the cruel, ironic, blue sky (in Lowell's translation): "Water, when will you fall? When will you burst, oh thunderclouds?" Either the weather changes in the course of the poem (in which case the swan gets his wish) or people all lack different—and sometimes contradictory—things. To portray the impossibility of satisfaction as a universal condition, Baudelaire risks the possibility that *someone else* will want what torments *you*. The image of universal exile cannot be contradicted by empirical facts: that would be to admit that there can be no universal lack. And thus no universal melancholy. Yet the poem is intent on convincing us that there *is* universal melancholy, and it will continue to do so *even if* there is no universal lack.

The poet may be lamenting some timeless universal lack, but he is also prompted to these reflections by a very precise moment in Parisian history. One day as Baudelaire is walking past one of Haussmann's transformations, he suddenly realizes that old Paris no longer exists. He feels a familiar sense of loss, and is haunted by the thought that everything he sees might be a sign of something that is no longer there:

Paris change! mais rien dans ma mélancolie
N'a bougé! palais neufs, échafaudages, blocs,
Vieux faubourgs, tout pour moi devient allégorie,
Et mes chers souvenirs sont plus lourds que des rocs.

In Lowell's translation:

Paris changes; nothing in my melancholy
stirs . . . new mansards, *arrondissements* razed *en bloc*,
glass, scaffolding, slum wards—all allegory!
My memories are heavier than rock!

Lowell again situates from the outside what could not have been situated from within. The mansard roofs that characterize Second Empire architecture for *us* could not have done so for Baudelaire, for
whom they were probably just "architecture." The "slum wards"
were both created and destroyed by Haussmann's unrespectful cuts.
("It is curious that every time we buy a house," remarked Madame
Haussmann, "a boulevard passes through it.") The scaffold that
gave way to the guillotine for Lowell returns as *scaffolding*—the
framework for an uncompleted building. At the same time, although
the revolutionary Assembly had in 1790 invented the word *arrondissement* (as part of a total reorganization of administrative units in
France), it wasn't until 1895 that Taride, originally an automobile
and bicycling club, began publishing its famous guides to Paris by
arrondissement. Baudelaire, in whose day the number of recognized
arrondissements was in any case far smaller than it is today, would
have been much more likely to use the word *quartiers*. For Walter
Benjamin, however, a good part of the magic of Paris inheres in
those guides, as it has for tourists (including, no doubt, Robert
Lowell) ever since.

It is a sad testimony to the underdeveloped *amour-propre* of most of
the great European cities that so very few of them—at any rate, none of
the German cities—have anything like the handy, minutely detailed,
and durable map that exists for Paris. I refer to the excellent publication by Taride, with its twenty-two maps of all the Parisian *arrondissements* and the parks of Boulogne and Vincennes. Whoever has
stood on a streetcorner of a strange city in bad weather and had to deal

with one of those larger maps—which at every gust swell up like a sail, rip at the edges, and are soon no more than a little heap of dirty colored scraps with which one torments oneself as with the pieces of a puzzle—learns from the study of the *Plan Taride* what a city map can be. People whose imagination does not wake at the perusal of such a text, people who would not rather dream of their Paris experiences over a map than over photos or travel notes, are beyond help.[9]

And so we return to that bad weather that afflicts Jeanne Duval as she makes her way along the street. It seems that the arcades were initially designed to protect pedestrians from the weather. In the very first paragraph of the first "Convolute," Benjamin writes:

"In speaking of the inner boulevards," says the *Illustrated Guide to Paris*, a complete picture of the city on the Seine and its environs from the year 1852, "we have made mention again and again of the arcades which open onto them. These arcades, a recent invention of industrial luxury, are glass-roofed, marble-paneled corridors extending through whole blocks of buildings, whose owners have joined together for such enterprises. Lining both sides of these corridors, which get their light from above, are the most elegant shops, so that the arcade is a city, a world in miniature, ☐ Flâneur ☐, in which customers will find everything they need. During sudden rainshowers, the arcades are a place of refuge for the unprepared, to whom they offer a secure, if restricted, promenade—one from which the merchants also benefit. ☐ Weather ☐" (*Arcades*, 31)

Escape from the weather was thus a commercial windfall, and the fact that the promenade was perhaps more restricted than the rain meant that particular care could be lavished on display. The buyer was at first inside the *vitrine*, and was not merely its spectator. That means that the flâneur, according to Benjamin, "is no buyer. He is merchandise" (*Arcades*, 42).

The flâneur may be merchandise, he may be on display, but the real unity between seller and wares is exemplified by the prostitute. The male streetwalker may be a flâneur, but a female flâneur is a streetwalker. The arcades presented such a spectacle of aroused desires that they lent themselves almost too well to the trade of prostitutes. Because both the saleswomen and the merchandise inflamed desire, in fact, the police had to issue an edict as early as 1830 banning streetwalkers from the arcades, and in fact from plying their trade outside of licensed brothels altogether (see *Arcades,* 499). One can see how the ideology of the "interior" invaded the house even of prostitution.

The poet could identify with the prostitute, but he could never let her speak. ("Baudelaire never wrote a whore-poem from the point of view of the whore," says Walter Benjamin [*Arcades,* 347]). What would the woman in "A une passante" have said if she had looked back? Stamping through puddles, then, Jeanne Duval has been expelled from the arcades and is forced to walk the streets in the rain, under the constant menace of vehicles. Benjamin notes the progress of pavement:

> Asphalt was first used for sidewalks. (*Arcades,* 427)

> With the steady increase in traffic on the streets, it was only the macadamization of the roadways that made it possible in the end to have a conversation on the terrace of a café without shouting in the other person's ear. (420)

The Parisian café is one of those thresholds between inside and out—like the arcade—that have had a long history of fostering cultural life, and might never have had a chance to do so without the macadamization of the roadways. Paris seems more than usually associated with such *rites de passage* in an entirely nonmythological sense. Here is how Benjamin describes modern man's lack of tolerance for the threshold experience *of the very link between myth and transport* in the midst of the proliferating commercialization of all passageways:

> Rites de passage—this is the designation in folklore for the ceremonies that attach to death and birth, to marriage, puberty, and so forth. In modern life, these transitions are becoming ever more unrecognizable and impossible to experience. We have grown very poor in threshold experiences. Falling asleep is perhaps the only such experience that remains to us. (But together with this, there is also waking up.) And, finally, there is the ebb and flow of conversation and the sexual permutations of love—experience that surges over thresholds like the chang-

ing figures of the dream. "How mankind loves to remain transfixed," says Aragon, "at the very doors of the imagination!" *Paysan (de Paris)*, 1926, p. 74. It is not only from the thresholds of these gates of imagination that lovers and friends like to draw their energies; it is from thresholds in general. Prostitutes, however, love the thresholds of these gates of dream.—The threshold must be carefully distinguished from the boundary. A *Schwelle* (threshold) is a zone. Transformation, passage, wave action are in the word *schwellen*, swell, and etymology ought not to overlook these senses. (*Arcades*, 494)

The "rites de passage," which seemed to be pathways to the domain of mythic "correspondences," have become the *correspondances* that let you move around inside the transit system. These modern rites of passage promise just to get you from one place to another. For Benjamin's *Arcades Project*, the privileged modern vehicle was indeed the Métro (the negotiation of whose intricate *correspondances* necessitated the use of a *Plan Taride*). For Lowell, in 1960s America, the privileged vehicle was no doubt the private car. Not only did those strange finned creatures "slide by on grease," but the whole Boston construction site in "For the Union Dead" existed for the sake of a parking garage in the first place.

One change made by Lowell at the end of "The Swan" seems to depart entirely from the original. Where Baudelaire writes:

Ainsi dans la forêt où mon esprit s'exile
Un vieux Souvenir sonne à plein souffle du cor!
Je pense aux matelots oubliés dans une île,
Aux captifs, aux vaincus! . . . à bien d'autres encor!

Lowell translates:

and in this forest, on my downward drag,
my old sorrow lets out its lion's roar,
I think of Paris raising the white flag,
drowned sailors, fallen girls . . . and many more!

The sailor forgotten on the island has finally come home and surrendered in Paris. The lion can roar in the forest of "Correspondances," but the remaining lost sailors are given up for drowned. The unsatisfying, unfinished business started by Baudelaire is now clearer, but no less heartbreaking for being readable. The defeated city has almost destroyed the world before its surrender. There is nowhere left to go.

But neither can one stand still. The form of a city, alas, changes faster than a human heart, but therefore everything for me can become an allegory. My own memories of what is gone can get in the way of seeing what is there. No one feels at home, even people who have never been elsewhere. Urban renewal projects have stopped holding out the promise of heart-transforming renewal, but it is in the midst of both *them* and our own recalcitrant memories and rhetorical departures from reality that we must go on living. Baudelaire's poem "Le Cygne" and Lowell's poem "For the Union Dead" are both, finally, realizations of just how hard—and yet how inescapable—it is to share a sidewalk with Milton's Sin and Death, Haussmann's asphalt, and Baudelaire's Jeanne Duval.

SEVEN

Doing Time

Mal informé celui qui se crierait son propre contemporain.

[He who would proclaim himself his own contemporary is misinformed.]

—Stéphane Mallarmé, "L'Action restreinte"

No, not yet . . . No, not there.

—E. M. Forster, *Passage to India*

This chapter is an attempt to reread Paul de Man's essay "Literary History and Literary Modernity," now that his wartime writings for a collaborationist journal have come to light. What difference does de Man's own history make now to the things he said about history then? But when was that? In the history of the things his writings made possible, *he* was presumably in a position to know something that his readers did not. The "before/after" structure that is so seductive now for readers cannot coincide with the before/after structure that can be postulated for de Man then as writer, but some such structure has become unavoidable for readers of his work. What puts those who have learned from him in a bind is the fact that he is somehow *both* the Nazi father *and* the recoil from him. It is certainly possible to see de Man's post-1960 work as an attempt to avoid being duped at all costs, but the earlier de Man, the ghost of the dupe, is all the more haunting.

Thus, the question becomes: "In what he says about history in those essays, how has the knowledge that he was concealing/repressing/rethinking *then* become newly readable *now?*" And—depending on whether the unblinded reader now thinks the right word here is "concealed," "repressed," or "rethought"—what can be said about de Man's statements about history, now that his history has rendered those statements themselves part of history?

Such questions inevitably focus on the last sentence of "Literary History and Literary Modernity," which reads: "If we extend this notion beyond literature, it merely confirms that the bases for historical knowledge are not empirical facts but written texts, even if these texts masquerade in the guise of wars or revolutions."[1] The present chapter will work toward a reading of that sentence.

"Literary History and Literary Modernity," like many of de Man's essays, takes the inauspiciousness of its beginning as a way to begin. There are three terms in the title that behave like two or four: the title either contrasts "history" and "modernity," using "literary" as a constant, or it uses "literature" as a way of putting the contrast between "history" and "modernity" in question. If it is impossible to choose between the two, then de Man has his inauspiciousness just where he wants it.

The problems involved here derive from the fact that the two sets of underlying oppositions do not perfectly overlap: these could be called "synchronic" versus "diachronic," on the one hand, and "constative" versus "performative," on the other. As has often been pointed out, "modernity" is an act or quality; "modernism" is a historical movement; and "modernness" is a contrastive relation to the past. "Modernism" and "modernness" are thus descriptive, constative, diachronic terms: "modernism" is an element of literary history; "modernness" names the fact of diachrony itself. And "modernity" would be synchronic as opposed to diachronic, but it is always perceived as performative (indeed, impossibly so: see Rimbaud's "Il faut être absolument moderne") rather than constative. Hence the paradox de Man formulates: "One is soon forced to resort to paradoxical formulations, such as defining the modernity of a literary period as the manner in which it discovers the impossibility of being modern" (144).

De Man's essay strongly marks itself as a timely (as opposed to Nietzsche's "untimely") meditation by its frequent recourse to words like "again," "of late," "not so long ago," and "now." What characterizes the present moment, says de Man, is on the one hand the return of the term "modernity" in Germany ("banned for political reasons" [143]), and, on the other, in France and the United

States the transfer of methods from the social sciences to literary studies. At first, this doesn't seem to promise much. But if his essay was first delivered as a lecture in 1969, the French social sciences at the time were being transformed by a revolution that today would hardly be associated with them: the Saussurean revolution, or "linguistic turn." Linguistics, anthropology, and sociology, at that moment, had begun to transform the disciplines of philosophy, psychoanalysis, and literary studies. There may thus be a link between the "linguistic turn" in France and the return of "modernity" in Germany.

Having established the starting paradox—that the modernity of a literary period might consist in the way in which it discovers the impossibility of being modern—de Man introduces his essay's project as follows:

> It is this complication I would like to explore with the help of some examples that are not necessarily taken from our immediate present. They should illuminate the problematic structure of a concept that, like all concepts that are in essence temporal, acquires a particularly rich complexity when it is made to refer to events that are in essence linguistic. (144)

"Events that are in essence linguistic." This is the crux of the essay, I think. What does it mean? What does it mean to speak of an event that is "in essence linguistic"? The expression is being contrasted with "temporal." In 1969, de Man published his first well-known essay, entitled "The Rhetoric of Temporality." But in that essay, "temporality" refers to mortality, not history. The "temporal" is the impossibility of stasis, symbol, simultaneity, eternity: de Man calls this impossibility "allegory." As the essay famously puts it: "Whereas the symbol postulates the possibility of an identity or identification, allegory designates primarily a distance in relation to its own origin, and, renouncing the nostalgia and the desire to coincide, it establishes its language in the void of this temporal difference."[2]

"Temporal," here, therefore, in a way means "linguistic." That is, what de Man calls "temporal difference" is an understanding of the importance of noncoincidence in the structure of signs—Saussurean "difference" or, later, Derridean "différance." What he calls "temporal" in "Literary History and Literary Modernity," however, is necessarily but contingently—rather than by definition—diachronic. The question he is asking, then, is: What happens when the hidden temporality of the sign is analyzed within the overt temporality of history? In its efforts to achieve a coherent interpretive narrative, the second (historical) kind of temporality actually seems to depend on the repression of the first (linguistic). The critique of those efforts leads most directly toward the kind of running in place about which de Man writes in his preface to *Allegories of Reading:*

> *Allegories of Reading* started out as a historical study and ended up as a theory of reading. I began to read Rousseau seriously in preparation for a historical reflection on Romanticism and found myself unable to progress beyond local difficulties of interpretation.[3]

De Man cautions, however, that the historical framework of the questions might be intrinsic to the inability to get beyond them; the inability to progress, in other words, cannot be taken for granted apart from the literary history it displaces. What does the "literary modernity" in this chapter have to do with the "literary history" de Man went on to fail to write?

In a quick survey of the French seventeenth-century "Quarrel between the Ancients and the Moderns," de Man notes two paradoxes: first, the defenders of the ancients were better readers than the defenders of the moderns because what they were defending was the ancients' modernity; and second, the defenders of the moderns were symptomatic of "the alacrity with which modernity welcomes the opportunity to abandon literature altogether" ("Literary History," 156). And yet, the modern always wins out in the long run. "Literature, which is inconceivable without a passion for modernity," de Man observes, "also seems to oppose from the inside a subtle resistance to this passion" (156).

De Man's essay thus establishes literature not as a contested object but as the sign that something is being contested. The fact that a real contest is taking place can only, however, be lived as "unbearable" (162) or "an incandescent point" (147). But in Nietzsche's "Use and Abuse of History for Life," the text to which de Man first turns for insight into the problem, the same unbearable conflict is figured, paradoxically, as animal serenity. In animals, the self-coincidence so desired by man is not an achievement but a condition. The animal's radical forgetfulness is what Nietzsche—who does not use "modernity" in this sense—calls "life."

> Man says "I remember," and envies the animal that forgets at once, and watches each moment die, disappear in night and mist, and disappear forever. Thus the animal lives unhistorically: It hides nothing and coincides at all moments exactly with that which it is; it is bound to be truthful at all times, unable to be anything else.[4]

"It hides nothing." Does "It hides nothing" in fact hide something? De Man has actually introduced several invisible elisions into this passage. The translation by Adrian Collins says, "The beast lives *unhistorically;* for it 'goes into' the present, like a number, without leaving any curious remainder. It cannot dissimulate, it conceals nothing; at every moment it seems what it actually is, and thus can be nothing that is not honest."[5] What de Man has thus left out is the "curious remainder" and the "dissimulation." What he has added is the self-coincidence that allegory, in "The Rhetoric of Temporality," renounces. In "Literary History and Literary Modernity," too, non-coincidence is a fundamental characteristic of writing in general: "The ambivalence of writing is such that it can be considered both an act and an interpretive process that follows after an act with which it cannot coincide" (152).

At first, the elisions do not seem to matter much in de Man's translation: what is left out is, in any case, a negative characteristic of "man" as contrasted with "beast." But the difference between men and animals—between biology and language—is at the heart of the problem of modernity. For the relation cannot be one of simple contrast: "Since 'life' has an ontological as well as a biological meaning, the condition of animality persists as a constitutive part of man" (146). But when "life" and "forgetfulness" become that without which nothing "truly human" can come into being, we are confronted with a paradox in Nietzsche's text that is not immediately remarked in de Man's: man can be "truly human" only when he is truly animal. De Man summarizes Nietzsche's thought without bringing out the paradox: "Moments of genuine humanity thus are moments at which all anteriority vanishes, annihilated by the power of an absolute forgetting" (147).

In many of de Man's early texts, this moment would be marked not as "absolute forgetting" but as "renunciation" ("*renouncing* the nostalgia and the desire to coincide"). Is self-coincidence, then, *renounced* or produced by *forgetting?* In order to renounce something, you have to remember it. In order to forget something, you cannot renounce it. The human relation to the past would seem to have something to do with the relation between forgetting and renouncing.

In a remarkable essay included in the 1985 volume of *Yale French Studies* entitled "The Lesson of Paul de Man" (published at the height of the phase of mourning following de Man's death in 1983, but before the revelation of his wartime collaborationist journalism), Minae Mizumura analyzes the word "renunciation" in de Man's texts. She writes, "The question of renunciation arises in de Man only when literature comes into the scene. . . . Literature—or the self constituted by and in language, the very condition of literature, comes into being in the renunciation, not of the empirical self, but of the temptation to reconcile itself with the empirical self."[6] According to Mizumura, the word "renunciation," so central to the earlier texts, drops out of the later texts to the extent that the later texts translate an existential into a rhetorical vocabulary. As de Man writes with hindsight in the preface to the second edition of *Blindness and Insight,* "This [older] terminology is still uncomfortably intertwined with the thematic vocabulary of consciousness and of temporality that was current at the time, but it signals a turn that, at least for me, has proven to be productive" (xii). In moving from problems of consciousness to problems of language, de Man, in effect, renounces renunciation. "In renouncing the notion of renunciation," Mizumura concludes, "what de Man renounces is above all the notion of renouncing and hence of the knowing subject" (Mizumura, 92).

The serenity of renunciation in "The Rhetoric of Temporality" is assumed by a personification, not a person: "renouncing the nostalgia and the desire to coincide, *allegory* establishes its language in the void of this temporal difference." The rhetorical subject of the knowledge of the impossibility of knowledge is a subject that can belong only to language. This problem becomes, in fact, the subject of "Literary History and Literary Modernity":

> The distinctive character of literature thus becomes manifest as an inability to escape from a condition that is felt to be unbearable. It seems that there can be no end, no respite in the ceaseless pressure of this contradiction, at least as long as we consider it from the point of view of the writer as subject. The discovery of his inability to be modern leads him back to the fold, within the autonomous domain of literature, but never with genuine appeasement. As soon as he can feel appeased in this situation he ceases to be a writer. His language may be capable of a certain degree of tranquillity; it is, after all, the product of a renunciation that has allowed for the metaphorical thematization of the predicament. But this renunciation does not involve the subject. (162)

In other words, the subject inheres in the unbearable *only*. Tranquillity can be achieved, but only when language has taken over the renunciation the subject cannot accomplish. "As soon as he can feel appeased in this situation he ceases to be a writer." The immediate self-doubling of "the representation of the present" (an expression de Man takes from Baudelaire's "Painter of Modern Life") is not simply a logical problem but the creation of similarity where there may be total difference. "Fashion (mode) can sometimes be only what remains of modernity after the impulse has subsided, as soon— and this can be almost at once—as it has changed from being an incandescent point in time into a reproducible cliché, all that remains of an invention that has lost the desire that produced it. Fashion is like the ashes left behind by the uniquely shaped flames of the fire, the trace alone revealing that a fire actually took place" (147). Ashes, of course, in no way resemble flames. They are a sign, a *trace*, of the fire that produced them. While there may be a necessary relation between the "desire" and the "invention," there is none between the desire and the trace.

The appeasement of the writer's language is thus a tranquillity of ashes. "As soon as he can feel appeased in this situation he ceases to be a writer." Literature is the space where the fire and the ash come together. But that space cannot be inhabited by "the writer," who can find such a space only either "unbearable" or "too tranquil." "Baudelaire states clearly," concludes de Man, "that the attraction of a writer toward his theme—which is also the attraction toward an action, a modernity, and an autonomous *meaning* that would exist outside the realm of language—is primarily an attraction to what is not art" (159). The specificity of art is thus its desire to get outside of art. The much-misused sentence by Derrida—"il n'y a pas de hors texte"—refers to this structure. Far from reinforcing the inside/outside boundary between the text and the real, Derrida defines "text" as the attempt to get beyond that boundary. The text has no "inside" that has not been constituted through the attempt to get outside: and there is no outside of *that*. There is no attempt to get outside that is not a repetition of the structure one is attempting to escape.

Memory, in the Nietzsche passage quoted above, is nothing other than such a repetition. De Man truncates the passage he quotes beyond the elisions already noted. Why does man envy the animal? Not just because he remembers, but because something returns:

> A leaf is continually dropping out of the volume of time and fluttering away—and suddenly it flutters back into the man's lap. Then he says, "I remember . . . ," and envies the beast.[7]

The original German text of the whole passage then reads:

> Fortwährend löst sich ein Blatt aus der Rolle der Zeit, fällt heraus, flattert fort—und flattert plötzlich wieder zurück, dem Menschen in den Schoss. Dann sagt der Mensch "ich errinere mich" und beneidet das Tier, welches sofort vergisst und jeden Augenblick wirklich sterben, in Nebel und Nacht zurücksinken und auf immer verlöschen sieht. So lebt das Tier *unhistorisch:* denn es geht auf in der Gegenwart, wie eine Zahl, ohne dass ein wunderlicher Bruch übrigbleibt, es weiss

nicht zu verstellen, verbirgt nichts und erscheint in jedem Momente ganz und gar als das, was es ist, kann also gar nicht anders sein als ehrlich.[8]

It is because the "volume of time" has always already been structured like a purloined letter (on its first publication, the essay that is now called "Excuses" was entitled "The Purloined Ribbon") that the past can come back. In other words, it cannot with certainty be renounced. But what is it that has now returned after having been ripped out of the volume of time? Perhaps it is precisely the word "modernity," now making a comeback in Germany after having been "banned for political reasons." It would probably be an exaggeration to attribute the existence of this essay to the return of the purloined letter of modernity, but at least we can begin to suspect that when man (or de Man) murmurs "I remember . . . ," something more complicated than a mere contrast between man and beast is going on.

In an early essay quoted by Mizumura on the difference between Madame de Staël and Rousseau, de Man says something that resonates now with his silence about the inability to escape the past:

> To move from self-justification to self-knowledge, the reflection must be able to *renounce*, not only the hope of overcoming the sorrow, but also the hope of justifying oneself by means of this sorrow, of making it subserve the glorification of oneself. . . . The priority of fiction is established in the *renunciation* of oneself.[9]

The play between the "reflection" and the "self" is once again resolved at the expense of the "self." Rousseau is better than Madame de Staël, de Man argues, because Madame de Staël does not reconcile herself to the priority of fiction, while Rousseau (in *La Nouvelle Héloïse*) does. "The world of Clarens is a world that is entirely fictive and founded on a difficult knowledge" (quoted in Mizumura, 85). Both Rousseau and Madame de Staël, he implies, are now all text, but whereas Rousseau planned for this, Madame de Staël did not. She writes as though something that is not text ("oneself") can be served by the text. Her refusal to renounce herself resists the priority of fiction. The "difficult knowledge" that inheres in the fiction can be obtained only at the expense of the writer. This is the "death of the author" that the text requires. But Madame de Staël's refusal to renounce may be precisely the modernity that, if she had simply acceded to it, her text could not have achieved. A text can kill off its author too late or too soon, but it cannot do so at exactly the right time. De Man's lifelong fascination with Rousseau inheres in the suspicion that what is renounced will always come back somewhere. Rousseau remains important because the definitiveness of his renunciation ("May I never have to speak about it again") guarantees that return. The "renunciation of oneself"—like the "death of the author"—can never be completed because, although every text proclaims it, no one can write it.

Let us return now to the final moves of de Man's essay. Modernity and literature turn out to be two poles of a noncoincidence that keeps both in existence:

> In describing literature, from the standpoint of the concept of modernity, as the steady fluctuation of an entity away from and toward its own mode of being, we have constantly stressed that this movement does not take place as an actual sequence in time; to represent it as such is merely a metaphor making a sequence out of what occurs in fact as a synchronic system. . . . It follows that it would be a mistake to think of literary history as the diachronic narrative of the fluctuating motion we have tried to describe. Such a narrative can be only metaphorical, and *history is not fiction.* (163, my emphasis)

Diachronic narratives can plot out metaphorically as sequential only what is in fact simultaneous. If history is not fiction, it is something other than a diachronic narrative. Sequential narratives may correspond to entities, but not to "events": "The sequential, diachronic structure of the process stems from the nature of literary language as an entity, not as an event" (163). It is thus diachronic narrative that is the fiction, the metaphor. Far from claiming that history is a "mere" text, de Man seems to be claiming that the moment one has a text, one loses history.

> Could we conceive of a literary history that would not truncate literature by putting us misleadingly *into* or *outside* it, that would be able to maintain the literary aporia throughout, account at the same time for

the truth or falsehood of the knowledge literature conveys about itself, distinguish rigorously between metaphorical and historical language, and account for literary modernity as well as its historicity? (164)

De Man does not so much answer this question as overturn the assumptions on which it is based. "The need to revise the foundations of literary history may seem like a desperately vast undertaking; the task appears even more disquieting if we contend that literary history could in fact be paradigmatic for history in general, since man himself, like literature, can be defined as an entity capable of putting his own mode of being into question" (165). The distinction between "literature" and "man himself" disappears. Both are entities capable of putting their own mode of being into question. But they are not simply analogous. Both have something fundamental to do with "events that are in essence linguistic." Their capacity to put their own modes of being into question can arise only if the linguistic is experienced *as* an event.

At the end of the essay, de Man seems to content himself with offering advice for "the much more humble task of reading and understanding a literary text."

> To become good literary historians, we must remember that what we usually call literary history has little or nothing to do with literature and that what we call literary interpretation—provided only it is good interpretation—is in fact literary history. (165)

Literary history has nothing to do with an entity that puts itself into question, but literary interpretation will have to confront literature's self-questioning and make sense of it. Thus, to aim at a sequential narrative is to miss the object altogether, but to grapple with it will end up producing a sequential (or at any rate coherent) narrative in the end. This is where de Man drops his final sentence:

> If we extend this notion beyond literature, it merely confirms that the bases for historical knowledge are not empirical facts but written texts, even if these texts masquerade in the guise of wars or revolutions. (165)

A war or revolution is a text in the form of history, not history in the form of a text. It is inscribed in human historicity instead of on paper. The interpreter is therefore *inside* the text, not outside it. "Empirical facts" pretend that they are outside the text, but if wars or revolutions are inconceivable outside the domain of linguistic events, then the text has no outside in which they can exist as facts.

Paul de Man contributed a great deal to the pervasiveness of the "linguistic turn" in the field of theory, moving from the "social sciences" into literary studies. But the social sciences in question were those borderline fields, like history, linguistics, philosophy, and anthropology, whose categorization as social sciences was always, in fact, contested. They would not be central today to the social sciences, which, in the United States at least, are largely focused on quantification rather than signification. But in those early days of the structuralist revolution, many breakthroughs came about if one tried to see where the linguistic model would lead. I think the limitation of the Saussurean model was not, however, its focus on the sign at the expense of the world, but rather its tendency to make a universal model of language based on properties derived from the fact of diversity. Saussure pictured language as pure speech (not tainted by writing, which he considered secondary), but he structured his linguistic model like a dead language, to which no further change could occur (and thus, nothing but writing). Saussure took into consideration the multiplicity of languages, but only insofar as that diversity made the arbitrariness of any one language apparent. But he was still able to make the fact of diversity into a universal model. This is not unlike the problem of diversity in today's American universities, in fact. This, too, is a pre-Babelian fantasy. And however central to de Man's theory an ultimate aporia always was, he, too, wanted to make impossibility into a new Oneness. It was just that, unlike the latter-day defenders of the referent over the sign, he didn't eliminate the linguistic in order to get there.

"Beyond literature" is exactly where literature is found. There is no fire escape. "As soon as he can feel appeased in this situation," writes de Man about the literary subject, "he ceases to be a writer." Whether or not de Man himself ever "ceased to be a writer" in this sense, he at least made clear the stakes involved in remaining one.

EIGHT

Animate Alphabets

By the end of supper my mother had convinced me I should study short-hand in the evenings. Then I would be killing two birds with one stone, writing a novel and learning something practical as well. I would also be saving a whole lot of money.

That same evening, my mother unearthed an old blackboard from the cellar and set it up on the breezeway. Then she stood at the blackboard and scribbled little curlicues in white chalk while I sat in a chair and watched.

At first I felt hopeful.

I thought I might learn shorthand in no time, and when the freckled lady in the Scholarships Office asked me why I hadn't worked to earn money in July and August, the way you were supposed to if you were a scholarship girl, I could tell her I had taken a free shorthand course instead, so I could support myself right after college.

The only thing was, when I tried to picture myself in some job, briskly jotting down line after line of shorthand, my mind went blank. There wasn't one job I felt like doing where you used shorthand. And, as I sat there and watched, the white chalk curlicues blurred into senselessness.

—Sylvia Plath, *The Bell Jar*

There is a striking and unexpected parallel between Walter Benjamin and Sylvia Plath—two people whom one would not normally think to compare—in their perpetual deferral of learning a foreign language despite their reiterated intentions to do so. The fact that they both ended up committing suicide has been obscured by the seemingly very different reasons they did so: betrayal by husband and father, perhaps, in Plath's case, and despair of escaping the Nazis, in Benjamin's. But perhaps *both* suicides are related to the Holocaust, which has been a hot issue—for different reasons—in the critical literature surrounding the two writers.

I. *Correspondences*

I have sent the piece to "Muttersprache," the journal of the General Language Association, but I have not actually heard anything back from them as yet.
—Theodor Adorno to Walter Benjamin, April 21, 1934

In Benjamin's case, the foreign language never learned was Hebrew, and it was accompanied by the deferral of his emigration to Palestine, and, beyond that, by his complex relation to being a Jew. In Plath's case, the foreign language was German. German was the native language of both her parents—and the native language of Benjamin as well. The attraction was, therefore, to occupy the place that was intimately *addressed;* the resistance was perhaps that *addressing* it was different from *being* it. Learning a language is itself an act of addressing someone, but addressing the world in that language might have entailed changing a default setting that each considered too vital a part of the self. What changing that position entailed, I think, has everything to do with the Holocaust.

When people complain that Plath has not "earned" the right to claim "familiarity with the hellish subject," that "whatever her father did to her, it cannot be what the Germans did to the Jews,"[1] they are forgetting that Plath's father *was* a German. The "gothic"[2] elements in Plath's poetry have been criticized as melodramatic, her references to the Holocaust "monstrous" (Irving Howe),[3] a "subtle larceny" (George Steiner) caused by rampaging "so permissively in the history of other people's sorrows that it simply overdraws its rights to our sympathy" (Seamus Heaney).[4] "This penchant for the Gothic effect seems to me to weaken much of Sylvia Plath's earlier verse," writes Steiner, who nevertheless praises Plath as one of a generation of writers "in no way implicated in the actual holocaust." Later, he makes more of this distance by calling Plath "plump and golden in America." "I may be mistaken," he writes, "but so far as I know there was nothing Jewish in her background."[5] But critics have been misled, I think, by focusing on the ethics of Plath's identification with the Jews as the Nazis' victims. They forget that without Germans, the Holocaust could not have happened. Of course, nothing mandated that European anti-Semitism would take the form that it took in Germany. The Holocaust could easily have happened else-where—in France, for example—or nowhere, and it was not enough to speak German to be a Nazi. But there is nothing metaphorical about Plath's identification of her father as German. And the devas-tation caused by the Holocaust may have had a broader impact than we are used to believing—an impact on the family, on the nature of authority, on the nature of evil, and on the political relations be-tween "same" and "different."

"Gothic," of course, is also a type of German font, one that makes the familiar letters of the alphabet themselves take on an uncanny ap-pearance:

> A yew hedge of orders
> Gothic and barbarous, pure German.[6]

Otto Plath died in November 1940, so he had plenty of time to de-clare his sympathy for or against the Nazi Party. Although he was a pacifist, there is some evidence in Plath's diary for the former:

> He wouldn't go to a doctor, wouldn't believe in God and heiled Hitler in the privacy of his home.[7]

Assia Weevil, the woman with whom Plath's husband, Ted Hughes, had the affair that provoked his separation from Sylvia, *was* half Jew-ish. Her family spent the war years in Palestine. So Daddy (in Plath's mind at least) was a real Nazi, while Assia was a real Jew. The opposi-tion between German and Jew becomes reinvested for Plath with negative energy from the overlay of the opposition between male and female. Nazi and Jew become an infernal couple; the true victim is the third. It is she who dies gassed in an oven.

Small wonder that Plath would find it difficult to learn German:

> I could never talk to you.
> My tongue stuck in my jaw.

> It stuck in a barbed wire snare.
> Ich, ich, ich, ich,

I could hardly speak.
I thought every German was you.
And the language obscene

An engine, an engine
Chuffing me off like a Jew.
A Jew to Dachau, Auschwitz, Belsen.
I began to talk like a Jew.[8]

What does Plath mean, "I began to talk like a Jew"? How does a Jew talk? Does she mean Yiddish? Hebrew? But maybe the line should read: "I began to talk / like a Jew." Maybe the girl who cannot address her father finds herself a Jew the moment she begins to talk. It is astonishing how harshly Plath judges her own daily speech. It is as though she is capable only of *blithering, burbling, gibbering, jittering, gushing, blasting off, "giving out,"* or *blatting.* (These are all words from her diaries.) The insectlike sounds emanating from the overly expressive but inarticulate daughter very much resemble the sounds heard by the witnesses to the gruesome murder of mother and daughter in Poe's story *The Murders in the rue Morgue:*

> But in regard to the shrill voice, the peculiarity is—not that they disagreed—but that, while an Italian, an Englishman, a Spaniard, a Hollander, and a Frenchman attempted to describe it, each spoke of it as that *of a foreigner.* Each is sure that it was not the voice of one of his own countrymen. Each likens it—not to the voice of any individual of any nation with whose language he is conversant—but the converse.[9]

When it turns out that the murders were committed by an "Ourang-Outang," it becomes clear that the foreign sounds—and the self's deepest fears—were not even human. Faced with the uncomprehending Nazi father, in other words, every speaker would represent some totally rejected otherness.

As Hughes himself puts it in his late, autobiographical book of poems, *Birthday Letters,* he was powerless against the dead father:

> I did not
> Know I had made and fitted a door
> Opening downwards into your Daddy's grave. . . .

My incomprehension
Deafened by his language—a German
Outside my wavelengths.[10]

In presenting the poem "Daddy" to a BBC audience, Plath explained:

Here is a poem spoken by a girl with an Electra complex. Her father died while she thought he was God. Her case is complicated by the fact that her father was also a Nazi and her mother very possibly part Jewish. In the daughter the two strains marry and paralyze each other—and she has to act out the awful allegory once over before she is free of it.[11]

If the daughter has an Electra complex, she desires the dead father and wants to kill the unfaithful mother. "Every woman adores a Fascist,"[12] though, implies that the desire of "every woman" is for the Nazi father, not the Godlike father. This says something about desire itself, not just about Plath's particular biography. To desire that which is most undesirable—that against which life itself should rebel—has a certain fascination despite all arguments to the contrary. In his preface to Deleuze and Guattari's *Anti-Oedipus,* Michel Foucault calls the book an *Introduction to the Non-Fascist Life.* "Last but not least," he writes, "the strategic adversary is fascism. . . . And not just historical fascism, the fascism of Hitler and Mussolini . . . but also the fascism in us all, in our heads and in our everyday behavior, the fascism that causes us to love power, to desire the very thing that dominates and exploits us."[13]

The mystery of desiring one's own domination, however, may not be so easy to separate from what the self most values. And the passage from "historical fascism" to "the fascism in us all" may represent just that metaphorization of the Holocaust that critics—ignoring the historical situation of the real Otto Plath—have held against the poet. But it is not that family life *is like* fascism, but that, after fascism, family life is not the same. Desiring one's own death may be a structure of desire that can indeed be exploited by fascist parties, but it is too closely tied to ecstatic experience to be confined to them. If moral codes always begin with prohibitions, then the desire to do away with a contradiction between nature and humanity cannot be accomplished once and for all. To eradicate the desire to be annihilated in favor of a more life-affirming way of being just instates the war within the self that such an eradication would terminate.

For Plath (and not only for Plath), the desire for annihilation was precisely the proof of strong sexual feeling: "There is a panther stalks me down: / One day I'll have my death of him," she wrote in a poem immediately after meeting Ted Hughes. As she writes in her diary at that time, "Love turns, lust turns, into the death urge. My love is gone, gone, and I would be raped" (*Journals*, 234).

The poem written for Hughes, "Pursuit," is the only one in Plath's *Collected Poems* to begin with an epigraph in a foreign language:

> Dans le fond des forêts votre image me suit.
> —Racine

Plath was enjoying her French class at Newnham College, in which she was reading Racine. With French, she seemed to experience none of the friction that prevented her from learning German:

> I was struck, even in a tedious session in a dark cubicle in Newnham with Miss Barrett lisping sweetly to those immature girls performing an autopsy on "Les Fleurs du Mal," that I could translate Baudelaire by sight, almost immediately, except for the obvious vocabulary words I didn't know: I felt the sensuous flow of the words and meanings, and plunged in them alone, longing to read him and live with him. Maybe someday French will actually be natural to me. (*Journals*, 226)

This fantasy of French seeming "natural" and "sensuous" is, even though a fantasy, quite different from the Gothic barbed wire of the German language that always sticks in the throat.

Here is a partial record of Plath's attempts to learn German, taken from her journals:

> [Summer 1954, took an elementary German course at Harvard's summer school]

> [February 25, 1956, looking forward to the St. Botolphe's party where she will meet Ted; thinking back to visit to a psychiatrist that morning] Now, you have to begin somewhere, and it might as well be with life; a

belief in me, with my limitations, and a strong punchy determination to fight to overcome one by one: like languages, to learn French, ignore Italian (a sloppy knowledge of 3 languages is dilettantism) and revive German again, to build each solid. (209)

[February 27, 1956] I have such a damned puritanical conscience that it flays me like briars when I feel I've done wrong or haven't demanded enough of myself: I feel I've cheated myself on languages: I haven't really worked at learning it, and I must be tutored in German next year, instead of Italian. (215)

[July 4 (3?), 1958, finished with year's teaching at Smith; about to spend a year in Boston writing] I began German—two hours a day, on July 1st. (399)

[July 4, 1958] Wickedly didn't do German for the last two days, in a spell of perversity & paralysis. (400)

[January 20, 1959] Will study German. (464)

[January 27, 1959] Learn German, Italian. Joy. (465)

[January 27, 1959] I do no German, no French. Is this because it is easier to complain I don't do it than to do it? (465)

[March 20, 1959, starts Robert Lowell's poetry workshop] Have not touched German: to learn that would be a great triumph for me. (375)

[October 1959, at Yaddo writers' colony] Did launder clothes yesterday. Must do handwash today. Go over Ted's two stories. Either draw or do German. (513)

[October 10, 1959] German and French would give me self-respect, why don't I act on this. (517)

[October 13, 1959] At least I have begun my German. (517)

[October 19, 1959] Worked on German for two days, then let up when I wrote poems. Must keep on with it. It is hard. So are most things worth doing. (519)

[November 4, 1959] Take German lessons wherever I am, and read French. (523)

[November 7, 1959] Dangerous to be so close to Ted day in day out. I have no life separate from him, am likely to become a mere accessory. Important to take German lessons, go out on my own, think, work on

my own. Lead separate lives. . . . I am inclined to go passive, and let
Ted be my social self. Simply because we are never apart. Now, for example: the several things I can do apart from him: study German,
write, read, walk alone in the woods. . . . (524)

As this last entry suggests, studying German was a way of getting
some distance from Hughes. Ted Hughes was a perfect complement: many entries in Plath's diary describe him as a yin to her yang.
Plath suffered not because she never found her male counterpart but
because she was sure she had. It was simply that perfect complementarity was stifling. In a perfect fit between two people, there is
really only room for one. But everything depends on who we think
that one is. In July 1957 she had written: "My danger, I think, is becoming too dependent on Ted. He is didactic, fanatic. . . . Between
us there are no barriers—it is rather as if neither of us—or especially
myself—had any skin, or one skin between us & kept bumping into
and abrading each other" (401). At the same time, "O, only left to
myself, what a poet I will flay myself into," she sighed on Mother's
Day in 1958. When she says that Hughes is "closer, warmer, dearer
than I ever was to myself" (*Journals*, 361), this is no exaggeration.
Fusing with another was easier for Sylvia Plath than dealing with the
self-difference of being alone.

But the English language, which all English-speaking countries
supposedly have in common, could itself turn into a foreign language. Picking up James Joyce's *Finnegans Wake*, Plath takes as a
sign of impending madness the unreadability that Joyce must have
courted. Squinting at a 100-letter word, Esther Greenwood, in *The
Bell Jar*, thinks:

Why should there be a hundred letters?
Haltingly, I tried the word aloud.
It sounded like a heavy wooden object falling downstairs, boomp
boomp boomp, step after step. Lifting the pages of the book, I let
them fan slowly by my eyes. Words, dimly familiar, but twisted all awry,
like faces in a funhouse mirror, fled past, leaving no impression on the
glassy surface of my brain.
I squinted at the page.
The letters grew barbs and rams' horns. I watched them separate,
each from the other, and jiggle up and down in a silly way. Then they

associated themselves in fantastic, untranslatable shapes, like Arabic or Chinese.

I decided to junk my thesis.[14]

If, as Aurelia Plath reports in her introduction to *Letters Home,* the young Plath was fed the letters of the alphabet in place of the mother's body when her brother Warren was born, then it stands to reason that Plath would be unusually struck by the strangeness of other alphabets. Neither Arabic nor Chinese is read from left to right—nor, for that matter, is Hebrew. To learn to read not only in another alphabet but in another direction was more than just learning a foreign language. For both Plath and Benjamin, it was internalizing an intimate foreignness that they never wanted.

II. Benjamin's Hebrew Lessons

I have come to know living Judaism in absolutely no form other than you. The question of my relationship to Judaism is always the question of how I stand—I do not want to say in relation to you (because my friendship will no longer depend on any decision)—in relation to the forces you have touched in me. But whatever this decision may depend on, it will be made soon—however much, on the one hand, it is embedded in circumstances that seem to be totally alien to it and, on the other hand, in that procrastination that has been stretched to the limit and that is second nature to me when it comes to the most important situations of my life. Having begun to loosen the extremely tangled knot of my existence in one place—Dora and I have since gotten a divorce—this "Gordian knot," as you once justifiably called my relationship to Hebrew, will also have to be unraveled.

—Walter Benjamin (in Berlin) to Gershom Scholem (in Jerusalem), April 25, 1930

There seems to be a male-female opposition somewhere behind Benjamin's story too. The woman who occasioned the breakup of Benjamin's marriage to the (Jewish) Dora—the woman who uncannily seems to bear the same first name as Plath's "other woman"—was a Christian Bolshevist named Asja Lacis. Benjamin seems to have fallen in love with Asja and Marxism at the same time, and while the affair with Asja was short-lived, the affair with Marx lasted for the rest of his life.

Indeed, Benjamin seems unusually bisexual in his passions—and unusually multilingual. His gradual backing away from Hebrew sounds in his correspondence like an infidelity to Gershom Scholem, who had emigrated from Germany to Palestine and hoped that Benjamin would do the same. Scholem's doubts about both Benjamin's Judaism and Benjamin's materialism sound like the poutings of a jilted lover. The fact that we don't have edited volumes of his correspondence with Dora or Asja has made the rivalry between Judaism and Marxism seem like a pull between Scholem and Theodor Adorno, but both of them seem piqued that he doesn't in fact tell them much about the "other scene" involving the women.

What happened when Walter Benjamin tried to learn Hebrew? The transition between German and Hebrew had already been established, of course, by Yiddish. How much Yiddish did Benjamin know? He seems to have learned "family Yiddish" only orally in quite an assimilated family (he mentions celebrating Hanukkah later with his son, but then celebrating Christmas with his parents). He addresses most of his (few) Yiddish and Hebrew words to Scholem, but also to the scholar Florenz Christian Rang, to whom he tries to present his "Jewish self."[15]

To what extent did the fantasy of confronting Judaism exist for Benjamin independently of his relation to Scholem? In my reading of their correspondence, I think it began as a genuine desire on Benjamin's part, and only later did his relationship with Scholem begin to diverge from his interest in "things Jewish." This was partly caused by his infatuation with Asja and with communism, but also partly caused by his inability to leave a Europe that was rapidly leaving *him*. The appearance of *The Arcades Project* just as Benjamin was ready to emigrate to Palestine offered a way of leaving Germany without leaving Europe. The fact that "The Paris Arcades: A Dialectical Fairy Play" ballooned from "a project that will take just a few weeks" (*Correspondence*, 322) to a huge pile of notes still uncompleted at his death indicates that something unconscious needed not to let it go.

In any case, Benjamin was still unacquainted with the Hebrew alphabet as late as 1928:

My trip to Palestine is a settled matter, as is my intention to strictly observe the course of study prescribed by Your Heirojerusalemitic Excellency. Let me moreover avow that the awestruck undersigned will be able to read the alphabet common to the country before he sets foot on the soil of Eretz Israel. (Benjamin to Scholem, August 1, 1928; *Correspondence,* 338)

His only use of Hebrew letters in his correspondence occurs in a letter to Scholem written on June 6, 1929, at the moment he had started serious Hebrew lessons with Max Mayer: "*beracha gam le-Escha,*" he writes at the end of his letter. A note tells us that this greeting to Scholem's wife is written in Hebrew characters, but it does not reproduce them. Since on page 220 of the edited *Correspondence* a word is printed in the Greek alphabet, the mere foreignness of the alphabet cannot solely account for this. There are two possible explanations: either Benjamin made mistakes, or he was writing in mock-printed letters instead of the cursive writing that Hebrew speakers use in daily life. In either case, Scholem's non-reproduction coincides with the difference between the dead language of Scripture and the living language of "Eretz Israel." It is interesting that Benjamin uses—twice—the Hebrew expression for "ignorant": *Amhaaretz.* Literally, it means "country people" or "illiterates." To the "people of the book," the people of the land were illiterate. But in "Eretz Israel," the land suddenly became the unifying force for "the people." *Amhaaretz* might mean "ignoramus," but it also means "the people of the land" that Palestine had come to be. Scholem was already worried in 1925 about what was happening as the dead language came alive. Benjamin writes to him, "Your observations on the 'seemingly dead' transmitted language, which, as the Hebrew living and being transformed in the mouths of the new generation, threatens to turn against those who speak it, are not clear to me in every respect" (*Correspondence,* 268).

For Benjamin, then, Hebrew was not a native language. Indeed, it was never defined as a "mother tongue." As a book about Yiddish puts it:

> Since Jewish women were not taught Hebrew, the "sacred tongue," they spoke *Yiddish* to the children—who, in turn, spoke it to their parents and, later, to their own children. So *Yiddish* became known as *Mame-loshen,* "mother's language," to distinguish it from *loshen-ha-kodesh,* "the sacred language."[16]

Learning Hebrew involved a voyage to the sacred, not a voyage to the origin. And transforming a dead language into a living one entailed transgressing a long-standing gender divide and moving the patriarchs from the text into life. It is no wonder Scholem was not sure life was such a good place for Hebrew. At first, though, for Benjamin, the origin and the sacred appeared to coincide, and a voyage to the one appeared to open up the other. He writes to Scholem:

[July 23, 1920] Perhaps your June letter, which thoroughly grasped my situation, is what led me to start Hebrew—a decision I would not have dared make on my own. (*Correspondence,* 165)

[December 1, 1920] It would be impossible for me to succeed in getting my bearings simultaneously in two different areas, scholasticism and Hebrew, which are both so difficult, unfamiliar to me, and at a great remove from each other. . . . I would for the last time have to let Hebrew take a back seat. (168)

[December 29, 1920] I am unable to devote myself to things Jewish with full intensity before having derived from my European apprenticeship what may result at least in some chance of a more peaceful future, family support, etc. (169–170)

[February 19, 1925] And, finally, if ever, I soon have to take seriously my study of Hebrew. (265)

[April 8, 1925] I intend to begin taking Hebrew lessons in the near future. (265)

[January 30, 1928] This is perhaps my last chance to devote myself to the study of Hebrew and to everything we think is connected with it. But this is also a very propitious time for it. First and foremost, in terms of my being ready for the undertaking, heart and soul. Once I have, one way or another, completed the project on which I am currently working, carefully and provisionally—the highly remarkable and extremely precarious essay "Paris Arcades: A Dialectical Fairy Play." (322)

At this point, Scholem notes: "Hebrew ultimately lost out in its conflict with the *Arcades* project. The *Paris Arcades,* WB's uncompleted major work, is mentioned here for the first time (but was called this already in a conversation in 1927)" (325). But Benjamin had clearly not read that note. He met (twice!) with Judah Magnes, the chancellor of the newly founded University of Jerusalem, and obtained a subsidy to learn Hebrew—possibly with a view to getting an appointment there after he emigrated to Palestine. "My way is clear to begin Hebrew lessons," he wrote. Desperate for money, he was very grateful for Magnes's subsidy—but he still failed to learn Hebrew. He took lessons for about a month, but was unable to continue when his teacher departed. Scholem adds in a note to Benjamin's letter of June 1929 describing his Hebrew lessons to Hugo von Hofmannsthal, "He discontinued his lessons in July and this was essentially the end of his study of Hebrew" (351).

III. A Change of Address

> "Do as you like with me. I'm your parcel.
> I have only our address on me.
> Open me or readdress me."
>
> —Ted Hughes, "The Inscription"

Benjamin wrote to Scholem on May 24, 1928:

> The work on the *Paris Arcades* is taking on an ever more mysterious and insistent mien and howls into my nights like a small beast if I have failed to water it at the most distant springs during the day. . . . In any case, it gives me no respite. . . . It was a very lucky coincidence that, within certain limits, [Hofmannsthal] was in the know—obviously only in terms of my plans for *Hebrew*—. . . .
> I have firmly put an autumn visit to Palestine on my agenda for the coming year. . . . I do, in fact, intend to bring actual production to a temporary halt once I am finished with my current project, in order that I may *just* learn. (*Correspondence*, 335)

Scholem's account of the rivalry between Hebrew and *The Arcades* was not exaggerated. In March 1929, Benjamin wrote to Scholem, "This work [his essay on Surrealism] is, in fact, a screen placed in front of the *Paris Arcades*—and I have many a reason to keep secret what goes on behind it. . . . A perilous, breathtaking enterprise, re-

peatedly put off over the course of the winter, not without reason—
also because of the terrible competition with Hebrew—thus sometimes paralyzing me, and as I have discovered, it was just as impossible to postpone as it is to complete at this time" (*Correspondence,*
348).

The "paralysis" that Sylvia Plath described within the couple Ger-
man-plus-Jew is the same paralysis that Benjamin feels here—*within*
German. Benjamin couldn't leave German and enter Hebrew, since
for him there was no separation possible between being German
and being Jewish. For Plath, there was an *absolute* contradiction.
Benjamin could not assume his identity as a Jew if it meant giving up
his identity as a European. Plath identified totally with the Jew she
wasn't.

For Benjamin, the difficulty of leaving Europe altogether for Israel
is perhaps best expressed in an earlier letter to Hofmannsthal: "A
more profound treatment would of course require me to leave the
domain of German and enter that of Hebrew, which, in spite of my
best intentions, I have yet to set foot in" (October 30, 1926; *Correspondence,* 309).

In a beautiful letter to Benjamin written on February 20, 1930,
Scholem, aware of his friend's stalling and plunging bravely into
what he himself thought it meant, wrote:

> I am surely someone who will be able to accept with composure and,
> perhaps, with some comprehension if you reveal that you can no
> longer, and will no longer, in this life consider a true confrontation
> with Judaism that lies beyond the medium of our friendship. I some-
> times believe that, when speaking about these matters, you do so with
> more concern for me than for yourself—as paradoxical as that may
> sound, I truly believe it to be an accurate description of your attitude in
> some instances and I would not feel the way I do about you if I did not
> suffer on account of this situation. I occasionally say, Walter does not
> dare to give a clear accounting of his situation out of friendship for me.
> He avoids "getting to the heart of the issue, comprehending it"[17]—but
> I assure you that this can and should not be a valid reason, in either a
> moral or symbolic sense. It is much more important for me to know
> where you really are than where you perhaps hope to venture at some

future time, since, of course, given how your life is constituted, it is certain that you, more than any other person, will always arrive someplace other than where you intended. (*Correspondence,* 363–364)

"You will always arrive someplace other than where you intended." One can only admire Scholem for his loving renunciation of knowing where.

Benjamin's constant deferrals of his departure for Palestine and its nevertheless constant imminence resemble uncannily Baudelaire's similar deferrals and promises to go to Honfleur to be with his mother after the death of Jacques Aupick. Although Baudelaire did make it for a few months to Honfleur, whereas Benjamin never made it to Palestine, Baudelaire nevertheless spent the last ten years of his life assuring everyone he wrote to (and not just his mother) that he was just about to make the trip. He had just published *Les Fleurs du Mal,* which he surmised (probably correctly) would offend and embarrass his mother, but he had overcome his desire to keep his book and his mother apart and had sent her one of the luxury volumes of his poetry when the first edition came out in 1857. The occurrence of his trial and his condemnation must have made the task of defending his work to his mother quite a lot harder. Some trace of the mixed feelings he must have had about the prospect of writing new poems in the house of a Second Empire widow to replace the ones removed by a Second Empire court remains, perhaps, in Baudelaire's difficulties in writing the word "fleur" at the end of "Honfleur" in a letter to his mother written December 7, 1860:

> Je ne stationnerai dans ce logement que huit jours et puis j'irai [à Honff *biffé*] [à Honff *biffé*] à Honfleur.[18]
>
> [I will only stay here a week and then I'll go to [Honff crossed out] [Honff crossed out] Honfleur.]

Nevertheless, during the short period in which he lived by her side, he had an uncharacteristic burst of creativity:

> Je commence à croire qu'au lieu de six *fleurs,* j'en ferai vingt. (To Poulet-Malassis, November 5, 1858; *Correspondance* 1: 522)

[I'm beginning to think I'll do twenty new *flowers* instead of six.]

J'ai fait une nouvelle *fleur; Les Voyageurs* [now called *Le Voyage*], à Max. Du Camp. (To Poulet-Malassis, February 4, 1859; 1: 546)

[I wrote a new *flower; The Travelers* dedicated to Max. Du Camp.]

Nouvelles *fleurs* faites, et passablement singulières. Ici, dans le repos, la faconde m'est revenue. (To Sainte-Beuve, February 21, 1859; 1: 553)

[New *flowers* done, and some quite singular. Here, with rest, my volubility has come back.]

Nouvelles *Fleurs du Mal* faites [note: Le Cygne, Sept Vieillards, Petites Vieilles]. A tout casser, comme une explosion de gaz chez un vitrier. (To Poulet-Malassis, April 29, 1859; 1: 568)

[New *Flowers of Evil* done. To beat the band, like a gas explosion in a glass factory.]

Baudelaire's famous city poems about Paris were thus written in the country: the painter of modern life was perhaps able, for the only time in his life, to write genuinely about what he was not at that moment experiencing.

In Benjamin's case, the difficulty of leaving may have led to a situation in which he could no longer escape. When the spread of Nazism had definitively made Europe unsafe for him, Benjamin finally prepared to leave—this time for New York. True to form, he wrote on January 17, 1940, to Gretel Adorno, "My English lessons are going to start next week." But, finally, despite so many plans, Benjamin never left Europe.

IV. Foreignness

I need an outsider: feel like the recluse who comes out into the world with a life-saving gospel to find everybody has learned a new language in the meantime and can't understand a word he's saying.
—Sylvia Plath, *Journals*

It may seem that Baudelaire's postponements of his move to Honfleur lack the dimension of foreign-language learning we have discussed in the deferrals of Plath and Benjamin. But perhaps there is a way in which the vestige of a foreign language inheres in the one word remaining to him after the onset of his aphasia. That word was *crénom*, which interpreters have identified as part of the exclamation "sacré nom de Dieu!" But "sacré nom de Dieu" was how he translated the "national swearword" of those detestable Belgians about whom he was writing his last, and unfinished, book.

> Il y a plusieurs mois, je me suis trouvé, la nuit, égaré dans un faubourg que je ne connaissais pas; j'ai demandé mon chemin à deux jeunes filles, qui m'ont répondu: *Gott for damn!* (ou *domn!*) (j'écris mal cela; jamais un Belge n'a pu même me dire comment on devait orthographier le juron national; mais cela équivaut à *Sacré nom de Dieu!*). Deux jours après, je rencontre un Belge qui me dit "Ah! çà, vous allez donc à la messe, vous! *Gott for domn!* (toujours le même juron que je ne sais pas écrire). Qu'en est-ce que vous allez à la messe, PUISQUE VOUS N'AVEZ PAS DE LIVRE DE MESSE?" Ceci est un raisonnement essentiellement belge. (To Mme Paul Meurice, February 3, 1865; *Correspondance,* 2: 449)

> [A few months ago, I found myself, at night, lost in an unfamiliar area; I asked two girls which way I should go, and they answered: *Gott for damn!* (or *domn!*) (I don't know how to write it; no Belgian has ever been able to tell me even how to spell the national swearword; but it's equivalent to *God be damned!*) Two days later, I meet a Belgian, who says, "Ah! oh, so you're going to Mass, are you! *Gott for domn!* (that same curse I still don't know how to spell). How could you be going to Mass, SINCE YOU DON'T HAVE A PRAYER BOOK?" That is an example of Belgian reasoning.]

In addition, there is a way to see Baudelaire resisting the task not of learning a foreign language but of *un*learning the specificity of his own. In an age of universal progress and utility, language was stripped down to its bare essentials. In the "Projets de Préface" that he drafted in self-defense at the time of the trial of *Les Fleurs du Mal,* he proclaimed:

> Je sais que l'amant passionné du beau style s'expose à la haine des multitudes. Mais aucun respect humain, aucune fausse pudeur, aucune coalition, aucun suffrage universel ne me contraindront à *parler le patois incomparable* de ce siècle, ni à confondre l'encre avec la vertu.[19]

[I know that the passionate lover of beautiful style opens himself up to the majority's hatred. But no human respect, no false modesty, no coalition, no universal suffrage will constrain me to *speak the incomparable dialect of this century*, nor to conflate ink with virtue.]

The political Esperanto derived from the French Revolution courted, in fact, the same danger Plato warned against: the danger— or, here, the hope—of mimesis. The patois of utopian thinking was based on a mimetic correlation between language and the world. Indeed, the very reason Baudelaire was being prosecuted was that all the horrors he depicted were attributed to him: "On m'a attribué tous les crimes que je racontais [I was credited with all the crimes I recounted]" (*Correspondance*, 2: 182).

But in another sense, I think there is a fundamental relation between mothers and foreignness that is not confined to literal foreign languages. The binding relation the child sometimes maintains with the mother can result in her seeming *not foreign enough*. If both Baudelaire and Plath were not sure of the difference between themselves and their mothers, their choice of love object seems to guarantee the foreignness that might be lacking. Baudelaire's lifelong mistress was not only foreign but also black, and Ted Hughes's Englishness was part of his appeal for Plath. And in *Birthday Letters*, Hughes makes it clear that Plath's Americanness was part of *her* appeal for *him*. He writes, for example, in a poem called "Your Paris":

Your Paris, I thought, was American.
I wanted to humour you.
[. . .]
I kept my Paris from you. My Paris
Was only just not German. The capital
Of the Occupation and old nightmare.
[. . .]
My Paris was a post-war utility survivor,
The stink of fear still hanging in the wardrobes,
Collaborateurs barely out of their twenties,
Every other face closed by the Camps
Or the Maquis.
[. . .]

              Your practised lips
Translated the spasms to what you excused
As your gushy burblings—which I decoded
Into a language, utterly new to me
With conjectural, hopelessly wrong meanings—
You gave me no hint how, at every corner,
My fingers linked in yours, you expected
The final face-to-face revelation
To grab your whole body. Your Paris
Was a desk in a *pension*
Where your letters
Waited for him unopened. Was a labyrinth
Where you still hurtled, scattering tears,
Was a dream where you could not
Wake or find the exit or
The Minotaur to put a blessed end
To the torment.

More often than not, his poems tell us that Hughes was keeping to himself any mention of how differently he and his wife were experiencing something. In other words, he is telling the *reader* something he did not tell his wife. Who mandated this? Even if in "Your Paris" he ultimately confesses that he did not know what was really going on in his wife's head, neither did she know what was going on in his. By placing the dead father as the unknown center of Plath's labyrinth, Hughes still leaves unspoken his own.

After Plath's death, the grieving husband must have discovered in her diaries many things written in that "utterly new" language. He imagines that Paris, for her, must have conjured up her frantic search for Richard Sassoon, and the utter aloneness she must have felt when she realized that the man with whom she was so infatuated had left Paris. The looming ghost of the dead father then comes in to explain all unbearable losses, all betrayals. Killing oneself in order to join him makes perfect sense. But blaming the Big Bad Ghost for everything the husband failed to understand enables Hughes to treat both Plath and himself as innocent children, manipulated by a force over which they had no power. This leaves in the shadow any possible complaints they might have had about each other.

It also leaves in the shadow their very different experiences of the Second World War. The Vichy government would forever come to an Englishman's mind as an indictment of just how much France had participated in the Holocaust. Genteel anti-Semitism had long been a fundamental part of Frenchness: Baudelaire himself provides an example of this casual ruthlessness. He writes in his journal, "Belle conspiration à organiser pour l'extermination de la Race Juive [Fine conspiracy to organize for the extermination of the Jewish Race]" (*Oeuvres complètes*, 1: 706). As German planes bombed London, Hughes had plenty of reason to associate France with betrayal.

What went through his mind, then, when he thought about his wife's German ancestry? Aurelia Plath, it will be recalled, was a language teacher. And it was while she was taking a course in Middle High German from her future husband, Otto, that the two of them fell in love. She seemed to have relished recounting to her children the story of her first attempt at learning English:

> Both my children were always asking me to "tell us about the olden days when you were a little girl," and I shared with them the unforgettable memory of my first day in school. Although my father spoke four languages and had lived in England two years before migrating to the United States, he and my mother spoke German at home. There were no children nearby to play with, so I too spoke only German. I told my children how isolated I felt at recess as I stood by myself in a corner of the schoolyard, listening intently to what the children were shouting to each other. The two words I heard most frequently were, "Shut up!" so when I went home at the end of the school day and met my father, I answered his greeting proudly and loudly with "Shut up!" I still remember how his face reddened. He took me across his knee and spanked me. Weeping loudly over that injustice, I sobbed out, *"Aber was bedeutet das, Papa? Was bedeudet das?"* (What does that mean?) Then he realized I had not understood what the words meant; he was sorry, hugged me, and asked me to forgive him. It was my first and last spanking.[20]

This is an interesting story from a number of points of view. It is a subtle defense: "I did nothing wrong"; "I was unjustly punished." This was clearly a defense Aurelia Plath needed in order to deal with both her brilliant daughter's suicide and the portrait of the mother painted in *The Bell Jar*. It also makes the ancestral German more fraught for Plath, who, in the notes to her poem "Lorelei," writes:

> Pan [the spirit in the Ouija board] said I should write on the poemsubject "Lorelei" because they are "my own kin." So today [July 4], for fun, I did so, remembering the plaintive German song Mother used to play and sing to us beginning "Ich weiss nicht was soll es bedeuten. . . ." (*Collected Poems*, 287)

The English expression "shut up!" commands a silence that only people who understand English can obey. But this expression, "shut up," seems to have stuck with Sylvia. In a poem called "The Courage of Shutting Up," she writes:

> So the discs of the brain revolve, like the muzzles of
> cannon.
> Then there is that antique billhook, the tongue,
> Indefatigable, purple. Must it be cut out?
> It has nine tails, it is dangerous.
> And the noise it flays from the air, once it gets going!
>
> No, the tongue, too, has been put by,
> Hung up in the library with the engravings of Rangoon
> And the fox heads, the otter heads, the heads of dead
> rabbits.
> It is a marvelous object—
> The things it has pierced in its time.

Many times she tells herself, "I think the worst thing is to exteriorize these jitterings & so I will try to shut up & not blither to Ted. His sympathy is a constant temptation" (*Journals*, 409). Then of course there is that moment in *The Bell Jar* when Esther, hospitalized for mental illness after her suicide attempt, comes across fellow patients Joan and DeeDee together in bed, and later asks her therapist Dr. Nolan, "What does a woman see in a woman that she can't see in a man?"

> Doctor Nolan paused. Then she said, "Tenderness."
> That shut me up. (231)

V. Plath's "Queerness"

Publisher's Note: . . . These journals contain Sylvia Plath's opinions and not those of the publisher. Readers should keep in mind the colloquial meanings of words appropriate to the time period of the journals. For example, Plath used the word "queer" to denote an eccentric or suspicious person, according to her annotated dictionary, and not a homosexual.

—*The Unabridged Journals of Sylvia Plath*

To suggest that Sylvia Plath was anything but heterosexual, Ted Hughes wrote to Jacqueline Rose, would be, in some countries, "grounds for homicide." Rose had written, in a chapter called "No Fantasy without Protest" in her book *The Haunting of Sylvia Plath*, a reading of the fantasies enacted in Plath's poem "The Rabbit Catcher." Hughes was afraid that Plath's children, realizing that a reader of Rose's book might be forced to think "about their mother the thoughts Professor Rose has taught," could be mortally damaged by that reading of the poem.

To show that Rose's reading does not imply that, even *in fantasy,* sexual identity involves anything definite, I will quote it in its entirety:

> For the sexuality that it writes cannot be held to a single place—it spreads, blinds, unreels like the oil in the sea. Most crudely, that wind blowing, that gagging, calls up the image of oral sex and then immediately turns it around, gagging the speaker with her own blown hair, her hair in her mouth, her tasting the gorse (Whose body—male or female—is this? Who—man or woman—is tasting whom?), even while "black spikes" and "candles" work to hold the more obvious distribution of gender roles in their place. For Freud, such fantasies, such points of uncertainty, are the regular unconscious subtexts—for all of us—of the more straightforward reading, the more obvious narratives of stable sexual identity which we write.[21]

Although this sounds like a dispute about Sylvia Plath's sexual identity, I think that what we find in Hughes and Rose are not two different readings of sexual orientation but, rather, two different theories of sexuality. Children are always disturbed by their parents' sexuality, but Hughes seems unusually protective of his wife's heterosexual reputation. For him, heterosexuality *is* sexuality; for Rose, heterosexuality is underpinned by "regular unconscious subtexts . . . of uncertainty." In other words, it is almost as though, for Hughes, without heterosexuality there is no sexuality; for Rose, there is no sexuality if there is *nothing but* heterosexuality. These are both, in a way, defenses of heterosexuality. And in cases where heterosexuality is to be at all costs protected, any suggestion otherwise might indeed be "grounds for homicide."

Janet Malcolm, who spends quite a lot of time on this exchange, writes that, in a letter to the *Times Literary Supplement*, Rose indignantly quoted Hughes's remark: "I was told . . . that to speculate on a mother's sexual identity would in some countries be 'grounds for homicide.' If this is not illegitimate pressure (it did not—I of course checked with Virago's lawyer—legally constitute a threat), then I would like to know what is." Hughes protested, as if innocently, that his intention had been to arouse her "common (even maternal) sensibility," and continues:

> "I cast about for some historical example, a situation in which what is perceived as a fanciful, verbalized, public injury to a mother's 'sexual identity' strikes into her children with a pain that is not only violently real, but is also well recorded, documentary, believed by Professor Rose. I lit on the obvious case, and asked her to imagine how it would be, to interpret some local mother's 'sexual identity,' publicly (even publishing it to the world), as she had interpreted Sylvia Plath's—in one of those pride and honour societies of the Mediterranean."[22]

"Common (even maternal) sensibility." Here is another example of the opposition between mothers and lesbians. As if it were impossible to be both at once.

In an article about *The Bell Jar* and the death of Julius and Ethel Rosenberg, Marie Asche quotes the first sentence of the novel:

> It was a queer, sultry summer, the summer they executed the Rosenbergs.[23]

In her article, Asche points out the insistence of lesbian possibilities:

> The pursuit of satisfactory heterosexual relationships against a backdrop of interesting or seductive lesbian possibilities is apparent throughout the novel. (223)

But although the reader might look for more about these "other-than-heterosexual" relationships, the emphasis in the article is really on why Ethel Rosenberg was executed. At first, the fact that she would be abandoning two children seemed to move her judges to clemency. But when they learned that her political activities had in themselves demonstrated that she was a bad mother, they were adamant about inflicting on her the maximum punishment. Ethel Rosenberg was executed, in other words, not for stealing atomic secrets but for violating every code of behavior expected of a wife and mother. Asche's attempts to equate lesbians with bad mothers makes some sense: both are proscribed by the fifties' ideal of healthy heterosexuality. But Rosenberg was certainly no lesbian, and lesbians are certainly no spies.

However, the opposition between lesbians and mothers remains deeply embedded in our cultural assumptions. Ted Hughes speaks to Jacqueline Rose as though she has only to imagine properly, and she will be convinced. Think like a mother, he tells her, and not like a lesbian . . . or an English teacher ("the thoughts Professor Rose has *taught*"). I think this is less a form of homophobia (although it is perhaps that) than an opposition between *life* and *reading*.

Janet Malcolm quotes Hughes's anger at English teachers several times. For example:

> "Critics established the right to say whatever they pleased about the dead. It is an absolute power, and the corruption that comes with it, very often, is an atrophy of the moral imagination. They move onto the living because they can no longer feel the difference between the living and the dead. They extend over the living that licence to say whatever they please, to ransack their psyche and reinvent them however they please. They stand in front of classes and present this performance as exemplary civilised activity—this utter insensitivity towards other living human beings. Students see the easy power and are enthralled, and begin to outdo their teachers. For a person to be corrupted in that way is to be genuinely corrupted." (Malcolm, 47)

This is a very powerful moral statement. It implies that there is an absolute distinction between life and death. And indeed, we would all like to believe this. But reading writings departs from the clarity of that distinction. To want to keep control is to forbid any reading that the author's consciousness would not recognize. But Sylvia Plath *is* dead, and to forbid critics from saying things she would not say is ultimately to prevent them from reading altogether, at least without a censor looking over their shoulder. To read is indeed to treat as dead. That the surrender of control that this implies is uncomfortable is indubitable. Anyone who has ever had a book reviewed knows how uncomfortable it is to be read. That Sylvia Plath's death left behind many people who could still feel that pain, and whose lives *could* be affected by readings is indeed a matter of sensitivity. But to write is to hand over control to writing, and to let someone else decide how to put the pieces together. There is just no way to make sure that the process will be painless.

Readers of *The Bell Jar* have found undeniable traces and symptoms to prove that Plath was repressing a lesbian possibility. These are the teachers Hughes fears, who pounce on Plath's texts to convict her of things she would have consciously refused. Such readers live in a Freudian universe where ambiguity is expected and is not incompatible with normative health. The mechanism of psychoanalysis depends on the possibility that there might be a discrepancy between the testimony of consciousness and the testimony of the unconscious. If that discrepancy is read for the benefit of the analysand, relief can be obtained. But if that discrepancy is read against the person whose unconscious is giving testimony to what she is repressing, then "reading" can indeed be felt as an aggressive act, and the difference between life and death is the difference between talking to an analyst and talking to a tape recorder. In her journals, Plath shows herself to be a child of the Freudian fifties: ambiguity and normativity were somehow both expected. But her English husband held to older forms of irrationality, according to which ambiguity was a form of bad faith. As A. Alvarez wrote on the occasion of the publication of *Birthday Letters:* "It didn't matter that sometimes he used mumbo-jumbo to get where he wanted to be—astrology, hypnosis, Ouija boards, or the dottier forms of Jungian magical thinking."[24]

Sylvia Plath both believed in and relied on the unconscious as a source for other people's writing. But she refused to let her own join the conversation. She inspected her own behavior, named the symptoms, and could not let a symptom become a source of writing. The moment blood or anger came up, she passed beside it with minute description. But perhaps the problem lies elsewhere. A true unconscious symptom would be a shock, something disowned, not expected. In many ways, Freud was part of Plath's *consciousness*, not her unconscious. Being analyzed was itself a social act for women of her class, generation, race, and educational level. Might it not be that the clues she lets drop ("I wondered what I thought I was burying") are a little *too* obvious to be the truth?

So what *does* Sylvia Plath mean by "queer"? At first I assumed this was simply an Englishism, used rather indiscriminately to mean "strange" or, as contemporary Americans often say, "weird." I looked in Virginia Woolf's diaries (which Sylvia Plath read closely while she was writing her own), expecting to find it in this sense. But actually, I didn't. The relatively few occasions on which Virginia Woolf uses the word, however, are significant: they all have to do with the nature of writing:

> [April 8, 1921] As I write, there rises somewhere in my head that queer and very pleasant sense of something which I want to write; my own point of view.[25]

> [February 18, 1922] My only interest as a writer lies, I begin to see, in some queer individuality. (52)

> [September 10, 1929] Really these premonitions of a book—states of soul in creating—are very queer and little apprehended. (141)

> [March 28, 1930] Yes, but this book is a very queer business. (151)

> [January 26, 1940] How queer the change is from private writing to public writing. (300)

Virginia Woolf tried to trust the queerness of writing, even if it seemed to lead to madness: "Never be unseated by the shying of that undependable brute, life, hag-ridden as she is by my own queer, difficult, nervous system" (September 5, 1925; 84–85).

She is, in fact, another Holocaust suicide; she walked into a river as

German bombers buzzed overhead. Woolf had recourse to the word "queer" even to describe her wartime experience: "Yes, I was thinking: we live without a future. That's what's queer . . ." (January 26, 1941; 335).

As the example of Virginia Woolf indicates, "queer" is a word for all the things—conscious and unconscious, rational and irrational— that make up an individual's creative process; things learned from the "elsewhere" of the self. This is what, in Plath, was perhaps "shut up" until the very last months of her life.

VI. Lessons

> You stand at the blackboard, daddy,
> In the picture I have of you . . .
> —Sylvia Plath, "Daddy"

In his essay "The Storyteller," Benjamin writes: "'And they lived happily ever after,' says the fairy tale. The fairy tale, which to this day is the first tutor of children because it was once the first tutor of mankind, secretly lives on in the story."[26] The "happily ever after" ending of fairy tales also seems like something that excludes ambiguity, and it is constantly urged on Plath by her mother:

> My enemies are those that care about me the most. First: my mother. Her pitiful wish is that I "be happy." Happy! (*Journals*, 98)

As a result, the number of her letters in *Letters Home* that begin with some version of "I've never been so happy in my life" is very great— until a letter of October 1962 in which Sylvia tells her mother:

> Don't talk to me about the world needing cheerful stuff! What the person out of Belsen—physical or psychological—wants is nobody saying the birdies still go tweet-tweet, but the full knowledge that somebody else has been there and knows the *worst*, just what it is like. (*Letters Home*, 473)

Aurelia Plath seems to conform to this either/or logic when she adds the note we have already discussed about the mother-hating moments in Plath's abridged diaries:

Much of the material in these pages relating to Sylvia Plath's therapy is of course very painful to me, and coming to the decision to approve its release has been difficult. I have no doubt that many readers will accept whatever negative thoughts she reveals here as the whole and absolute truth, despite their *cancellation* on other, more positive pages. In any case, the importance of this material to Sylvia Plath's work is certain, and in the interest of furthering understanding of her emotional situation, I have given my consent to the release of this material.[27]

Negative and positive thoughts seem locked in a struggle in which only one can stand. The coexistence of contradictory feelings does not seem like a possibility.

Yet, in general, the best stories are those that distract the listener with a binary world—a lure—which the story then proceeds to transgress. The challenge is to portray an event in which the listener thinks he knows where justice lies, and then to pull it out from someplace else. So although it ends up confirming the values it seemed to transgress, it can do so only through a detour that at first seems to contradict them. Order is restored, and it is all the stronger for the temporary deviation.

Sylvia Plath's poems about her mother try to oppose domains beyond her influence to the cheery storyteller and teacher she had always been. Yet the result is strangely ambiguous. The poem "The Disquieting Muses" begins:

> Mother, mother, what illbred aunt
> Or what disfigured and unsightly
> Cousin did you so unwisely keep
> Unasked to my christening, that she
> Sent these ladies in her stead
> With heads like darning-eggs to nod
> And nod and nod at foot and head
> And at the left side of my crib?
>
> Mother, who made to order stories
> Of Mixie Blackshort the heroic bear,
> Mother, whose witches always, always
> Got baked into gingerbread, I wonder
> Whether you saw them, whether you said

Words to rid me of those three ladies
Nodding by night around my bed,
Mouthless, eyeless, with stitched bald head.

The silent, sinister Muses surround the poet's bed and, despite all
the lessons the mother paid for,

I learned, I learned, I learned elsewhere,
From muses unhired by you, dear mother.

That Plath learned things her mother preferred her not to know is
perfectly plausible. But if a Muse is an object of address and an in-
spirer of speech, the poem is still addressing the mother, and the
mother is still the master of "words." Only silence and blankness
come from "those ladies." Yet their very presence invokes a well-
known fairy tale: in "Sleeping Beauty," the sleep is the thirteenth
fairy's revenge for not being invited to the christening. The Muses
would not have appeared if the mother, too, had not failed to invite
someone. Again, the apparent violation of the values proclaimed in
the tale becomes that without which there would be no tale. This is
the double bind of the storyteller.

The mother's tale telling, then, is responsible for the presence of
what it excludes. In the end, the mother floats off in a cheerful bubble, leaving the daughter to face her blank traveling companions.
The poem ends:

And this is the kingdom you bore me to,
Mother, mother. But no frown of mine
Will betray the company I keep.

"Bore" could mean "carried off" or "birthed." If it is the mother
who floats off as the speaker faces her fellow travelers on earth, then
life itself is that dark secret the mother is ignorant of. But "betray"?
It means both "reveal" and "be false to." Something like "traduce."
In other words, any expression that reveals what is inside can be
harmful. To show to the mother any face but the one she has put
there exposes the "muses unhired by you."

This poem is one of a series commissioned by *ARTnews* in which
Plath was also supposed to speak of works of art. In this case, her

subject is a painting by Giorgio de Chirico called *The Disquieting Muses,* in which "three dressmakers' dummies in classical gowns" are waiting with luggage in the setting sun. It is astonishing how well Plath describes both the painting and her childhood. But her note on the poem treats it as having yet a third, archetypal, meaning, having to do with the same triad of women (the Fates, the witches) that Freud studied in his essay "The Three Caskets." Part of the richness of the poem lies in the ways all three readings are justified.

But let us pursue the question of painting further. On February 16, 1958, Sylvia Plath wrote to her brother:

> I have received a letter from a New York magazine, *ARTnews,* offering me from $50 to $75 for a poem on a work of art, so I'm hoping to go to the Art Museum and meditate on Gauguin and Rousseau and produce something this week—it's so tantalizing to have the outright assignment, I just hope I'm not all dried up. (*Letters Home,* 235–236)

A month later, she wrote to her mother:

> Just a note to say that I have at last burst into a spell of writing. I was rather stunned Thursday morning, my first real day off after a week of correcting 70 papers, averaging midterm grades and writing a report on another senior thesis, but I had about seven or eight paintings and etchings I wanted to write on as poem-subjects and bang! . . . A total of about 90 lines written in one day.
>
> These are easily the best poems I've written and open up new material and a new voice. I've discovered my deepest source of inspiration, which is art: the art of primitives like Henri Rousseau, Gauguin, Paul Klee, and de Chirico. I have got piles and piles of wonderful books from the Art Library (suggested by this fine Modern Art course I'm auditing each week) and am overflowing with ideas and inspirations, as if I've been bottling up a geyser for a year. Once I start writing, it comes and comes. . . . I feel like an idiot who has been obediently digging up pieces of coal in an immense mine and has just realized that there is no need to do this, but that one can fly all day and night on great wings in clear blue air through brightly colored magic and weird worlds. Even used the dregs of my inspiration to write about six of those Dole Pineapple Jingles! We could use a car, or $5, or $15,000! (*Letters Home,* 336–337)

The inside/outside opposition figured by a Muse is posed here in terms of inspiration, or perhaps we might call it arousal: the source of inspiration comes from outside and releases a geyser from within. An opposition is set up between depth and height, wetness and dryness, blackness and color: where Plath had feared she was "dried up" (which in fifties girlhood always preceded "old maid"), she now "comes and comes." Where she had been obediently digging, now she flies. Is it the paintings, or is it the fact of the assignment? Why is an assignment a liberation from obedience? And what about the financial incentive? Like Baudelaire, Plath associated her mother with money, but instead of not giving enough, Aurelia Plath had already given more than she could afford. As a result, all money Plath earned from writing was a trophy to lay at her mother's feet.

What I have just quoted begins and ends with money: *ARTnews* will pay for the poems, and the Dole Pineapple company was running a contest for jingles that could win you money, or even a car. There was no end to the financial possibilities poems on paintings might open up.

On March 28 Plath writes in her diary that her "paralysis" has really ended:

> I was taken by a frenzy a week ago Thursday, my first real day of vacation, and the frenzy has continued ever since: writing and writing: I wrote eight poems in the last eight days, long poems, lyrical poems, and thunderous poems, poems breaking open my real experience of life in the last five years: life which has been shut up, untouchable, in a rococo crystal cage, not to be touched.
>
> [Description of walking past a fire] I dragged Ted to it, hoping for houses in a holocaust, parents jumping out of the window with babies. . . . The fire was oddly satisfying. I longed for an incident, an accident. What unleashed desire there must be in one for general carnage. I walk around the streets, braced and ready and almost wishing to test my eye and fiber on tragedy—a child crushed by a car, a house on fire, someone thrown into a tree by a horse. (*Journals,* 356–357)

Plath's move from "I" to "one" ("What unleashed desire there must be *in one* for general carnage") seems a disavowal of the violence she covers here through generalization. Anyone who watches the local evening news on TV, though, can recognize that the desire to see accidents, houses on fire, dead children, and violence committed by animals *can* be generalized. Plath's estranging of this desire from herself through generalization is a way of acting as though it *is* actually particular to her. And Plath criticism follows suit. The unleashing of poetry and the unleashing of the desire for carnage do seem to occur together.

Something that has been "shut up" in a crystal cage has been liberated. But like the Janus-faced "bell jar," the image can never be simple. Either it means being silent or it means keeping oneself from blurting out to another what one should keep for oneself. Either it means that one is imprisoned or it means that one is protected. Sylvia Plath knew that she would never be able to decide which.

Ted Hughes seems naturally to have taken up the role of teacher that Aurelia Plath had once played. In one of her "happy" letters to her mother, Sylvia writes:

> He is educating me daily, setting me exercises of concentration and observation. (*Letters Home,* 267)

And we recall her comment in her journal:

> My danger, partly, I think, is becoming too dependent on Ted. *He is didactic,* fanatic. . . . Between us there are no barriers—it is rather as if neither of us—or especially myself—had any skin, or one skin between us & kept bumping into and abrading each other. (*Journals,* 401)

The enchantment of the perpetual teacher even came in a recognizable form: that of the storyteller.

> Living with him is like being told a perpetual story: his mind is the biggest, most imaginative, I have ever met. I could live in its growing countries forever. (*Journals,* 249)

Perhaps getting an assignment from a muse "unhired by" the primary teacher is the only way to satisfy the didactic libido and escape it at the same time.

In Walter Benjamin's correspondence, a fascination with fairy tales begins to take shape not only in his retelling of the story of Sleeping Beauty ("The Storyteller," 295), but also in the first version of the *Arcades* project: "The Paris Arcades: A Dialectical Fairy Play." As he writes to Scholem in May 1925:

> I secretly entertain the opinion that there must be new and surprising things to say about the beauty of fairy tales. Hardly anyone has as yet delved into this matter. In addition, this particular form of intellectual productivity is beginning to fascinate me. (*Correspondence*, 269)

It was not until 1936 that Benjamin got the journalistic assignment that enabled him to make public that fascination.

In his *Birthday Letters*, Ted Hughes offers a series of poems that respond to particular poems written by Plath. Every one of them responds to the binary opposition inherent in a Plath poem, and shows why the accused is not guilty, but without casting guilt back on Plath. Thus Hughes not only does not fight back, he bitterly laments the fight. He shares the guilt, but only the guilt of not knowing. In "The Minotaur," he describes a sin he has committed, and the overreaction it provokes in his wife:

> The mahogany table-top you smashed
> Had been the broad plank top
> Of my mother's heirloom sideboard—
> Mapped with the scars of my whole life.
>
> That came under the hammer.
> The high stool you swung that day
> Demented by my being
> Twenty minutes late for baby-minding.
>
> "Marvelous!" I shouted. "Go on,
> Smash it into kindling.
> That's the stuff you're keeping out of your poems!"
> And later, considered and calmer,
>
> "Get that shoulder under your stanzas
> And we'll be away!" Deep in the cave of your ear
> The goblin snapped his fingers.
> So what had I given him?

The bloody end of the skein
That unravelled your marriage,
Left your children echoing
Like tunnels in a labyrinth.

Left your mother a dead-end,
Brought you to the horned, bellowing
Grave of your risen father—
And your own corpse in it.

In describing the magnitude of his own loss—the smashing of his mother's heirloom table—Ted Hughes responds not with a cry of personal pain but with teacherly encouragement, shouting, "Marvelous!" The authority of the teacher will always amount to the equivalent of "teacher knows best." This can act as a form of censorship, even of self-censorship, if the student is never permitted to fail. The husband's investment in what is or isn't accessed by his wife's poems trumps his own loss completely. Violence toward him was perhaps "shutting up" Plath's real poetry: the pain he feels (or allows the reader to feel) is precisely a proof of unrepression. His loyalty to the poetry swallows up his own life. And indeed, students of literature should be more grateful than they are for the laborious hours he spent editing and finalizing Plath's poems—giving readers the fuel to attack him. Both he and Aurelia Plath, in fact, let their loyalty to literary history and "truth" take precedence over the devastation that Plath had caused in their own lives. Their defense is a failure of learning: "I didn't know" (used by Hughes eleven times in *Birthday Letters*). The only argument they both make about that pain is the argument, "It wasn't my fault." Which is why critics have so often thought that it was. The failure of the most gifted teacher is precisely to censor the student through the act of always being right.

The last line of "The Minotaur," describing Otto Plath's grave "And your own corpse in it," echoes the end of a happy childbirth poem written by Plath in 1960: "A clean slate, with your own face on" (*Collected Poems*, 141). It also describes Plath's search for Otto's grave and holds him as the center of her labyrinth. But it seems to me that the roles are reversed: Plath, like her father, Otto, died young; Hughes, like Plath's mother, Aurelia, was left with two children to care for. Plath's fusion first with her mother and then with Hughes indicates that oneness with the lone teacher was something Plath learned from the living parent, not the dead one.

Ultimately, both Aurelia Plath and Ted Hughes allowed their investment in Plath's writings—and the lessons that could be learned from them—to take precedence over the way in which she had affected their own lives. "It does not fall to every man to kill a genius," sighed Hughes. Although he had a vigorous, distinguished career himself, the wound would never heal. The fact that Assia killed herself (along with the child she had had with Ted) in the same way that Plath did must have added immeasurably to the pain, but it also demonstrates, somehow, that it was the only way she could compete with what must have been an indelible mark.

Despite the pain to themselves, Plath's survivors came to put forward what was able to express itself *through them.* Of them it could be said, as Benjamin says of the storyteller:

> Seen in this way, the storyteller joins the ranks of the teachers and sages. . . . For it is granted to him to reach back to a whole lifetime (a life, incidentally, that comprises not only his own experience but no little of the experiences of others . . .). His gift is the ability to relate his life; his distinction, to be able to tell his entire life. The storyteller: he is the man who could let the wick of his life be consumed completely by the gentle flame of his story. ("The Storyteller," 108–109)

Yet however seductive we might find this voice that belongs to no one, perhaps we have to renounce it in order to hear the cacophony around us. Perhaps it is precisely the unity of what is transmitted *through* us that prevents us from attending to the *un*-unifiable sounds of the particular voices that are close at hand.

Notes

1. Correctional Facilities

1. This is the argument Alexander Nehamas makes in "Plato and the Mass Media" (in *Virtues of Authenticity* [Princeton: Princeton University Press, 1999]), but he himself does not rest content with it (see his "Eristic, Antilogic, Sophistic, Dialectic: Plato's Demarcation of Philosophy from Sophistry" in the same volume).
2. Hazard Adams, ed., *Critical Theory since Plato* (New York: Harcourt Brace, 1992).
3. Edith Hamilton and Huntington Cairns, eds., *Plato: The Collected Dialogues* (Princeton: Princeton University Press, 1961).
4. Dominique LaCapra, *"Madame Bovary" on Trial* (Ithaca: Cornell University Press, 1982), p. 9.
5. See Paul de Man, *Wartime Journalism, 1939–1943,* ed. Werner Hamacher, Neil Hertz, and Thomas Keenan (Lincoln: University of Nebraska Press, 1988).
6. Quoted from Adams, ed., *Critical Theory since Plato,* p. 37.
7. Hamilton and Cairns, eds., *Plato,* p. 483.
8. "Sappho in the Text of Plato," in Page duBois, *Sappho Is Burning* (Chicago: University of Chicago Press, 1995), p. 87.
9. Hamilton and Cairns, eds., *Plato,* p. 43.
10. See "Dossier des Fleurs du Mal," in Baudelaire, *Oeuvres complètes,* ed. Claude Pichois (Paris: Gallimard, 1961), vol. 1, p. 1178; henceforth cited as "Dossier."
11. "Dossier," p. 1206.
12. Ibid., p. 1208.
13. Joan de Jean, *Fictions of Sappho, 1546–1937* (Chicago: University of Chicago Press, 1989), p. 2.
14. Baudelaire, *Oeuvres complètes,* 1:181.
15. "Dossier," pp. 1181–1182.
16. Jacques Hamelin, *La Réhabilitation judiciaire de Baudelaire* (Paris: Dalloz, 1952), p. 73.
17. Du Bois, *Sappho Is Burning,* p. 82.

18. *Sappho: A New Translation,* trans. Mary Barnard (Berkeley: University of California Press, 1958), p. vii.
19. Willis Barnstone, *Sappho* (Los Angeles: Sun and Moon Press, 1998), p. 11.
20. Jacques Derrida, *Dissemination,* trans. Barbara Johnson (Chicago: University of Chicago Press, 1981), pp. 71–72.
21. Franz Kafka, *The Trial,* trans. Willa Muir and Edwin Muir (New York: Modern Library, 1956).
22. Franz Kafka, *The Trial,* trans. Willa Muir and Edwin Muir; rev. and trans. E. M. Butler (New York: Schocken, 1968).
23. Franz Kafka, *Der Prozess* (Frankfurt: Fisher, 1992).
24. Walter Benjamin, *Selected Writings* (Cambridge, Mass.: Harvard University Press, 1996), p. 257.
25. A. C. Grayling, *Financial Times,* February 17, 2002, p. v, in his review of John McWhorter, *The Power of Babel* (New York: Times Books/ Henry Holt, 2001), a book that studies not the appearance but the disappearance of languages, which are becoming extinct as fast as endangered species in the rain forests.
26. Hélène Cixous and Catherine Clément, *The Newly Born Woman,* trans. Betsy Wing (Minneapolis: University of Minnesota Press, 1986), pp. 63–64.
27. For a study of the historicity of theories of reproduction, see the unpublished dissertation of Lilian Porten, "The *Mâle du Siècle:* Creation and Procreation in French Literature" (Harvard University, 1999), especially the discussion of the assumption of natural stability as vehicle in the section "An Equation with Two Unknowns," talking about the metaphor of the author as parent.
28. For a brilliant study of the relations between sexual difference, foreign languages, and the unconscious, based on a reading of the large number of parapraxes involving foreign languages in Freud's *The Psychopathology of Everyday Life,* see Mary Gossy, *Freudian Slips: Woman, Writing, the Foreign Tongue* (Ann Arbor: University of Michigan Press, 1995).

2. *L'Esthétique du Mal*

My epigraph and much of the framework for this part of my essay are taken from the brilliant article by Deborah Jenson, "Gender and the Aesthetic of 'le Mal': Louise Ackermann's *Poésies philosophiques,* 1871," *Nineteenth-Century French Studies* 23 (1994–95): 175–193. In her article, Jenson argues that while men make badness into an aesthetic value, women are often mentioned as prime examples of bad writing.

1. Anne Sexton, *The Complete Poems* (Boston: Houghton Mifflin, 1981), p. 126.
2. Arthur Rimbaud, *Oeuvres* (Paris: Garnier, 1960), p. 357.
3. Gordon Millan, *Mallarmé: A Throw of the Dice* (London: Secker and Warburg, 1994), p. 144.
4. Stéphane Mallarmé, *Oeuvres complètes* (Paris: Gallimard, 1945), pp. 382–383.
5. Ibid., p. 383.
6. Peter Brooks, "Must We Apologize?" in *Comparative Literature in the Age of Multiculturalism*, ed. Charles Bernheimer (Baltimore: Johns Hopkins University Press, 1995), p. 105.
7. "The Bernheimer Report, 1993," in *Comparative Literature*, ed. Bernheimer, p. 42.
8. "The Levin Report, 1965," in *Comparative Literature*, ed. Bernheimer, p. 25.
9. *Hegel's Encyclopedia of Philosophy*, trans. and annotated by Gustav Emil Mueller (New York: Philosophical Library, 1959), p. 1.
10. One letter to the editor read as follows: "*Sir,*—I will not, like your 'Constant Subscriber' of last week, protest against all foreign languages. I can read some of them myself, and have relations who can read others. But I shall take it very kindly if the next time M. Stéphane Mallarmé occupies your columns, you kindly append a French translation of his article, or what in Decadish might be called 'une française traduction.' I am, yours resignedly, *one who used to think he could read French*." *The National Observer*, April 9, 1892, p. 540.
11. Stéphane Mallarmé, "Crise de vers," in *Oeuvres complètes*, p. 368, my emphasis.
12. Jacques Derrida, "Letter to a Japanese Friend," in *A Derrida Reader: Between the Blinds*, ed. Peggy Kamuf (New York: Columbia University Press, 1991), p. 270.
13. *The Poetry and Prose of William Blake* (New York: Doubleday, 1965), p. 151.
14. Written and directed by Amy Heckerling, starring Alicia Silverstone as Cher Horowitz.
15. English translation by C. K. Cohen (London: Routledge and Kegan Paul, 1924).

16. W. E. B. Du Bois, *The Souls of Black Folk* (New York: Penguin, 1989), p. 5.

17. Joan Copjec, *Read My Desire* (Cambridge, Mass.: MIT Press, 1994), pp. 174–175.

3. The Task of the Translator

1. Claude Pichois and Jean Zeigler, *Baudelaire,* trans. Graham Robb (London: Vintage, 1989), p. 145.

2. Momme Brodersen, in his biography of Benjamin, puts his finger squarely on this point: "In addition, Benjamin's Baudelaire translations are primarily the aesthetic evocation and revocation of a man whom, for the whole of his life, he not only considered a great poet and translator, but in addition to whom he remained highly indebted for a long time on numerous accounts: in questions of literary taste and aesthetic judgement, indeed in his entire bearing as a writer. As such, these translations were a move to free himself from a man whose influence on his thought and creative output cannot be overestimated." Momme Brodersen, *Walter Benjamin,* trans. M. R. Green and I. Ligers (London: Verso, 1996), p. 111.

3. Walter Benjamin, *Selected Writings,* ed. Marcus Bullock and Michael W. Jennings (Cambridge, Mass.: Harvard University Press, 1996), vol. 1, p. 362; brackets are the editors'.

4. Stefan George, *Die Blumen des Bösen* (Berlin: Georg Bondi, 1918), p. 5; punctuation and capitalization are George's.

5. Brodersen, *Walter Benjamin,* pp. 111–112.

6. Walter Benjamin, *Charles Baudelaire: A Lyric Poet in the Era of High Capitalism,* trans. Harry Zohn (London: NLB, 1955), p. 125 ("The delight of the urban poet is love—not at first sight, but at last sight").

7. Walter Benjamin, *The Arcades Project,* trans. Howard Eiland and Kevin McLaughlin (Cambridge, Mass.: Harvard University Press, 1999), p. 205.

8. Ibid., p. 127.

9. Walter Benjamin, *The Origin of German Tragic Drama* (London: NLB, 1977), p. 166.

10. Benjamin, *Selected Writings,* 1: 263.

11. Stéphane Mallarmé, *Oeuvres complètes* (Paris: Gallimard, 1945), pp. 363–364.

12. Jacques Lacan, *Feminine Sexuality: Jacques Lacan and the École Freud-

ienne, ed. Juliet Mitchell and Jacqueline Rose, trans. Jacqueline Rose (New York: Norton, 1982), p. 144.

13. The Schocken Bible, trans. Everett Fox (New York: Schocken, 1995), p. 15.

14. Paul de Man, *The Resistance to Theory* (Minneapolis: University of Minnesota Press, 1986), p. 11.

15. Jacqueline Leiner, *Imaginaire, langage, identité culturelle, négritude* (Paris: Jean-Michel Place, 1980), p. 144.

16. See Carol Jacobs's remarks about Harry Zohn's translation of *Illuminations:* "His translation results in phrases such as 'the same thing,' 'the same object,' where the German speaks neither of things nor objects." Carol Jacobs, *In the Language of Walter Benjamin* (Baltimore: Johns Hopkins University Press, 1999), p. 81.

17. De Man, *Resistance,* p. 87.

18. Because this is the transcription of a lecture, it is impossible to say whether *Brot* or *brood* is the correct term, especially since de Man has just stated that they sound alike. The written hesitation cannot mirror the oral conflation.

19. Sigmund Freud, *The Interpretation of Dreams* (New York: Avon, 1965), p. 146.

20. Gershom Scholem, *Kabbalah* (New York: Meridian, 1974) p. 136.

4. The Poet's Mother

1. This use of the word "pregnant" is to some extent an overdetermination via translation here, since the French original just says "grosse de."

2. Jacques Lacan, *Ecrits,* trans. Alan Sheridan (New York: Norton, 1977), p. 286.

3. "Ode to the West Wind."

4. Barbara Johnson, *A World of Difference* (Baltimore: Johns Hopkins University Press, 1987), pp. 198–199.

5. See Sigmund Freud, *Beyond the Pleasure Principle* (New York: Norton, 1961), p. 11.

6. Sylvia Plath, *The Collected Poems,* ed. Ted Hughes (New York: Harper and Row, 1981), p. 226.

7. See especially Sylvia's notes on her 1958–1959 therapy with Ruth Beuscher, the therapist she had first met during her stay at McLean Hospital in 1953, in *The Unabridged Journals of Sylvia Plath,* ed. Karen V. Kukil (New York: Random House, 2000), pp. 429–438.

8. Plath, *Unabridged Journals,* p. 401.

9. Plath, *Collected Poems,* p. 245.

10. Plath, *Unabridged Journals,* pp. 469–470.

11. Charles Baudelaire, *Correspondance,* ed. Claude Pichois (Paris: Gallimard, 1973), vol. 1, p. 113.

12. Janet Malcolm, *The Silent Woman* (New York: Knopf, 1994), p. 33.

13. *The Journals of Sylvia Plath,* ed. Ted Hughes and Frances McCullough (New York: Ballantine, 1982), p. 265.

14. Simone de Beauvoir, *The Second Sex,* trans. H. M. Parshley (New York: Knopf, 1953), p. 237.

15. Jay Greenberg, *Oedipus and Beyond* (Cambridge, Mass.: Harvard University Press, 1991), pp. 6, 7, 9.

16. See *The Selected Melanie Klein,* ed. Juliet Mitchell (New York: Free Press, 1986).

17. Susan Suleiman, "Writing and Motherhood," in *The (M)other Tongue,* ed. Shirley Nelson Garner, Claire Kahane, Madelon Sprengnether (Ithaca: Cornell University Press), p. 355.

18. Serge Leclair, *On tue un enfant* (Paris: Seuil, 1981).

19. Jean-Paul Sartre, *Baudelaire* (Paris: Gallimard, 1963), p. 17; translation mine.

20. In *Baudelaire and the Poetics of Modernity,* ed. Patricia Ward (Nashville: Vanderbilt University Press, 2001).

21. D. W. Winnicott, *Playing and Reality* (London: Tavistock, 1971), pp. 10–11; emphasis in the original.

22. See Dominick LaCapra, *"Madame Bovary" on Trial* (Ithaca: Cornell University Press, 1982), p. 21.

23. Sylvia Plath, *Letters Home: Correspondence, 1950–1963,* selected and ed. Aurelia Schober Plath (London: Faber, 1975), p. 16.

24. Plath, *Collected Poems,* p. 38 ("Soliloquy of the Solipsist").

5. Passage Work

1. Benjamin's first mention of Baudelaire occurs in a letter of January 1915 to Ernst Schoen. In the published correspondence, it occurs between news of close friend Wolf Heinle's suicide and the letter of rupture Benjamin wrote to his former mentor, Gustav Wyneken, in March. Both of these events were directly concerned with the outbreak of World War I.

2. See, for example, editor Peter Demetz's well-known introduction to Benjamin's *Reflections* (trans. Edmund Jephcott; New York: Schocken,

1986) and Terry Eagleton's *Walter Benjamin, or Towards a Revolutionary Criticism* (London: Verso, 1981).

3. Walter Benjamin, *The Origin of German Tragic Drama,* trans. John Osborne (London: NLB, 1977). Walter Benjamin, *Charles Baudelaire: A Lyric Poet in the Era of High Capitalism,* trans. Harry Zohn (London: NLB, 1973).

4. Walter Benjamin, *The Arcades Project,* trans. Howard Eiland and Kevin McLaughlin (Cambridge, Mass.: Harvard University Press, 1999), p. 321 (henceforth referred to in the text as *Arcades*).

5. Walter Benjamin, *Baudelaire: Un poète lyrique à l'apogée du capitalisme,* trans. Jean Lacoste (Paris: Payot, 1979), preface, p. 9.

6. *The Correspondence of Walter Benjamin, 1910–1940,* ed. Gershom Scholem and Theodor W. Adorno, trans. Manfred R. Jacobson and Evelyn M. Jacobson (Chicago: University of Chicago Press, 1994), p. 557 (henceforth abbreviated *Correspondence*).

7. *Arcades,* p. 322.

8. Jean-Paul Sartre, *Baudelaire* (Paris: Gallimard, 1963).

9. Charles Baudelaire, *Correspondance* (Paris: Pléiade, 1966), vol. 1, p. 214.

10. Benjamin, *Correspondence,* p. xvii.

11. Baudelaire, "Un fantôme" ("Les Ténèbres").

12. Note the ways in which horror of conflation here is diametrically opposed to the search for conflation in the poem "Correspondances."

13. Charles Baudelaire, *Oeuvres complètes,* ed. Claude Pichois (Paris: Gallimard, 1976), vol. 1, p. 181.

14. Take, for example, the idea of "pricelessness" used to sell a credit card in a recent ad campaign: the illusion that something escapes exchange is used to market pure exchange value.

15. William Pietz, "The Problem of the Fetish, I," *Res* (Spring 1985): 5–11, here p. 5.

16. *The Marx-Engels Reader,* ed. Robert C. Tucker (New York: Norton, 1978), p. 98 ("Economic and Philosophic Manuscripts of 1844").

17. Benjamin, *Baudelaire,* p. 55.

18. Ibid., pp. 55–56.

19. Cf. Andrew Parker, "Why Western Marxists Don't Like Poetry," unpublished lecture.

20. Adam Christian pointed out the false cognates in *commodité* and, since the French translation of "false cognates" is *faux amis,* tied them to the prose poem "La fausse monnaie," which is about the falseness of a friend (unpublished junior essay, Harvard University, 1999).

21. Benjamin to Adorno, in Theodor W. Adorno and Walter Benjamin, *The Complete Correspondence, 1928–1940,* ed. Henri Lonitz (Cambridge, Mass.: Harvard University Press, 1999), p. 99 (henceforth abbreviated *Adorno Correspondence*).

22. Adorno to Benjamin, ibid., p. 282.

23. "Baudelaire," in Walter Benjamin, *Selected Writings,* ed. Marcus Bullock and Michael W. Jennings (Cambridge, Mass.: Belknap Press of Harvard University Press, 1996), vol. 1, p. 361.

24. Brand names.

25. Paul de Man, *The Rhetoric of Romanticism* (New York: Columbia University Press, 1984), p. 251.

26. Benjamin, *Baudelaire,* pp. 139–140.

27. My subtitle is taken from an essay written in honor of Paul de Man by Shoshana Felman entitled "Postal Survival, or The Question of the Navel" (*Yale French Studies* 69 [1984]: 68), alluding to the following letter Paul de Man wrote to the author the previous summer: "Rather than entrusting the (perhaps unique) copy of this text to the singularly decrepit mailman who insures postal survival in this place, I prefer to return it to you myself next week" (Paul de Man to Shoshana Felman, Maine, August 23, 1983).

28. Benjamin, *Selected Writings,* 2: 120.

29. Susan Buck-Morss, *The Dialectics of Seeing* (Cambridge, Mass.: MIT Press, 1989), pp. ix, x.

30. Pietz, "Problem of the Fetish, I," p. 6.

31. Stéphane Mallarmé, *Oeuvres complètes* (Paris: Gallimard, 1945), p. 647.

32. Benjamin on Kafka, quoted in Hannah Arendt, "Introduction" to Walter Benjamin, *Illuminations,* ed. Hannah Arendt (New York: Schocken, 1968), p. 17.

33. Félix Nadar, *Quand j'étais photographe* (Paris, 1900), p. 281. Quoted by Benjamin in *Arcades,* p. 90.

6. Construction Work

1. Robert Lowell, *Life Studies; and, For the Union Dead* (New York: Noonday Press, 1972), pp. 70–72.

2. See Lowell's two poems entitled "The March" reproduced in *The Norton Anthology of Poetry.*

3. My thanks to Jan Ziolkowski, for whose philological wisdom I am greatly indebted throughout these remarks.

4. Sigmund Freud, *Civilization and Its Discontents,* in *The Standard Edition of the Complete Psychological Works of Sigmund Freud,* ed. and trans. James Strachey (London: Hogarth, 1961), vol. 11, p. 70.
5. This is a spectacular example of historical irony!
6. Nathaniel Hawthorne, *The Marble Faun* (New York: Penguin, 1990), p. 37.
7. Richard Klein, *Cigarettes Are Sublime* (Durham: Duke University Press, 1993), p. 8. Duke University, of course, was built out of tobacco fortunes.
8. Charles Baudelaire, in "Enivrez-vous," *Oeuvres complètes,* ed. Claude Pichois (Paris: Pléiade, 1975), vol. 1, p. 337.
9. Walter Benjamin, *The Arcades Project,* trans. Howard Eiland and Kevin McLaughlin (Cambridge, Mass.: Harvard University Press, 1999), p. 85.

7. Doing Time

1. Paul de Man, "Literary History and Literary Modernity," in *Blindness and Insight: Essays in the Rhetoric of Contemporary Criticism,* 2nd ed., rev. (Minneapolis: University of Minnesota Press, 1983), p. 165.
2. Paul de Man, "The Rhetoric of Temporality," in *Blindness and Insight,* p. 207.
3. Paul de Man, *Allegories of Reading* (New Haven: Yale University Press, 1979), p. ix.
4. Nietzsche quoted and translated by de Man in "Literary History," p. 146.
5. Friedrich Nietzsche, *The Use and Abuse of History,* trans. Adrian Collins (New York: Liberal Arts Press, 1957), p. 5.
6. Minae Mizumura, "Renunciation," in "The Lesson of Paul de Man," *Yale French Studies* (1985): 87.
7. Nietzsche, *Use and Abuse of History,* p. 5.
8. Friedrich Nietzsche, *Vom Nutzen und Nachteil der Historie für das Leben* (Frankfurt: Insel, 1989), p. 13.
9. Quoted in Mizumura, "Renunciation," p. 85. De Man's essay was published later in a slightly different translation (by Richard Howard) as "Madame de Staël and Jean-Jacques Rousseau," in Paul de Man, *Critical Writings, 1953–1978,* ed. Lindsay Waters (Minneapolis: University of Minnesota Press, 1989).

8. Animate Alphabets

1. Leon Wieseltier, "In a Universe of Ghosts," *New York Review of Books,* November 25, 1976, p. 20.
2. Tim Kendall, *Sylvia Plath: A Critical Study* (London: Faber and Faber, 2001), p. 76.
3. Quoted in Jacqueline Rose, *The Haunting of Sylvia Plath* (London: Virago, 1991), p. 206.
4. Quoted in Kendall, *Sylvia Plath,* p. 121.
5. "Dying Is an Art," in *The Art of Sylvia Plath: A Symposium,* ed. Charles Newman (Bloomington: Indiana University Press, 1970), pp. 213, 216, 217.
6. Sylvia Plath, "Little Fugue," in *The Collected Poems* (New York: Harper and Row, 1981), p. 188.
7. *The Unabridged Journals of Sylvia Plath* (henceforth referred to as *Journals*), ed. Karen V. Kukil (New York: Random House, 2000), p. 430; see also p. 431: "He was an ogre. But I miss him."
8. Sylvia Plath, "Daddy," in *Collected Poems,* p. 223.
9. Edgar Allan Poe, *Selected Poetry and Prose* (New York: Modern Library, 1951), p. 178.
10. Ted Hughes, "The Table," in *Birthday Letters* (New York: Farrar, Straus and Giroux, 1998), p. 139.
11. Plath, Notes, *Collected Poems,* p. 293.
12. Plath, "Daddy," p. 223.
13. Michel Foucault, preface to Gilles Deleuze and Felix Guattari, *Anti-Oedipus: Capitalism and Schizophrenia,* trans. Robert Hurley, Mark Seem, and Helen R. Lane (Minneapolis: University of Minnesota Press, 1983), p. xiii.
14. Sylvia Plath, *The Bell Jar* (London: Faber and Faber, 1963), p. 131.
15. *The Correspondence of Walter Benjamin, 1910–1940,* ed. Gershom Scholem and Theodor Adorno, trans. Manfred R. Jacobson and Evelyn M. Jacobson (Chicago: University of Chicago Press, 1994), p. 215.
16. Leo Rosten, *The Joys of Yiddish* (New York: Pocket Books, 1968), p. 440.
17. Quoted from one of Benjamin's essays.
18. Charles Baudelaire, *Correspondance,* ed. Claude Pichois (Paris: Gallimard, 1973), vol. 2, p. 702, note.
19. Charles Baudelaire, *Oeuvres complètes,* ed. Claude Pichois (Paris: Gallimard, 1976), vol. 1, p. 181.

20. Aurelia Schober Plath, "Introduction," in Sylvia Plath, *Letters Home,* ed. Aurelia Schober Plath (New York: Harper Collins, 1975), p. 4.

21. Rose, *The Haunting of Sylvia Plath,* p. 138.

22. Janet Malcolm, *The Silent Woman* (New York: Knopf, 1994), pp. 187–188.

23. Marie Asche, "*The Bell Jar* and the Ghost of Ethel Rosenberg," in *Secret Agents,* ed. Marjorie Garber and Rebecca L. Walkowitz (New York: Routledge, 1995), p. 215.

24. *New Yorker,* February 2, 1998, p. 64.

25. Virginia Woolf, *A Writer's Diary* (New York: Signet, 1953), p. 40.

26. Walter Benjamin, "The Storyteller," in *Illuminations,* ed. and with an introduction by Hannah Arendt, trans. Harry Zohn (New York: Schocken, 1969), p. 102.

27. *The Journals of Sylvia Plath,* ed. Ted Hughes and Frances McCullough (New York: Ballantine, 1982), p. 265, emphasis added.

Credits

Index